MW00424356

Governing the
Metropolitan Region

Governing the Metropolitan Region

—

America's New Frontier

David Y. Miller and Raymond W. Cox III

Routledge
Taylor & Francis Group

LONDON AND NEW YORK

First published 2014 by M.E. Sharpe

Published 2015 by Routledge
2 Park Square, Milton Park, Abingdon, Oxon OX14 4RN
711 Third Avenue, New York, NY 10017, USA

Routledge is an imprint of the Taylor & Francis Group, an informa business

Copyright © 2014 Taylor & Francis. All rights reserved.

No part of this book may be reprinted or reproduced or utilised in any form or by
any electronic, mechanical, or other means, now known or hereafter invented,
including photocopying and recording, or in any information storage or retrieval
system, without permission in writing from the publishers.

Notices
No responsibility is assumed by the publisher for any injury and/or damage to
persons or property as a matter of products liability, negligence or otherwise,
or from any use of operation of any methods, products, instructions or ideas
contained in the material herein.

Practitioners and researchers must always rely on their own experience and
knowledge in evaluating and using any information, methods, compounds, or
experiments described herein. In using such information or methods they should
be mindful of their own safety and the safety of others, including parties for
whom they have a professional responsibility.

Product or corporate names may be trademarks or registered trademarks, and
are used only for identification and explanation without intent to infringe.

Library of Congress Cataloging-in-Publication Data

Miller, David Young.
  Governing the metropolitan region : America's new frontier / by David Y. Miller and
Raymond W. Cox III.
     p. cm.
Includes bibliographical references and index.
ISBN 978-0-7656-3983-7 (hardcover : alk. paper)—ISBN 978-0-7656-3984-4 (pbk. : alk. paper)
1. Metropolitan government—United States. 2. Municipal government—United States.
3. Urban policy—United States. I. Cox, Raymond W. II. Title.

JS422.M55 2014
320.8′50973—dc23   2013038334

ISBN 13: 9780765639844 (pbk)
ISBN 13: 9780765639837 (hbk)

Contents

Preface

This book is the result of a collaboration that began when the two of us agreed to serve on the then Urban Management Education Committee of Network of Schools of Public Policy, Affairs, and Administration (NASPAA) more than a decade ago. Over time both of us served as Chair of what would be renamed the Local Government Management Education Committee. That close working relationship yielded a number of joint efforts ranging from the review of standards for local government specializations in MPA degrees to panels at NASPAA. After preparing a paper for a symposium sponsored by the Section on Intergovernmental Administration and Management at the American Society for Public Administration conference in 2009, we began a serious discussion about how much had changed concerning urban and metropolitan governance since the publication of *The Regional Governing of Metropolitan America* (Miller 2002). We agreed that, while the issues had not changed, the broader landscape and political environment had. We decided that a new look was needed. Thus began the collaboration that would yield this work.

We engage this topic from a stance of both respect for the herculean efforts of those who strive to enhance metropolitan governance and a sense of frustration that few really seem to understand metropolitan regions in America and the cities that anchor them. The uneven but necessary recalibration of decision making by isolated local governments separated by large swathes of hinterlands to local governments that are so close together that name plates identifying boundaries are easily missed if one is not looking closely. The former is now a historical artifact although many Americans still try to think and act as if these separations still exist. The latter is a reality we are still learning about—a frontier. Our institutions of local governance were built for the former but really don't work for the latter. Indeed, new ways of doing the business of local governance continue to emerge. We capture these as the governance of the metropolitan region, a new scale for decision making. We build it by not throwing out old local governments, but by reframing them.

The recalibration is also occurring at the state level, the other "anchor" in the old state-local system. Unfortunately, the term "system" no longer seems to apply; at best it is a system in considerable disarray. Few states would even acknowledge the need for an urban agenda and still fewer have a sense of urgency about metropolitan regions. Local governments are pushed in two directions, funding from the states has declined yet the rules for spending those funds have expanded. Furthermore, while the state legislatures talk about the importance of regional solutions they are framed as money-saving efforts and are not relevant in and of themselves. This leads to short-term financial fixes that often emphasize the differences and conflicts across local governments.

Our self-appointed task was to explore the dynamics of the new relationships among local governments and between localities and the states in shaping policy in metropolitan regions. That exploration affirmed our concerns, but also suggested new pathways for collaborative governance.

We believe it was to our advantage that we both possess significant practical experience at the local and state levels. Dave started his career (with a newly minted MPA) as the Town Manager of Dover-Foxcroft, Maine (population, about 4,500), at the "still wet behind the ears" age of 24. Subsequently he managed several other towns in Maine and did a stint as Director of Management and Budget for the City of Pittsburgh. Raymond's practical experience is primarily on the political side of state government, with short stints in the federal government and service on the Akron City Council. His perspective from the "other side" helped shape and temper our conclusions about the future of Metropolitan America.

We could not have done our work without the help of many others, though we take full responsibility for any errors and omissions. Dave would like to acknowledge George Dougherty of the University of Pittsburgh, who collaborated with him in thinking through the difficult dilemma facing city managers in the balancing of local and regional interests—a topic explored in Chapter 11. Jenni Easton, a former student, honed her analytical skills developing the data that led to the analysis of the Pittsburgh regional revenue-sharing program discussed in Chapter 8. Kathy Risko, who serves as the Executive Director of CONNECT, had a role in coordinating the urban core building efforts in Pittsburgh, which is discussed in Chapter 7. Dave's thinking on both local and regional government has been shaped by the culture shock experienced after leaving the relative peace and quiet of small, intimate local governments in Maine for the hustle and often overwhelming complexity of modern urban America as practiced in Pittsburgh. During the transition and afterward, Dave Rusk's input helped develop the author's sense of how to meld the local with the regional.

Raymond's work in helping to shape state policy with regard to local government allowed him to work in the Massachusetts House of Representatives when an urban agenda was still viable, though focused on policy areas rather than governmental structures. Important lessons came from a year on the Akron City Council just as the Great Recession would exacerbate the growing rift between cities and states (2009).

Both authors owe thanks to their extraordinary students from the University of Pittsburgh and the University of Akron. We are indebted to Katherine Yoon, a doctoral student, and Dillon Moore, a masters' student, both at the University of Pittsburgh, who had the unenviable task of trying to keep us on schedule for more than a year. Two doctoral students from the University of Akron also provided vital assistance—Tricia Ostertag prepared much of the background material for the discussion on service sharing. The core discussions on service sharing in Chapter 5 are the product of her efforts. Beth Gersper took on the role of editor, challenging us to simplify our language to make it more accessible to a wider range of readers. Her work on our behalf was quite remarkable.

Commonly Used Acronyms

ACIR   Advisory Commission on Intergovernmental Relations
AMPO   Association of Metropolitan Planning Organization
AOG   Association of Governments
ARRA   American Recovery and Reinvestment Act
CAO   Chief Administrative Officer
CBSA   Core-Based Statistical Area
CEO   Chief Executive Officer
COG   Council of Government
CONNECT   CONgress of NEighboringCommuniTies
DOT   Department of Transportation
ED/GE   Economic Development/Government Equity
EU   European Union
FEMA   Federal Emergency Management Agency
FTE   Full Time Equivalent
FY   Fiscal Year
GAO   Government Accountability Office
GED   General Education Degree
HHI   Hirshmann-Herfindal Index
HUD   U.S. Department of Housing and Urban Development
ICMA   International City and County Management Association
IGR   InterGovernmental Relations
ILA   Interlocal agreement
ISTEA   Intermodal Surface Transportation Efficiency Act
JEDD   Joint Economic Development District
MA   Metropolitan Area
MARC   Mid-America Regional Council
MPDI   Metropolitan Power Diffusion Index
MPO   Metropolitan Planning Organization
MSA   Metropolitan Statistical Area
NACo   National Association of Counties
NARC   National Association of Regional Councils

NASPAA	Network of Schools of Public Policy, Affairs, and Administration
NASP-IV	National Administrative Studies Project IV
NCSL	National Conference of State Legislatures
OMB	U.S. Office of Management and Budget
PENNDOT	Pennsylvania Department of Transportation
RC	Regional Council
RGO	Regional Governing Organization
RPC	Regional Planning Commission
SMA	Standard Metropolitan Area
SMSA	Standard Metropolitan Statistical Area
SPC	Southwestern Pennsylvania Commission
SPRDC	Southwestern Pennsylvania Regional Development Council
SPRPC	Southwestern Pennsylvania Regional Planning Commission
TIF	Tax Increment Financing
TIP	Transportation Improvement Plan

Governing the
Metropolitan Region

1

Governing America's New Frontier

The Metropolitan Region

We understand the "city" to be an important institution around which virtually all modern societies are built. As academics, it is our explicit responsibility to study the city. However, we face a dilemma: there are two very different definitions of the term "city." In a sociological sense, a city is seen as an urban area where people live, work, and engage in interactions among themselves. Such a view is absent any legal context. When that legal context is added, a city becomes an entirely different concept. A city now has becomes a legal entity with chartered rights granted by the state, formal boundaries, and self-government. The second definition treats the city as a politico-legal institution: A "city" in the United States is "an incorporated urban center that has self-government, boundaries, and legal rights established by state charter."

As a sociological term, "city" is interchangeable with "metropolitan region" in that both terms mean an urbanized area with many jobs and people living therein. When "city" is used a politico-legal sense, the terms are not interchangeable, even though the need to make more public decisions at the regional level is becoming self-evident. Today's metropolitan regions have nascent characteristics of the politico-legal city. In this book, we will explore the use of the terms "metropolitan region" and "city" and how they are slowly converging into a hybrid concept of governance.

There are several reasons for this approach. First, the metropolitan region has replaced the city as the conceptual unit in which the majority of people live and business is conducted. Second, it allows us to better frame the discussion of the structured relationship between the institutions of government and governing. By that we mean there is a vertical relationship, in terms of the governing context created by the state in which the metropolitan region exists, and a horizontal dimension, or the relationship between the institutions of government that exist within a metropolitan region. As such, we offer the politico-legal definition of the metropolitan region as the formal and informal relationships between institutions of governing in the area. Brenner (2001) captures our perspective by calling the movement from city to metropolitan region a "new politics of scale." The state is too big, the city is too small, the region is just about right.

The study of the governing of our metropolitan regions is framed by acknowledging a conceptual distinction between government and governance. There have been broad societal changes over the last half century that have had pronounced effects on how we think about and operate in our world. As those changes relate to the public sphere, we are moving from a paradigm centered on government to one centered on governing or governance. Governing is the act of public decision making and is no longer the exclusive domain of governments. Indeed, governments at all levels, nonprofit organizations, and the private sector now work together in new partnerships and relationships that blur sectoral lines. Private businesses, under contract to governments, deliver a wide variety of governmental programs. Conversely, governments are often managing more private sector firms than public sector employees. Nonprofit organizations, often representing organizations of governments, are partnering with governments, private firms, and other nonprofits to deliver services. Private foundations in many metropolitan regions utilize revenues generated from the private sector to finance public, private, and nonprofit organizations in addressing important regional public problems. Although not everyone would agree (see Norris 2001), the study of the metropolitan region seeks to understand the governance of a region while recognizing that governments are important building blocks of the region's structure. From this perspective, each metropolitan region has a structure, and metropolitan regions, collectively, could be said to have different structures.

The metropolitan region exists within an older and more established framework of intergovernmental relations in which state and local governments have operated since before the founding of the United States. Think of a state government and the local governments within its borders as a complex network of parts and wires that somehow are supposed to work together, much like a sound system on which we listen to music, if all the wires are connected correctly. These systems, a sound system and governments, are similar in that they are complex sets of dynamically intertwined and interconnected elements. Each includes inputs, processes, outputs, feedback loops, all within an environment in which they operate and with which they continuously interact. Any change in any element of the system causes changes in other elements. The interconnections tend to be complex, constantly changing, and often unknown. This systems perspective is the overarching framework that will be used to explain state, local, and regional government in the United States.

A model of this traditional system is presented in Figure 1.1. In this simplified presentation, there are four principal actors—the citizen, local governments, state governments, and the federal government. When we use the term "citizen," we mean it in the broadest sense. It is meant to include citizens, local businesses, and other users of services, who also provide the

Figure 1.1   **The Traditional Four Principal Actors in the U.S. System of State and Local Government**

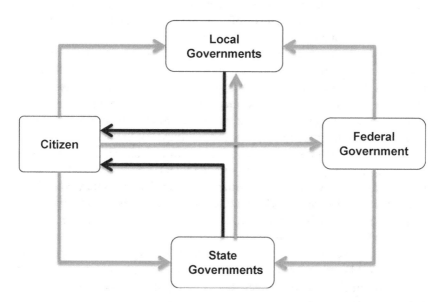

financial resources to those governments. The term "local governments" is used to define localized governmental entities such as towns, cities, counties, special districts, and school districts.

As depicted in Figure 1.1, there is a fundamental structure to the intergovernmental governing system. That structure is made up of expectations, administrative networks, financial flows, and authority relationships such as state and federal mandates. While this figure looks orderly, it is better viewed as loosely structured relationships among the actors.

Put yourself in the box that says "citizen." As a "citizen," you have a set of expectations about what the world around you should look like. You expect to have some say in what that world looks like for you and others around you. To that end, you provide resources to various levels of government in anticipation that the government will be able to match your desired world. If you are like most people, you are not necessarily concerned with which level of government delivers the services, as long as they are provided. More frequently, you are not particularly concerned with whether the public, non-profit, or private sector delivers the service. This is especially true for services generally considered as local.

Now, put yourself in the box that says "local governments." From this vantage point, you receive an allocation of funds in the form of taxes and fees from the "citizen," an allocation of resources from your state government, that may or may not have mandates attached, and some resources from the federal government. With those resources, you try to deliver a bundle of services that reflects the interests of your citizens, the state, and the federal government—not an easy task.

Move down and put yourself in the box that says "state governments." From this vantage point, as with local governments, you receive an allocation mostly in the form of taxes from the "citizen." You also get a fairly healthy allocation from the federal government that may or may not have mandates attached. With these resources you try to deliver a bundle of services to the citizens, either directly or through local governments. Sometimes, you make funds available to those local governments to be your agent in providing state services that you consider important. Other times, you provide funds to those local governments to help them provide local services they considered important. In either case, working with local governments, because they have their own resources, is complicated. Trying to maximize your resources from the federal government will help you achieve all your other goals.

Finally, move over to the "federal government" box. Here, you primarily administer a broad set of domestic policies through the provision of aid to state governments and, on a much more limited scale, to local governments. Under the constitution, you are in a compact with the states and the citizens. The states, each of which has its own constitution, have a legal relationship with their constituent local governments. As such, it is a challenge for you to deal directly with local governments without infringing on the role of the state government.

Life would be much easier if the simple model never varied. Although the model can generally be applied to each of the United States, there are 50 different and very distinct patterns of relationships—one for each state. Each state system has been evolving for centuries. They have become deeply institutionalized with relatively rigid formal and informal rules and expectations about how each government performs its responsibilities as a component in the system.

It is into this rich milieu of relationships that we now introduce a new player—the metropolitan region. The role of the metropolitan region is attached onto the existing patterns of relationships and is defined by them in the process. We have demonstrated this layering of the metropolitan region in Figure 1.2. We understand how the old system works, but we hardly understand the new system at all. We have used the oddly shaped depiction of the metropolitan region to reflect this lack of clarity in our understanding.

For instance, a line from the citizen to the metropolitan region is barely present, currently, in the system. Few, if any, regions have metropolitan-level officials and institutions that are known by citizens. The line from state

Figure 1.2   **The Traditional Four Principal Actors and a New Actor (the Region) in the U.S. System of State and Local Government**

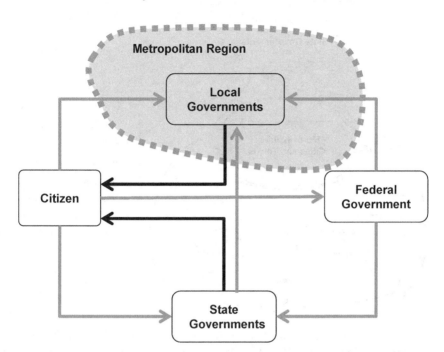

government to the metropolitan region usually goes through institutions of local governments. The line from the federal government to the metropolitan region varies from federal agency to federal agency. One agency of the federal government, the Office of Management and Budget, defines metropolitan regions, but then warns against using those definitions for anything other than statistical applications. Conversely, the Department of Transportation has forced the flow of federal highway dollars through a designated metropolitan organization, generally utilizing the definitions supplied by the Office of Management and Budget.

What we know about the metropolitan region could be answered as both "very little" and "fuzzy." In this way, it represents a frontier. Even though our research into a better understanding of the structure of governance in a metropolitan region is, at best, emerging, the discussion about what an appropriate structure of governance should be is not new. Battle lines have been laid out for more than 100 years, and skirmishes have moved the line back and forth between notions of regions of many governments and regions of few governments. Conceptually, today's discussion on how we manage a region is no different from yesterday's discussion on how we manage a city.

Figure 1.3 **The Three Dimensions of Metropolitan Regional Governance in the United States**

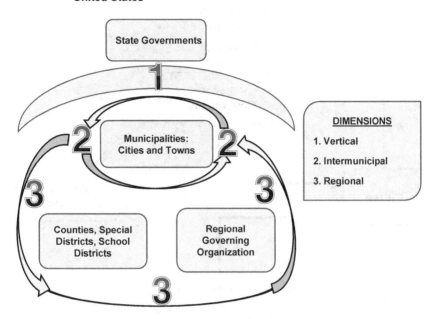

There is a structure to the patterns of relationships that exist within metropolitan regions (Miller and Lee 2011). This structure has three primary dimensions, as seen in Figure 1.3. The first is a vertical dimension represented by the number 1. We have used the symbol of the arch to reflect the overall responsibility that the state has for its territory. Virtually all of the activity that occurs under the arch falls within the domain of the state to define how it will work. As will be demonstrated, states have adopted a wide range of strategies relative to their treatment of local governing institutions. Some states take a relatively hands-off approach and leave much of the design and execution of local governing in the hands of localities. Other states take a relatively authoritarian approach and more directly control the design and function of local governments.

A second dimension is horizontal and involves the fundamental relationships between the municipalities within a metropolitan area. Municipalities, generally defined as cities and townships, are relatively equal in the eyes of the law and custom. They have grants of authority to undertake a number of functions, the power of taxation to implement the desires of its citizens, and the land-use authority to control the nature and direction of development within the community. Municipalities are the building blocks of metropolitan areas and their relationship (or lack thereof) to each other is the key variable in determining whether meaningful regional decision making can occur and how it will occur. We have represented this dimension by the number 2.

The third (represented by the number 3) is also horizontal but involves the fundamental relationships between important governing institutions within a metropolitan area. As such, it captures the emerging notion of metropolitan governance (see Foster 1997; Barnes and Foster 2012). In addition to local governments known as cities and townships, it includes the other principal types of local governments, such as counties, special districts, and school districts. Of the three, some county governments come closest to municipalities relative to function, taxation, and land-use authority. That said, and there are exceptions to the rule, it is seldom to the same degree of freedom as that of municipalities. The districts, special or school, will often lack at least two of the features associated with municipalities. First, they seldom have a broad functional role as they are most often confined to undertake one or two specific services. Second, few special districts have taxing authority and even fewer have land-use regulatory authority. Although special districts are qualitatively distinct, they are nonetheless as much a part of the fabric of metropolitan America as are municipalities.

In addition to traditional forms of local government, there has emerged over the last 50 years an institution born out of the "metropolitinizing" of America that we have named, for lack of a better word, the Regional Governing Organization (RGO). It is usually a single institution within a metropolitan area constituted primarily by local governments increasingly recognized as the place where regional issues and problems can be discussed and, hopefully, resolved. Such an institution exists in every metropolitan region under a wide and wild variety of titles with varying degrees of responsibility. Even though state and federal policies have driven the formation of the RGO, local actors and the willingness of local governments to accept its authority determines its role.

Taken together, these three dimensions play out differently in each metropolitan region, resulting in a wide variety of metropolitan governing structures throughout the United States. In this book we tell the story of the metropolitan region. It is a story that starts long before either of the words "metropolitan" or "region" were connected or even contemplated. Our first task, laid out in Chapters 2 through 6, is to summarize the rich, legal, and historical milieu in which local government has been developed and is practiced.

This task is complicated by the conflicted nature of local governments. Indeed, as demonstrated in Chapter 2, there are two distinct and diametrically opposed visions of local government. One holds local governments to be creatures of their citizens and the other that they are creatures of the state. Currently, a battle is playing out in a winner-take-all war wherein one vision will beat out the other. This is a senseless war because local governments are neither. Rather, they move back and forth between the two visions. Indeed, we want them to be both. That they can move back and forth is both necessary and essential to the success of local governing. The key to regional governing in America is the successful management of the competing visions those visions create separately and the tension they create collectively between them.

A Primer on State and Local Government in America

There are broad similarities and some generalizations that can be made about the roles that state and local governments play in delivering services. These are characterized in Chapter 3. The financial questions of "who between state and local governments delivers what?" and "who levies which type of taxes?" are addressed. The chapter reviews how these questions are currently answered, how they have been answered in the past, and why the answers have changed over time. Chapter 3 also demonstrates how unprepared America's state and local government systems were for the Great Recession.

Chapter 4 is a primer on local government. It breaks down the universe of local government into the primary types of local government, defined earlier as counties, municipalities (townships and cities), and districts (special and school). Each type of local government plays a relatively unique role in the overall system with different responsibilities, funding sources, and importance. After breaking out the local portion of the state-local financial relationships discussed in Chapter 3, each type of local government is examined in more detail.

General-purpose governments, defined as municipalities and sometimes counties, are, arguably, the most important local government players as they relate to building regional governing institutions. Their willingness, or lack thereof, is critical to the success of any such venture. As such, how they differ in their internal organization is also presented in this chapter. The various organizational designs include the mayor-council form, in which executive authority (mayor) and legislative authority (council) exist in an adversarial relationship; the council-manager form, in which executive authority (manager) and legislative authority (council) exist in a nonadversarial or unitary relationship; and the "adapted city" form, in which executive and legislative authority is allocated between council, mayor, and manager.

Chapters 2, 3, and 4 look at the American system taken as a whole, as if there was but one state with one set of local governments. Life should be so simple. Indeed, the American system of local government is, at times, seemingly incomprehensible by virtue of the 50 distinct variations of local government found in the United States. These 50 variations are a direct result of the authority that has been placed in the states (and not the federal government) to administer and govern their internal affairs. As a result, for instance, counties are the primary unit of local government in some states and are nonexistent in others. Chapter 5 is an exploration into these differences and their significance as they relate to building a cohesive set of strategies for regional governance across state systems.

Chapters 2 through 5 lay the foundation for our presentation of the metropolitan region in Chapter 6. For the purposes of this book, we follow the U.S. Office of Management and Budget (OMB) definition of the metropolitan region. OMB refers to a region as a metropolitan statistical area (MSA). We will leave the story of how and why the federal government made such determinations for later. MSAs constitute governable, identifiable urban areas of shared interests and concerns that serve as our focus. Surprisingly, we know a fair amount about these regions relative to how many types of local governments operate in each one and how that relationship varies across the United States. We also know the factors that aid in a region's ability (or resiliency) to react to stresses placed on their regional economies. Also introduced in Chapter 6 is the Metropolitan Power Diffusion Index (MPDI), a measure of the dispersion or concentration of local government power and authority within each MSA. This measure is useful in identifying how the structured relationship among local governments in a region is changing over time and in understanding how the distribution of power and authority fosters (or thwarts) regional governing.

Four Reform Initiatives on the Metropolitan Regional Governing Frontier

The Merriam-Webster Dictionary has two definitions of "frontier" and each has relevance as a descriptor of a metropolitan region. The first is "a region that forms the margin of settled or developed territory." Clearly, a metropolitan region is a set of political jurisdictions that have common interest among themselves that are separate and distinct from another set of political jurisdictions. The second definition is "the furthermost limits of knowledge or achievement in a particular subject." This definition suggests identifying not just the metropolitan region but those features of the metropolitan region that expand our knowledge and understanding a little farther.

Chapter 2 presents four current or potential institutional changes (reforms) that are frontiers on the frontier. Figure 1.4 identifies these reforms. In our view, these four developments balance the tension between the conflicted nature of local governments as identified in Chapter 2 and that build on the

Figure 1.4 **The Four Frontiers Defining the New Governance of Metropolitan Regions**

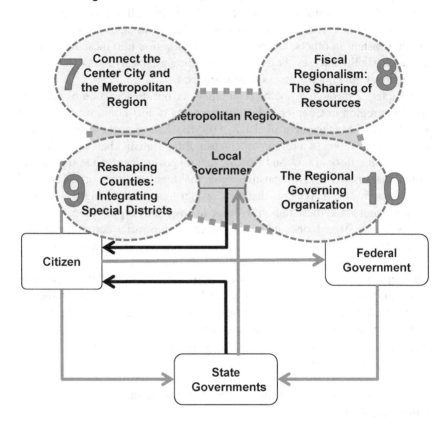

existing relationships of state and local governments identified in Chapters 3, 4, and 5.

Chapter 7 focuses on the political boundary that separates a city from the rest of the region. In addition to a legal distinction, it is also a psychological boundary that connotes the start of the suburbs, which have been created as refuges from the city. As a psychological border, it looms like a physical wall 5 feet wide and 100 feet tall. It has also become an extraordinarily meaningless line that has no value in today's urban world. Yet it remains a dysfunctional legacy of the past that stands in the way of building metropolitan regions. Rethinking city borders is the focus of Chapter 7. Rather than focusing on the differences between city and suburb, the border is used to identify the similarities that exist between the city and the municipalities that share its borders. Such an exercise reveals the potential of region building from the core out.

Chapter 8 is devoted to the simple idea of sharing within a metropolitan region. Coined "fiscal regionalism," the strategy has two distinct versions. The first is the sharing of a source of revenue such as the often-cited Tax-Base Sharing Program used in the Minneapolis-St. Paul metropolitan area. In that program, a percentage of each taxing jurisdiction's growth in taxable value (a measure of economic prosperity) is pooled and allocated based on each jurisdiction's relative fiscal capacity (a measure of need). The result is that tax resources are more evenly distributed across the metropolitan area.

The second is the sharing of the responsibility to provide public goods that are used by the citizens within the region. Examples include the Cultural Asset District in Denver and the Regional Asset District in Pittsburgh. In both metropolitan regions, services like the zoos, sports stadiums, parks, libraries, and arts organizations are financed by the region.

Chapter 9 takes one of the oldest local government types—the county—and repackages it as a type of regional government within a regional governing system. It also takes the newest of government types—the special district—and integrates it into the fabric of a metropolitan region. Counties have always had the potential to be regional governments, but, until recently, they have had neither the reason, capacity, nor interest to be cast in such a role. However, in many parts of the United States under the concept broadly characterized as the "urban county," counties once thought of as rural dead ends are transforming into players that have a major impact on and role in regional governing. These special districts have the potential to be important regional institutions. They also have the potential to create technical silos isolated and insulated from the region they are supposed to benefit. As with the first two frontiers (urban core and fiscal regionalism), the reshaped county and integrated special districts, as paths to metropolitan governing, build on the existing structure of local government relations within a metropolitan area.

The final institutional frontier is the subject of Chapter 10. To the degree that the metropolitan region is the "new kid on the block," the "kid" needs to be represented by an institutional arrangement that focuses on its interests. Such an institution now exists in every metropolitan region in the United States. It has been empowered by federal and, to a lesser extent, state dollars as well as the practical necessity created by problems and issues being oblivious to geopolitical boundaries. They go by wildly different names, engage in widely different activities, and represent wildly different potentials to glue a metropolitan region together. We refer to these institutions as Regional Governing Organizations (RGOs). Chapter 10 presents the state of RGOs in America with all of their potential, missteps, and current practices. That said, we also demonstrate that this frontier, like the others, aids in adjudicating the conflicting tensions between competing notions of local government.

Figure 1.5   **Obstacles and Issues Confronting the Emergence of Regional Decision Making**

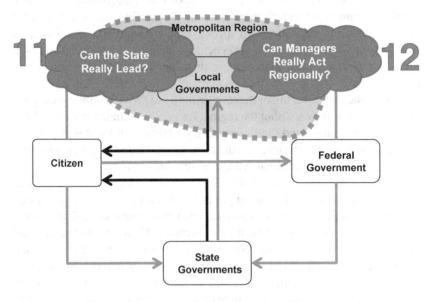

Unresolved Questions

The list of obstacles to the governing of metropolitan regions is formidable. Reducing the list to just a few is obviously difficult. However, our premise for this book is twofold. First, local governments are the building blocks of metropolitan regions, and second, we want local governments to serve a dual role. Sometimes we want them be a creature of the state and sometimes we want them to be a creature of the citizen. Being able to move back and forth between these two visions requires the resolution of two important questions. We have captured these two questions as the storm clouds in Figure 1.5.

The first question is straightforward: Can the state really lead in the movement to build metropolitan regions? This is a question of both capacity and will. As we examine these questions in more detail, we find that the states do have the capacity to help foster metropolitan governance. In truth, settled judicial law all but makes it mandatory for states to be an active and positive influence on metropolitan efforts. We will explore in Chapter 11 the more pressing question of whether the state legislature and the executive branch have apolitical interest in supporting efforts to revitalize and regionalize governance.

The second question is: Can managers really act regionally? Local governments need to move from regional consumers to regional citizens. A local government is a place where its citizens engage in making decisions about their community. It works best when citizens are working together for the good of the whole. How often do local government officials admonish its citizens when it appears they are showing unbridled self-interest? At the same time, those same officials will enter the regional arena and behave in exactly the same manner they just admonished their own citizens for. If local governments are to be the building blocks of the metropolitan region, they must behave and act like regional citizens. Citizenship is the ability to balance one's own interests with collective interests. Consumership is the act of transacting in the pursuit of one's interests while being benignly ambivalent to the impact those transactions may have on others.

Obstacles to moving from regional consumership to regional citizenship are the topic of Chapter 12. We focus on the professional managers and the norms, values, and education they receive, primarily as articulated through the International City/County Management Association (ICMA) and the graduate school curriculum offered by schools accredited by the National Association of Schools of Public Policy and Administration (NASPAA). Currently, those norms, values, and education are heavily skewed toward regional consumership, and regional citizenship is, at best, still at the margins.

In Chapter 13 we explore whether the concept of the metropolitan region as a governance model will occur. Without giving away the ending, we can say at this point that certain elements of regional governance are inevitable. That said, we also acknowledge that the level of interest among public officials in many suburbs, cities, and at the state level is low and nascent. While not always as hostile as it has been in the past, the prevailing attitude among those officials might be best described as benign neglect. Regional initiatives must be approved by the states, but those legislatures rarely take an active role in shaping metropolitan governance. Rather, state legislatures have not shown any interest in driving metropolitan reform. They merely react to efforts coming from the metropolitan areas. In this sense the "politics" of metropolitan and regional governance is almost exclusively local. Currently, metropolitan reform is the domain (some would say hostage) of local government officials based upon the collective decisions of those local officials.

The process of building regional decision making is messy and, as such, we see both encouraging and discouraging signs. As we career toward a new way of governance, we have organized our concluding thoughts and observations into three categories. The first broadly covers what we consider to be the encouraging signs in building a framework for regional decision making. The second covers the discouraging signs that continue to act as weights on the process. The third summarizes our recommendations for steps that important institutions and actors should take to move toward more effective means of true regional governance.

2
Creatures of Whom?
The Intentionally Conflicted Nature of Local Government in America

Practitioners of American public administration are familiar with the 1868 dicta of Justice John Dillon that local governments are "mere tenants at will of their respective state legislatures" and could be eliminated by the legislature with a "stroke of the pen" (1868). Specifically, the ruling was as follows:

> Municipal corporations owe their origin to, and derive their powers and rights wholly from, the legislature. It breathes into them the breath of life, without which they cannot exist. As it creates, so it may destroy. If it may destroy, it may abridge and control. Unless there is some constitutional limitation on the right, the legislature might, by a single act, if we can suppose it capable of so great a folly and so great a wrong, sweep from existence all of the municipal corporations in the State, and the corporation could not prevent it. We know of no limitation on this right so far as the corporations themselves are concerned. They are, so to phrase it, the mere tenants at will of the legislature.

For more than 140 years it has been settled law that the states establish the purpose and nature of the local governments within their boundaries. As little more than "mere tenants at will," local governments are subject to the dictates and views of the various legislatures. Issues from zoning to regionalization are matters left to the states. Nothing could be more straightforward.

Unfortunately, it is not that simple. Even Justice Dillon was more perceptive of the political realities than the stereotypical legacy his decision would imply. Consider his warning to those very legislatures he had just empowered. In his ruling, he states that if legislatures did exercise such authority it would be, "so great a wrong and so great a folly." He was saying, "you can, but you really can't."

Dillon's rule treads a hazy line that constitutes an unresolved but necessary tension between the legal nature of our local governments and their political-cultural nature. This tension has created two diametrically opposed foundational principles on which local government in the United States is organized.

Figure 2.1 **The Two Competing but Necessary Foundation Principles on Which Local Government Is Built in the United States**

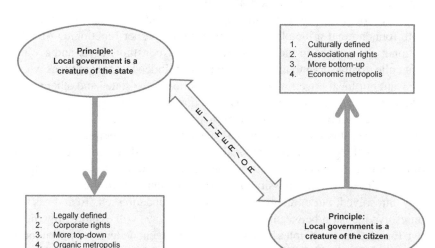

They are graphically presented in Figure 2.1. From a legal and administrative perspective, one foundational principle asserts that local governments cannot be sovereign; they are *creatures of the state*. They need to be, institutionally, subdivisions of the state, which is the sovereign. Someone or some institution has to be able to make the final decisions—in this case the centralized state. But from a political-cultural perspective, the other foundational principle asserts that local governments represent a citizen's constitutional right to freedom of association; local governments, no less than the states, are *creatures of the citizen*. The "wrong" and "folly" occur when the state exercises its power to take those associational rights casually. Then, as now, citizens guard their right to associate with great zeal and vigor. The Jeffersonian ideal/myth of the yeoman farmer embodying all that is best in democracy is deeply rooted in the American political psyche. The invocation of home rule was both a call for reform in the nineteenth century and an assertion of the superiority of small governments in the late twentieth century.

The halting pattern of political and institutional reform at the local level is a result of the tension between these two traditions. With few exceptions (the metropolitanization movement at the end of the nineteenth century and the boomlet of regionalization in the 1950s and 1960s), the political-cultural tradition has proven to be both powerful and resilient. Partly because of the twin financial crises of the first decade of the twenty-first century, we seem to be at the cusp of another rethinking of intergovernmental relations (IGR) (Cox 2009). The extent to which such changes will succeed and the general direction of the change will be a product of how the two foundational principles are captured in any new policies that emerge.

At the core of modernizing metropolitan regions is an understanding that both foundational principles are essential to the proper functioning of subnational governance in the United States. They constitute a yin and a yang that collectively serve to allow each to coexist. Indeed, there are times when we want our local governments to be "creatures of the state" and other times when we expect them to behave as "creatures of the citizen." Most efforts aimed to reform of the governance of metropolitan regions fail because they have ignored this basic tension. These foundational principles need to be first acknowledged as legitimate and important and then addressed in a set of policies that manage the tension and conflict between those two competing principles. It is not possible to resolve the tension. In the end, it must stay unresolved; but unresolved does not mean unaddressed. To address the unresolved tension between these two traditions, we will explore how these two foundational principles have led to such divergent understandings of local governance in the United States.

Theories of Local Government

It would be helpful for this discussion if there were a theory of local government. However, as William Mackenzie states, "There is no theory of local government. There is no normative general theory from which we can deduce what local government ought to be; there is no positive general theory on which we can derive testable hypotheses" (1961, 1). Roger Benjamin asserts, "The absence of theory must be identified as the major problem in the study of local government. Without theory, contradictory conclusions and policy recommendations may be reached, sometimes from the same data" (1980, 73–74). David Walker comments that "perhaps the greatest weakness of local government today is the absence of a theory that describes and interrelates the operational, political, and jurisdictional roles of local governments" (1986, 86).

Why the dearth of theory? Most of the earliest colonies were little more than villages or a cluster of villages (Plymouth, Providence, Massachusetts Bay, and New Amsterdam). From the standpoint of governance, the distinguishing feature of the early American colonies (especially the northern colonies) was the freedom to create new local governance models and to develop a theory of governance to justify and support these new forms. Even as the colonies spread west, the tension between the necessity and expectation of independence of governance and the development of supra-structures of governance that were more "distant" is striking. Local governments developed and flourished without input from any except those who were local (see, for example, Zuckerman 1970). The colony-level political structure had a limited effect on local practices, thus allowing for the independent development of both growing towns and growing colonies.

Anwar Syed (1966) observes that such a development leads to, on one hand, a popular image of local governments culturally traceable to Jeffersonian values of a "good" republic built from the bottom up and, on the other hand, a more centrist official image embodied in legal doctrine. Gerald Frug (1980) maintains that the American political system plays one image against the other based on changing values and fears. Jane Mansbridge (1980) considers the former image as face-to-face or unitary democracy and the latter as pluralistic or adversarial democracy. William Schambra (1982) sees the two images of governance in a dialectic and historical contradiction extending back to the positions of the Federalists and anti-Federalists in the late eighteenth century (see also Jillson 1988). The Massachusetts constitution of 1780 affirmed the inherent conflict between local and state interests by giving local governments a strong influence over the composition of the state House of Representatives, yet it also left to the legislature considerable and broad latitude over the structure and form of local and county governments. Thus, even the seven permissible forms of government are defined in statute, not in local charters.

The tension implied here is also observable as a tension between structure and process. Although the structures of government influence the administration of government, the core processes are shaped by political theory. The modern concept of democratic governance is associated with a set of principles of political philosophy focusing on relationships between the individual and the government. Max Weber defines a *democracy* as providing formal rights of equal opportunities (Weber 1946). Popularly, democracy is linked to the idea of participation and the right to vote, but there is also an organizational aspect. Critical for this analysis is the definition of process values of democracy that make initiating, inventing, and bringing about public policy possible. Three points are critical:

1. Practice is shaped by and, in turn, validates structure.
2. Values are related to the structure.
3. Structural elements overlap and reinforce one another.

The structural elements combine to form the internal logic of democracy. Democracy is identified as the interaction among the basic structures and values that frame the operational processes in a democratic form of government. Democracy is more than the sum of the processes that it invokes. Developing archetypal structures provides a methodology for contrasting that democratic structure with the way decisions are made in modern governments.

The values of democracy include equality, equity, and public interest. Each of these values, and the concerns they reflect, relate to another value— the interdependence of people and of institutions. A democratic structure reflects the values both as abstract goals (such as equity and equality) and as everyday practical realities (participation to determine the public interest). The values as goals are not met fully; rather, the structures and processes become approximations of what can be achieved. The structure provides the context for the processes, which are judged by the standards of the abstract goals. Understanding the relationship of the structures to both the goals and the processes permits an analysis of what manner of democracy has been, or can be, achieved.

Implicit in the idea of democracy in government is that some level of in- dividuality exists in a society or organization. People will see problems and, therefore, the solutions to those problems differently. The fact of individual differences is more critical than the reasons for those differences. The key is to create a structure that preserves the opportunity to be heard (makes oth- ers aware that you disagree). Further, the concept of being heard is one that begins at the point of defining problems, not with the subsequent process of shaping solutions.

The lesson of this structure is that three elements are critical: (1) a mean- ingful process of public discussion (including tolerance and a disposition to be persuaded, as well as to persuade), (2) a reliance on consensus building in decision making, and (3) a recognition of the importance of community (Cox, Buck, and Morgan 2011). Democracy emerges from a sense of the collective responsibility for the creation of mutually acceptable goals and mutually iden- tified problems. The intended government was organized to give the people the fullest opportunity to participate, directly or indirectly. We may disagree with the balance between direct and indirect participation chosen at the time, but the fundamental reason for desiring participation has not altered. Partici- pation is not a mathematical process but a subjective, qualitative relationship between individuals and society. The institutions of government were built on the use of consensus. The goal was to define what was best for society, not for any individual or group. The "best for society" did not emerge from a simple vote; rather, it emerged from a three-step process of open discussion, agreement on the scope of action, and then agreement on a temporary course of action. The focus was on collective social action, not on the implementa- tion of the top choice among rationally analyzed alternatives.

A government structured to make decisions through consensus was a government that prized diversity of ideas and opinions. The central purpose of any participative process is to permit the many views that may exist on a policy issue to be heard and considered. The eighteenth-century advocates of "harmony" (Zuckerman 1970) embraced the clash of interests because they believed that harmony emerged from successful completion of seemingly frantic and chaotic public discourse. Harmony results from knowing and understanding the views of others, not from suppressing them. Without toleration of contrary views, the introduction of additional views would appear to detract from, rather than contribute to, good decisions. Disagreement was expected, but so was a disposition to accept the possibility of being persuaded by opposing views.

Direct democracy is rare in the twenty-first century. The concept of representative democracy shares much with the ongoing debate about regional governance. The fundamental question is: What does it mean to represent others? Historically the answer has come from two dichotomous perspectives. The first model is the ideal of the representative as a delegate whose role is to give voice to the views of others; that is, the person is little more than a spokesperson who represents the opinions of others. John Adams referred to this model as a meeting of ambassadors (Adams 1856). The second model, most closely associated with Edmund Burke, calls on elected representatives to engage in a dialogue with others to learn their views for the purpose of creating a result that reflects a broader purpose (Burke 1949). Burke believed he owed his constituents his best judgment because, ultimately, as a member of Parliament he was to speak on behalf of his constituency but to act in the national interest. In the first model, the representative never veers from the perceived interests of a narrow constituency, operating as though the actions outside that geographical constituency are not relevant to defining problems. The second model focuses on presenting local interests as a first step toward defining the broader interest.

This is at the core of the tension as we see it today. We value independence above all else. Independence has become the end rather than a means. The opportunity to participate is an option we may or may not choose to exercise. As long as we can be materially successful in this "splendid isolation," we are content. We would rather not experience conflict. Thus, the core of democracy is to be abhorred; to be left alone is preferable. We seek communities of the like-minded so that conflict is unlikely. We participate with others to protect our isolation.

Often by invoking the spirit of Thomas Jefferson, Americans have come to understand the processes and values of democracy (governance) as possible only in small governments. Yet in this choice we have disconnected the structures of democracy from the processes. We do not take advantage of the opportunity to participate. In the community of the like-minded, we need not participate, confident that those who do participate speak with the same voice. A diversity of viewpoints is the problem. Even the possibility of debate is to be avoided. We grow impatient with mandates for debate and discourse. We want results but not commitment. We love cities for their endless variety, but we do not want to live in them. Democracy should be neat and tidy. We devalue government organizations. Government-led solutions are suspect. Our bias toward partnerships is in the impermanence of those partnerships.

For some 200 (in some sense, nearer 400) years, there has been no unifying theory of local government. The conflict has been resolved as we resolve all such matters—by politics. Not the politics of pluralism and discourse (Mansbridge 1980), but the politics of the market in which those who think alike cluster together. Just as the villages and towns found that the goal of harmony led to splintering communities into smaller and smaller units, we value homogeneous community in which harmony prevails and debate and discourse are unnecessary. We prefer small towns because we can contentedly avoid participation. These are self-governing communities, not in a democratic sense of self-governing but in the sense of the absence of government. This idyllic view of the small town dominates the American vision of proper government. This view is often manifested in the proliferation of gated communities that require conformity to a rigid set of rules of behavior (Blakely and Snyder 1997).

How Theory Impacts Metropolitan Government

Just as they have shaped our image of local government, the two notions derived from each foundational principle define how metropolitan regions ought to be governed. The first, the metropolitan region as an organic whole, sees a metropolitan region that happens to be made up of local governments. The second, the metropolitan region as a group of local public economies, sees a collection of local governments that happen to be in a metropolitan region. The former is reflected in a publication of the National Research Council (1999), and the latter in a series of readings edited by Michael McGinnis (1999) and another by Richard Feiock (2004).

The Organic Metropolis

The quest for a centralized metropolis as an organic whole comes and goes like the tide. Within the last century, there have been three distinct periods in which the notion has had its greatest currency. With the first wave of decentralization from the city in the early 1900s came a corresponding movement within planning circles that recognized inherent problems with the movement away from the central city. The solution, to planners, was self-evident and is embodied in George Hooker's statement, "the enlarging of the city to match the real metropolitan community is the natural method of dealing advantageously with metropolitan city planning problems" (1917, 343).

A second wave of interest in metropolitan regions took place in the 1960s and 1970s. It was rooted in the post–World War II scale of urban living that extended far beyond the existing metropolitan core and traveled deep into the periphery, so that the notion of an urban field was replacing the traditional concepts of city and metropolis (Friedman and Miller 1965). As suggested by Michael Keating (1995), this interest in the metropolitan area corresponded with the rapidly expanding role of government and the establishment of the American version of the modern welfare state. As a result, this interest bundled together political theories of metropolitan organization and an activist social welfare role of the state into a single theory. To advocate one was to advocate the other.

The third wave of interest occurred in the mid-1990s. It surfaced primarily as a reaction to the globalization of the world economy, to the perceived decay of center cities and the inner ring of suburbs surrounding those cities, and to the growing disparities in economic wealth between jurisdictions in those metropolitan areas (National Research Council 1999). This "iron law of urban decay," it is argued, is an artifact of our system's design (fragmentation) and not as the natural order of events (Luria and Rogers 1999). More recently, the nonsustainability of rapidly sprawling regions has buttressed this argument (Katz 1998; Berube et al. 2010; Muro and Katz 2010).

Much of the regionalist movement of the latter part of the twentieth century and early part of the twenty-first is built on the notion that an emerging world economy exists in which new organizations of different scale are needed. It is built on the assumption that a great paradox is shaping the organization of society on a global basis. "The planet is falling precipitously apart and coming reluctantly together at the very same moment" (Barber 1995, 5). On one hand, there is a deconcentration of society occurring that can be referred to as a return to tribes; on the other hand, the new economic order is forcing a new globalism, in that it is creating a planet of metropolitan regions.

Why metropolitan regions? The answer is complicated, but the imperative is to drive economic competitiveness and in the process to maintain community by addressing efficient service delivery and social equity (Katz 1998; Benjamin and Nathan 2001; Berube et al. 2010; Muro and Katz 2010). The economic imperative is derived from assumptions about the emerging global economy. Michael Porter (1998) has coined the term *clusters* to describe how businesses will prosper in the future. Unlike prior economic periods when businesses simply moved to areas with low production costs, businesses must now seek out areas where a critical mass of businesses in a particular field enjoy competitive success through the geographical concentration of interconnected companies and institutions. Silicon Valley and Hollywood are examples of clusters (see also Florida 2002, 2004, 2007). Clusters are supported by "local things" that further serve the existing clusters, the monopoly that the clusters have in the world economy, and the ability of the clusters to expand and support the local economy.

Douglas Henton, John Melville, and Kimberly Walesh (1997) have identified four features of clusters, or regional habitats, that make them valuable to businesses. The first is easy access to specialized workforces. Obviously, where there is a high concentration of jobs in a particular field, it is easier for businesses to obtain the workforce necessary to undertake their functions. Second, clustering enhances the research and commercialization capacities of businesses in the cluster. Third, clustering creates important innovation networks that allow local businesses to retain a competitive advantage over their competition. Finally, clustering creates a locally contextual business infrastructure that supports the companies in ways that create a working relationship between the institutions within a region and the agglomeration of businesses in that region.

Several of the essential ingredients of a successful cluster require the political institutions of the region to work together in ways that enhance the competitive position of the cluster. For instance, Porter (1998, 80) identifies the need for a high-quality transportation infrastructure, well-educated employees, and a tax and regulatory environment that addresses the specific needs of the cluster. Richard Florida (2002, 2004, 2007) suggests a more diversified and environmentally self-conscious approach to make a region attractive to innovative and creative individuals. Hence, the need for regionalism to support any cluster is established. Logically, a new geopolitical structure is necessary to match the cluster structure of the global economy. That matching structure is the metropolitan region.

The organic-whole argument has been supported by research that attempts to establish an interdependent link between the central city and the surrounding suburbs (Ledebur and Barnes 1993; Savitch et al. 1993; Downs 1994; National Research Council 1999). The essence of the argument is that the success of a metropolitan region is based on the improving economic health of both the center city and the suburbs: the stronger the economic growth of the center city, the stronger the economic growth of the suburbs. Conversely, an economically distressed center city adversely impacts the economic growth of the suburbs. The image portrayed is of a heart pumping oxygen to the body. The center city serves as the place to which people migrate from outside the region. As center city residents become more affluent, they move to the suburbs. Successful suburbs are therefore dependent on new immigrants to the metropolitan region as their future residents. Charles Adams and colleagues (1996) demonstrate that the outmigration from economically weaker center cities tends to be to suburban areas in other metropolitan regions. Conversely, outmigration from economically stronger central cities tends to be to the suburbs of that metropolitan region.

The economic reasoning behind the metropolitan region as an organic whole has a social equity counterpart. David Rusk (1993, 1999, 2003a) asserts that poverty and its resulting social dysfunctions are made worse by its concentration and that the elimination of poverty is a necessary end of any society. Poverty begets poverty. Governments with the highest concentrations of poor are becoming increasingly unable to cope with the costs of that concentrated poverty. Deconcentrating poverty, according to Rusk, is a regional responsibility that requires regional institutions, particularly in the areas of land use planning, fair-share housing plans, and revenue-sharing programs.

Generally, the preferred organizational design of the metropolitan region that follows from this model is one in which the integration of local governments is maximized. This can be accomplished either through reducing the actual number of governments or by increasing the mandated coordination of those governments by a higher level of government. The metropolitan region is a well-oiled machine that has minimized its disparities and maximized its external competitiveness. It can be logically deduced from the first foundational principle that, as "creatures of the state," local governments can be reorganized to better serve the interests of the state.

The Economic Metropolis

The application of economics to the study of political institutions has emerged as an increasingly sophisticated analytical approach (Frey 1978; Mueller 1979; Oakerson 1999). As it relates to local government, Charles Tiebout (1956) advanced the proposition that the more governments that exist in a metropolitan area, the more choices consumers have in selecting a community in which to reside that matches their preferences for the public goods they would like to receive and for which they are willing to pay (or, as seems to be the case today, not pay). After all, local governments are "creatures of the citizen."

As it relates to conceptualizing the nature of local government, three new ideas are derived from such a framework.

First, that market forces fueled by competitive processes are the optimal means to achieve efficiency and effectiveness. Application of this notion to a local government is both new and controversial. Local governments would become less like body politics and more like stores in a shopping mall selling a particular bundle of public goods and services at a particular price. Ideally, as a business, each local government would select and price a bundle of services that a sufficient number of voter-consumers would be interested in receiving such that they would elect to reside within the boundaries of that local government (Ostrom, Tiebout, and Warren 1961; Ostrom 1972).

Second, local governments are in competition with other local governments for voter-consumers. As such, municipalities must make their bundle of services and the price they charge for those services attractive. If there are a number of local governments in an area, the ones with the lower cost per unit of desired services delivered would be more successful than the others. Such competition would force less effective local governments to either replace their bundle of services or reduce what they charge for it (Peterson 1981; Schneider 1989).

Third, it is possible to separate the question of the provision of services from the production of those services. Although it may be a government's responsibility to provide a particular service, there is a wide array of means by which that service can be produced. Contracting with another public, nonprofit, or private entity; entering into an intergovernmental partnership; or providing the service directly are simply different modes of delivery that can be assessed on the basis of their efficiency and effectiveness in serving the interests of the local government responsible for the provision of that service (Oakerson 1999, 2004; Feiock 2004).

From this perspective local governments (or homeowners associations, special districts, and other public service delivery institutions) become a form of public household representing a group of citizens who share a common sense of purpose or want. In essence, each of these public households is a local public economy (Oakerson 1999). These local public economies engage in collective action and behave in a way that mirrors how individuals act as they seek their self-interests. In this manner, true voter-consumer preferences can be revealed, fiscal equivalence—in the sense that there is a strong relationship between who pays for and who receives a public good—can be identified, and accountability can be maximized.

A metropolitan area becomes an arena in which local public economies engage in rational collective behavior. Metropolitan governance is the act of making the rules and setting the framework that allows local public economies to engage in rational action. *Rational action* refers to actors creating arrangements that are mutually beneficial and in the enlightened self-interest of each of the local public economies. From these postulates, an abundance of research on how actors behave has emerged. Research on behavior has been used to understand how different rules and frameworks adjust the manner in which actors negotiate (Feiock and Carr 2001; Post 2004; Steinacker 2004; Carr and LeRoux 2005), how IGRs are a form of self-promotion for local officials seeking more regional offices (Bickers, Post, and Stein 2006), the role of reciprocity in fostering different arrangements (Lubell and Scholz 2001), and how norms and traditions of cooperation impact the willingness of actors to engage in cooperation (Olberding 2002).

The idea of local public economies derived from the field of economics is not without a political science companion. American political theory at the time of the American Revolution and the founding of the nation was based on a contract theory of the state (Syed 1966; Wickwar 1970; Frug 1980). During the nation-state building process of the last thousand years, Western political theorists have struggled with understanding how the state came into existence (Fukuyama 2011). To theorists such as John Locke (1632–1704) and Thomas Hobbes (1588–1679), before civilization, humans lived in a "state of nature." Both Locke and Hobbes theorized that humans needed to leave the state of nature and form a society. In the process of forming this society, humans entered into a contract with each other. As such, the governing of this new society was sometimes by, but always for, the individuals who had agreed to the contract. The American founders were very familiar with contracts, such as the Magna Carta and the Mayflower Compact, and reflected this perspective in the Declaration of Independence. Indeed, the first words of the U.S. Constitution are "We the people of the United States."

Polycentricity, as an economic theory, and the contract notion of the state, as a political theory, have combined to offer a powerful set of working assumptions bolstered by the analytics of economics. Generally, the preferred organizational design of the metropolitan region, which follows from this model of the region, is one in which the structure of local government has been designed to maximize individual preferences through the enhancing of competition among local governments. This can be accomplished by maintaining a significant number of local governments. It flows logically from the second foundational principle that, as "creatures of the citizen," local governments should be autonomous from the state to better serve the interests of the citizens.

Reconciling the Two Foundational Principles

Unfortunately, neither foundational principle alone can be used to organize our metropolitan regions. Both need to be accommodated in defining the relationship between the local governments and regional institutions that are created. Those institutions cannot be simple extensions of constituent local governments. Conversely, they cannot be created in spite of local government. Rather, they must be explicitly designed to be simultaneously local and regional (see Frug and Barron 2008).

Having a regional institution that is a simple extension of local governments means that local governments can do anything collectively that they can do individually. Because such actions are voluntary, the agenda will be restricted to a few activities that can generate unanimity of action. Further, the local governments can and will act collectively only when it is in their individual private interests to do so. In their critique, Frug and Barron (2008) argue that creating a functional division of power based on the idea that governmental functions can be divided into those that serve a parochial conception of self-interest and those that serve the greater good is a formula for failure. Such a model merely enables localities to advance a privatized notion of self-interest. Scott Bollens's (2008) study of special district formation in Southern California concludes that representation on regional policy boards by local government officials does not necessarily create regional constituencies, but merely allows local governments to operate in a regional forum to protect and enhance local interests even at the expense of regional goals. The notion of two-tiered government presumes that the tension between the local and regional can be solved through indifference. Rather than address the relationship between local and regional, the strategy is to divorce them and create separate domains.

Creating regional institutions that are divorced from local governments or are created in spite of local government institutions is an equally flawed approach. As the distance grows between the regional organization and the local governments within the region, the regional institution lacks the underlying credibility necessary to be effective.

Regions as Networks

One way to begin sorting through this dilemma is to think of our metropolitan regions as networks. Such a perspective accommodates both foundational principles and represents a way of thinking about how we govern as opposed to the study of governments (Agranoff 1990, 2001).

H. George Frederickson, in his 1999 John Gaus Lecture at the American Political Science Association, noted the growing use of interdepartmental agreements across municipalities. Under this arrangement, department heads (whether public works, parks and recreation, police, or fire) developed formal or informal cooperative agreements with their counterparts in other communities within a region. This behavior was attributed to the need to create economies of scale to make certain services more affordable and/or to improve the overall quality of service delivery. Mutual aid agreements for public safety units have been in place for several decades, but Frederickson also noted two aspects of this practice that he defined as new or innovative. The first was that the impetus for the arrangements came from within the departments, not from the political side of government; that is, it was viewed as simply an extension of "good" service delivery. The second was that the arrangements were viewed by the city managers as economically vital for their individual communities. This regionalization of services was touted as a significant step precisely because it came from within the professional community. It was argued that it avoided the political contentiousness that other regional proposals often engendered and that it permitted those who could benefit from cooperation to do so without getting the permission of those who might be opposed to the arrangements (Thurmaier and Wood 2003). In counterpoint, O'Toole and Meier (2004) expressed concern about the dark side of these management-dominated arrangements, in that the socially and politically powerful have an advantage.

These arrangements are of interest in part because they take for granted most of the foundational principles of the economic vision of the metropolitan area. It is as much self-interest as it is better services that drives this practice (Howell-Moroney 2008). Even when the search for better service is the goal, it is done through a search for like-minded departments and governments. It becomes a way to sell the uniqueness or distinctiveness of a community even as it cooperates with others. It ducks the entire issue of governance and presumes that what is being done is some kind of politically neutral, professionally driven administrative practice.

The tactics for expanded intergovernmental cooperation continue to straddle the line between the visions of the metropolis. As has been true for much of our history, the economic model predominates. Concerns about that model abound, if for no other reason than its historical links to polycentric models that challenge the need for metropolitanization of any type.

The European Union

An interesting development in Europe might help us think through how we design our governance systems in metropolitan regions in the United States. The European Union (EU) has been called "an ongoing experiment in fashioning a new structure of governance" (Sbragia 1993, 23) and "a current experiment with regional governance without regional government" (Sbragia and Stolfi 2012). Without knowing that the context for these statements was the EU, it would have been easy to presume the author was discussing metropolitan regions in the United States.

Before proceeding with this argument, a large disclaimer is in order.

Analogies between the EU and metropolitan regions in the United States can be taken only so far. For instance, the creation of a common market was an important outcome that cannot easily be replicated in metropolitan regions in the United States. The perceived necessity to minimize the military threat of a reconstituted Germany proved to be a powerful early incentive for the EU that has no corollary in the United States. Indeed, the EU emerged as a top-down political instrument only after the common market proved to be an extremely successful economic instrument. Trading a little bit of one's sovereignty for prosperity may truly underlie the apparent willingness of many to engage in this experiment in regional governance. Further, the EU's governmental restructuring is neither complete nor without serious structural problems. Among the unresolved issues is that the vast majority of the citizens of the individual states in Europe have yet to fully embrace even a modest notion of European citizenship (Judt 2010).

With those caveats, the EU does stand as testimony that the two competing foundational principles can be harmonized. Indeed, the EU, unlike American metropolitan regions, has had to overcome the added problems of language differences, currency incompatibility, and centuries of wars and military occupations. The EU's success in dealing with those added complexities should signal to America's metropolitan regions that seemingly insurmountable obstacles can be overcome.

At the core of the transformation of Europe into the European Union is the transfer of partial sovereignty from the constituent governments to a regional authority. Such power sharing is a form of dual sovereignty, a political concept familiar to and embodied in U.S. political institutions. The regional authority (the EU) can impose rules and regulations on the constituent governments when a supermajority of those constituent governments decides it is in the best interests of the whole. As such, the EU is not simply an aggregation of each government wherein each government has the ability to veto actions unilaterally. Conversely, the associational rights connected with each nation allow each member to manage its own affairs.

Certainly, the transformation of the EU was made possible by the institution of qualified majority voting as a substitute for the veto power of any particular government. *Qualified majority voting* is an ambiguous term that is used in the EU context. We abandon it here in favor of a more descriptive explanation, a supermajority. As practiced in the EU, each member receives a number of votes approximately equivalent to population but weighted to give smaller members greater voice. In this manner, 345 votes are allocated with 29 each to Germany, France, the United Kingdom, and Italy as the largest members. Malta, the smallest, receives three votes. Generally, for a law to pass, it must be backed by a majority (in some cases, a two-thirds majority) of the members, receive 255 of the 345 votes, and be supported by 62 percent of the total EU population. It should also be noted that this form of voting is reserved to a specific number of policy areas. In practice, the policy areas that are covered by supermajority voting are ever-expanding, as members grow more comfortable with it as a way to make decisions. Further, there are a number of key policy areas that still require unanimity. Significantly, the list of covered areas is growing as the list of sensitive areas is shrinking.

As we have noted earlier, democratic governance is more than the sum of its processes. The EU as a representative institution offers insights on more than a way to structure and organize a set of intergovernmental relationships. Although still in a nascent form, the EU has created, through the introduction of a partially universal currency and broad-ranging regulations through its administrative agencies, the possibility of a transcendent interest. Reinforced by supermajority voting and other protections for national interests, the members of the EU Parliament and its administrative agencies have the opportunity to function based on the Burkean model of representation. There is an identifiable European interest manifest in its decisions.

Concluding Thoughts and Things to Ponder

Three classic political theory questions are "who should rule?"; "where does the locus of authority lie?"; and "is that authority sufficient to the task of governance?" In the context of local governments in the United States there are no easy answers to any of these questions. Dillon's Rule at the very least implies that the locus of authority is with the states. However, in the development of home rule statements in state constitutions and/or broad statutory grants of authority, local governments on some service delivery and policy matters have considerable leeway within which to operate. The answers to the other two questions are yet more ambiguous. The question of who should rule is influenced by political ideological perspectives on the nature of government itself. As the discussion in this chapter points out, local governments in the United States are organized and operate upon two conflicting founding principles (see Figure 2.1). The halting pattern of political and institutional reform at the local level is a result of the tension between these two traditions. With few exceptions, the political-cultural tradition has proven to be both powerful and resilient. Partly because of the twin financial crises of the first decade of the twenty-first century, we seem to be on the cusp of another rethinking of intergovernmental relations. The extent to which such changes will succeed and the general direction of the change will be a product of how the two foundational principles are captured in any new policies that emerge. One thing seems certain; to organize metropolitan areas around either the

organic or economic model does not work. The economic metropolis has
been the primary driver of regional service delivery. These efforts are at best
a starting point, and are not sufficient. On the other hand, the organic model of
the metropolitan region is one in which the integration of local governments
is maximized. This can be accomplished either through reducing the actual
numbers of governments or by increasing the mandated coordination of those
governments by some higher level of government. Such a perspective demands
a strong interest from state government in reorganizing these "creatures of
the state" to better serve the interests of the state. There is no evidence that
the states wish to become the catalyst for such wholesale reorganization of
local government.

The question of who should rule has many layers. When treated as a legal
issue, models such as the EU are relevant. On the other hand, the precepts
of an economic metropolis suggest that the answer lies with the lowest common denominator government—meaning the answer is either everyone or
no one.

We are a long way from answering these questions. To even begin requires
that we step back and examine the relationships as they have evolved over
the last two centuries to tease out some lessons and ultimately judge where
we will go in the future.

Things to Ponder

1. Explain the tension between local government as a creature of the
   citizen and local government as a creature of the state and why the
   tension should and shall remain.
2. What are the three elements critical for democracy to remain alive
   and well in society? Discuss the importance of consensus and collective social action.
3. What are the dichotomous views of representative democracy?
   Discuss the effect these views have on the actual development of
   communities. How are these views effecting the participation of citizens within local government as well as the development of regional
   government?
4. What are clusters? What are their features and how do they relate to
   regionalism?
5. Metropolitan governance becomes a hub of local public economies.
   Explain local public economies and how this reflects local government as a creature of the citizen.
6. Compare and contrast the European Union experiment and the development of American metropolitan regions.

3

The Evolution of the Financial Relationship Among State and Local Governments

The American concept of governance is one of shared power, such as between the executive and legislative branches. Nevertheless, the concept is most fully developed in our intergovernmental system. The federal government and the states share duties and responsibilities, and the states and their constituent local governments reflect this same approach. Over the last 200-plus years this approach to governance has created a set of interrelationships, and particularly fiscal relationships, that set this American system of governance apart. Since the middle of the twentieth century fiscal federalism has produced a system in which governments may raise money to implement policy, but they may not actually implement the policy, instead relying upon other governments to be the service providers. Uniquely, political debate in the United States may be about who implements a program or policy, not merely how it is to be implemented. Much of the academic literature on intergovernmental fiscal relations has focused on the financial relationship between the states and the federal government (Wright 1988; Posner 1998; Salamon 2002; O'Toole 2007). This chapter emphasizes state-local financial relations (Chapter 5 focuses on the nonfiscal aspects of this relationship).

The Public Sector as a Financial Engine

State and local government in America is big business. In 2007, state and local governments received $2.782 trillion in combined operating revenues, spent about that amount, and employed close to 15 million individuals in the execution of their collective responsibilities (see Figure 3.1). The distribution of personnel reflects a system heavily dependent on the local governments for the delivery of public services. In 2011, there were 1,747,536 full-time employees in federal nondefense agencies. State governments employed 3,779,258. Those numbers pale in comparison to the 10,781,323 employed at the local government level. Even when defense employees are added to

Figure 3.1   **Summary of 2007 Total Operating Expenditures and Revenues for all U.S. State and Local Governments** (in billions of U.S. dollars)

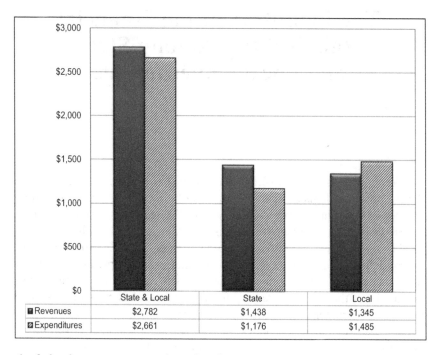

	State & Local	State	Local
■ Revenues	$2,782	$1,438	$1,345
▨ Expenditures	$2,661	$1,176	$1,485

the federal government numbers, local government employment is still twice that of the federal government.

Within each state, the state and local governments form a complex partnership in which power is both legally (more heavily skewed to the state) and culturally (more heavily skewed to local government) derived. The states dominate the framing of policy, but the local governments carry the burden of the delivery of services and, therefore, of policy implementation. Just as in the relationship between the federal government and the states, the responsibility for policy implementation means that interpretation of policy rests with those who implement the policy. What is done with the money is partly a statement of capacity. On the other hand, fiscal patterns may also reflect intentional policy variations. Most of the flow of state revenue from the state to local governments is done on formulae that account for more than population or other arithmetic ratios. Those formulae mean that certain local governments benefit or lose revenue based on the policy choices of the state. For example, the assumption that primary and secondary education is more complicated to deliver in urban areas and in poor communities means that funding for public schools is skewed toward more support for the urban and rural poor.

Revenue raising responsibility is surprisingly quite equally shared. In 2007, the states collected $1.4 trillion while all local governments combined collected $1.3 trillion. Nevertheless, relatively equal revenues paint a somewhat distorted picture of the governance system in the United States. State governments transfer a significant portion of their own revenue in direct aid (often referred to as local government funds) or for specific activities, such as public schools and transportation costs.

State and Local Revenues

Before looking in more detail at the intergovernmental relationship between state governments and the local governments within their borders, an examination of the sources and forms of taxation generating those revenues is necessary. Heading the list of revenues for both state and local governments is intergovernmental aid (see Figure 3.2). The largest single source of this revenue for states is the federal government and the largest single source for local governments is their respective state governments. Federal aid to the states is not necessarily a pass-through of funds to the local governments. Indeed, the federal government and state governments operate between themselves and the flow of federal dollars helps to operate the interstate system. Each state operates and finances its own intrastate system, primarily with different revenue sources than those used by the interstate system,

Various forms of taxation serve to fuel state and local governments. That said, the mix of taxes between state taxes and local government taxes is very different. In 2007, more than 82 percent of state tax revenues ($619 billion) were collected through sales and income taxes. Conversely, 72 percent of local tax revenues ($377 billion) were from property taxes. The dedication of particular types of revenues to particular levels of government has deep historical roots.

When new communities were developing in the eighteenth century, they required a set of public services generally related to property—roads built in and between new settlements, property protected through police and fire services, and a system to define where one's property ended and the neighbor's property began. The amount of land an individual owned was a fairly reliable measure of one's wealth, such that a tax on the value of property served the purpose of raising public dollars fairly and equitably while being used for property-related services. As a result, property taxes became the domain of local governments. As state governments grew in the scope of their responsibilities, so did their need to find additional financial support. Given that those increasing responsibilities had less to do with property, they staked out a tax base of sales and, to a lesser degree, income taxes. By the middle of the

Figure 3.2   **Summary of 2007 Major General Revenues for all U.S. State and Local Governments** (in billions of U.S. dollars)

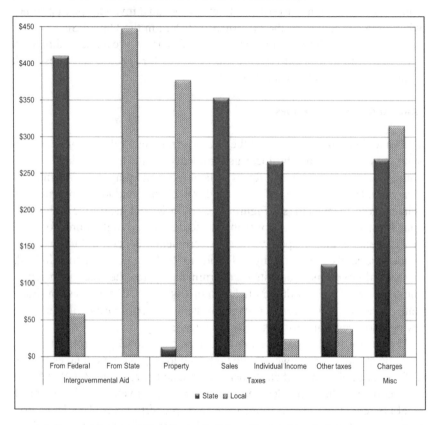

twentieth century virtually all states (New Hampshire being the exception) used either a sales tax, an income tax, or both to generate revenue.

Figure 3.2 demonstrates how local governments rely predominantly on revenues that have been raised from their constituents. Indeed, more than 65 percent of local government revenues are collected through assessing a tax, charging a fee, or other forms of local revenue generation. These revenues can be classified as "own-source" revenues. Heavy reliance on own-source revenues is a two-edged sword that is a significant and signature feature of the American system.

On one hand, it empowers. It makes citizen participation meaningful as the actions of local governments do affect where one lives. It allows communities and its citizens to meaningfully decide which issues are important enough to allocate resources. It creates ownership in the process of governing in that no higher level of government is dictating to communities what should be done or is providing resources so that needs are met through "someone else's money." On the other hand, it has created a fiercely competitive battle among governments (see Peterson 1981). According to Tiebout (1956), when local decisions to raise own-source revenues create a tax and fee package that is not competitive with other communities' tax and fee packages, that government is vulnerable. Resulting disinvestment and flight from the noncompetitive community are highly likely to set in motion a downward economic spiral for that community. Choice for communities with adequate resources is both engaging and empowering. Choice for communities without adequate resources sometimes is neither and approaches mere survival.

State and Local Expenditures

Generally speaking, state and local governments engage in different but compatible activities. Figure 3.3 represents the total expenditures by all state and local governments ranked by the type of service provided. Heading the list are costs for social services and income maintenance at $583 billion, which is primarily a state activity (73 percent of total expenditures). The second highest area of expenditure is elementary and secondary education at $535 billion, which is overwhelmingly a local activity (98 percent).

Although local governments deliver elementary and secondary education, state aid to local governments for education constitutes close to 60 percent of all aid given by the states. As a result, elementary and secondary education in America is locally delivered but state and locally funded. This relationship dramatizes the dual nature of local governments that exists in a number of policy areas: that of administrator of state programs and provider of locally originated and financed programming.

Social services and education (including higher education) constitute half of all the expenditures made by state and local governments. Those services account for 52 percent of all state expenses. Whereas local governments are the dominant service deliverers for primary and secondary education, state governments make up 83 percent of the expenditures for higher education.

The local government spending portfolio is more diverse than that of the state governments. Topping the list of local services is primary and secondary education, constituting close to 36 percent of all local government expenditures. Another 37 percent of local government expenditures are allocated to what can be considered property-related services. The list includes utilities (sewer, water, energy), environmental and housing, public safety, and transportation. Local governments make 71 percent of total state and local government expenditures in these four areas.

Figure 3.3 **Summary of 2007 Major Direct Expenditures for all U.S. State and Local Governments** (in billions of U.S. dollars)

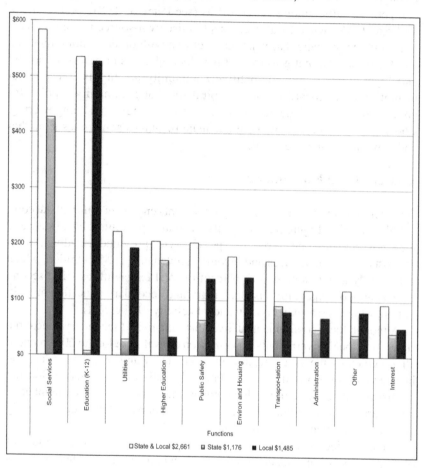

The Evolution of the American Fiscal System

The Depression is remembered as a deep shock to the economic psyche of Americans. Our always tenuous trust in "institutions and organizations" underwent a transformation. We have never had much faith in government, but in general adhered to a simple "local is best" mentality. After World War II, we embarked upon a four-decade period of reorganization of the fiscal structure of government. In 1900, local governments consumed the vast majority of government resources (about 90 percent). Even with the introduction of the federal income tax in 1913 and the broad regulatory reforms of the Progressive Era, the states and the federal governments still represented less than a fifth of government expenditures at the start of the Depression. By the mid-1950s the federal government was the dominant partner in fiscal matters. The only constant was the irrelevance and fiscal insignificance of the states.

The late 1950s into the early 1980s was a period of renaissance for state government. States sought to assert their role as partners to the federal government. Never an important fiscal actor and not particularly important on national issues after the Civil War, the states reformed, reorganized, and reshaped themselves in the latter part of the twentieth century as partners of both the federal and local government on a variety of fiscal policy issues. Five reforms in this period are indicative of the changes occurring in the states:

- Massive increases in state funding for public education
- A systematic policy of expansion of post-secondary public education
- Assumption of both the cost and administration of the "local" share of social services
- Major reorganization and restructuring reforms
- Transformation of state tax policy to generate funds to finance the above and other new initiatives across a wide range of policies

Three of these changes are important to the broader understanding of the role of the states in metropolitan governance, but for purposes of this chapter it is the last item that is most important. Just as the federal government could never become an important part of the expansion of social services in the twentieth century without a shift from unreliable and inconsistent revenues from customs duties to the graduated personal income tax as the prime revenue source, the states could not remake themselves without creating a more equitable and reliable revenue system. From the mid-1950s into the mid-1970s states debated, refined, and expanded their tax systems, focusing on two issues: tax equity and revenue redistribution. While in 1950 relatively few states used an income tax as a source of revenue, by 1975 more than 40 states used that method. Furthermore, states sought, though not always successfully, to substitute state dollars raised through sales and income taxes for regressive local property taxes. The basis for the shift was a belief that taxation should be as equitable (i.e., progressive) as possible and that revenue systems should be elastic.

Realigning the Political Relationships

The last two decades of the twentieth century were an economic and financial disaster for all levels of government, especially states and municipalities. The willingness of the public to support tax change other than tax cuts is nonexistent. Each level of government operates on the assumption that their fiscal policy decisions have no consequences for others. The downward spiral of budget cuts goes beyond the expectations of doing more with less and seemingly has a momentum of its own. Most devastating for recipient governments is that these cuts occur in programs that are most visibly their responsibility—schools, roads, and public safety.

The collective wisdom of the last two decades is that the states have shifted from a stance of partnership with local governments in the 30 years following World War II, which was marked as an effort to help urban governments address the problems created by social and economic changes in the postwar period. Aid for housing, social services, and public schools was greatly expanded by the states. In the last two decades or more a shift has occurred whereby the states have refocused their attention to their own interests and goals. Where ideas such as revenue sharing and formula funding for a variety of policy areas and programs were once common, now funding was grudging and shrinking. The states were much more interested in their own bottom line than in sharing revenues.

At least until the Great Recession (2008–2011), the overall financial structure of America's state and local government system was relatively stable during the last quarter of the twentieth century and first decade of the twenty-first century. That said, important shifts and potential trends can be observed. In 1982, state governments raised 61 percent of combined state and local government revenues. In 2007, the total was 52 percent. The greater utilization of sales taxes by local governments accounts for most of the change in the state's share. In 1982, states collected 84 percent of all sales tax receipts compared to 80 percent in 2007. More importantly, as measured by tax collections, the states had not been playing a greater financial role in the overall system even prior to the Great Recession. As such, the fiscal meltdown that would occur in 2008–2011 at the state level left no room for the states to expand their financial role during this crisis.

Of local government tax revenues, the property tax constituted 76 percent in 1982 and 72 percent in 2007 (see Table 3.1). Although often maligned as an unfair and difficult tax to administer, the property tax continues to dominate as the primary source of revenue for local governments. To the degree that local governments have looked to other tax revenue sources, the sales tax is the tax of choice. Whereas sales taxes constituted 14 percent of 1982 local government tax revenues, they were 17 percent of 2007 total tax revenues.

State governments were more apt to concentrate their tax revenues in sales and income taxes in 2007 than they were in 1982. Whereas those sources

Table 3.1

Comparison of Principle Revenue Sources for State and Local Governments, 1982, 1996, 2007
(in billions of 2007 U.S. dollars)

Type of Revenue	FY 2007			FY 1996			FY 1982		
	Total	State	Local	Total	State	Local	Total	State	Local
Federal Aid	$468	$410	$58	$275	$239	$36	$187	$142	$45
State Aid	$447	—	$447	$322	—	$322	$198	—	$198
Total Intergovernmental	$915	$410	$505	$597	$239	$358	$385	$142	$243
Per Capita	$136.41	$168.01	$89.13	$133.51	$61.43	$105.12			
% of Personal Income		0.35%	0.44%		0.27%	0.41%		0.24%	0.42%
Sales Tax	$440	$353	$87	$329	$272	$57	$202	$170	$32
Property Tax	$390	$13	$377	$276	$13	$263	$176	$6	$170
Income Tax: Individual	$290	$266	$24	$194	$177	$17	$110	$99	$11
Income Tax: Corporate	$61	$53	$8	$42	$38	$4	—	[a]	
Other Taxes	$83	$54	$29	$50	$36	$14	$73	$62	$11
Motor Vehicle Licenses	$21	$19	$2	$18	$16	$2	$13	$13	
Total Tax Collections	$1,285	$758	$527	$909	$552	$357	$574	$350	$224
Per Capita		$252.18	$175.33		$205.85	$133.13		$151.41	$96.90
% of Personal Income		0.65%	0.45%		0.63%	0.41%		0.60%	0.38%
Charges and Utility Fees		$287	$432		$185	$233			
Per Capita		$95.48	$161.10		$68.99	$86.89			
% of Personal Income		0.25%	0.42%		0.28%	0.35%			

Source: U.S. Department of Commerce. Bureau of Census. Census of Governments: Finance Summary Statistics, 1982, 1996, and 2007.
[a] 1982 data includes individual and corporate tax revenue.

constituted 88 percent of 2007 collections, they were only 77 percent of 1982 collections.

User fees or charges for current services are primarily the domain of local governments. In 2007, local governments collected 63 percent of all current charges and 95 percent of all utility revenues. State government charges are primarily in the area of higher education—56 percent of state current charges are related to that area. Local governments are the dominant revenue collectors for funding hospitals, sewerage, solid waste, and other activities.

The revenue area that has experienced the most significant change over the last several years is intergovernmental transfers. The 1960s and 1970s were highlighted by increasing involvement of the federal government in local government. As a result, by 1982, 24 percent of federal aid to state and local governments went to local governments. This experiment in federal lo-cal relations ended with the election of Ronald Reagan, although it took his administration until the mid-1980s to officially wind it down. By 2007, local governments received 12 percent of total federal aid allocated to state and local governments.

While the revenue-generation systems in the United States were never self-consciously tied together, by the last quarter of the twentieth century certain assumptions and expectations dominated intergovernmental relations. These assumptions and expectations were:

- In the name of effective tax administration, tax capacity and equity rev-enue collections should be pushed upward through the intergovernmental system, sometimes twice (local to state and state to federal). Unofficially and informally "they" were collecting money for "us."
- The money collected "above" was returned/redistributed based upon shared expectations that reflected mutually agreed-upon policy goals. The sense was that this was *our* money being collected by *one of us*, and then returned.
- Policy implementation represented broad policy goals with the ability at the local level to tailor the funding to reflect specific needs within the goals.

While the trilateral relationship among local, state, and federal govern-ments has remained the same over the last two decades, increasingly the politics of those relationships and the fiscal dynamics of those relation-ships have changed. The interactions among governments that had been marked by cooperation began to disintegrate. The new relationship was to be defined by the conflict and controversy associated with "unfunded" mandates.

Realigning the Tax Structure

The 1980s did not get off to an auspicious start. A recession that would push unemployment to 10 percent by December 1982, the cancellation of the last vestiges of federal revenue sharing, and a series of statutes and citizen-driven initiatives to limit the capacity of state and local governments to increase taxes changed, if not yet significantly, the dollars flowing through the intergovernmental system.

The public attitude about government had shifted. While there had not been a great deal of trust in state and local government for many decades, the trust in the federal government born in the Depression now evaporated. The federal tax cuts of 1982 focused on reducing the top end of the tax structure. Even when tax increases were enacted (as in 1986, 1992, and 1998) the tax debate was of a very different character than that of the 1960s and 1970s. Increases were as likely to affect middle-class Americans as they were the poor or the wealthy. Deductions for health care expenditures were curtailed by applying a net income deduction, but deductions for income tax payments and mortgage interest on multiple homes were preserved. The result of the tax changes in the 1980s and 1990s was a federal personal income tax system that was less progressive, yet it was still targeted as too high at the top end of the scale.

The debate in the states was even more stilted. Starting with the approval of Proposition 13 in California and Proposition 2.5 in Massachusetts, the policy focus was on limiting the capacity of state and local governments to increase taxes and/or to mandate an outright cap on tax rates. In other states, the focus was almost exclusively on retrenchment and reduction of business taxes. In parallel, the new model for economic development was the offer of "tax incentives" to convince businesses to relocate. Quite literally tens of millions of state and local taxes were not collected. Funding for a wide variety of programs, and especially the programs that were the crowning achievements of the state renaissance, such as social services, public education, and local government revenue sharing, was cut or at least limited in growth. "Reform" became synonymous with cuts to programs and taxes.

Fiscal Policy in the New Century

For most of the first decade of the twenty-first century public opinion was decidedly against any governmental action. The response to the recession of 2001 was not to increase spending, but rather to make more cuts. A good example of this mentality is the reaction of the Ohio state legislature to an Ohio supreme court decision in 1999 that concluded the state was in violation of the state constitution because it was not funding public primary education at the required level. Since that time, the original complainants have returned to the state supreme court four times because the legislature simply refused to change the funding formula to address the court decision. In part because of little outcry from the public, the legislature ignored all five court rulings. Clearly, there was little sentiment to adjust state expenditures upward, even though it should have been apparent to everyone that local property taxes were increasing to make up for the state dollars not appropriated. Even as the nation entered a second recession of the decade in 2008, public sentiment and legislative actions favored even further cuts. In 2013 the Ohio state budget called for a reduction in the income tax, replacing it with increased tolls on highways and broadening of the sales tax. Where counties had piggy-backed on the state sales tax with small taxes of their own, the tax changes recommended by the governor required a county by county reduction in the sales taxes collected for those counties, lest the county substitute those revenues for an alternative revenue source (i.e., the property tax). In other words, as part of a shift in the sources of taxes for state use, Ohio was specifically prohibiting counties from doing the same.

Unlike most states and almost all local governments, the federal government can conclude a fiscal year with a deficit. At various times that deficit has been a politically important issue. Yet, except in the 1990s, there has never been a time when tax changes were given serious consideration to slow or eliminate the annual federal deficits. From the 1990s into the current century, the response of Congress was to squeeze federal programs and especially make cuts in programs delivered by states and local governments. Unlike the 1990s these program cuts were not during a period when the general revenues of governments were growing. In the beginning of the twenty-first century, federal program cuts were being made at a time when those funds represented the difference between a balanced budget and a deficit for many states. The fiscal house of cards had collapsed by the middle of the decade. Yet the demand for further cuts at the federal and state levels, even though it potentially meant higher local property taxes, continued. The public simply did not believe that taxes would or should go up, and given the reluctance of all politicians to even discuss tax increases, they were correct. Cries for new funding, especially for school districts, fell on deaf ears.

The New Rules of the Game

The rules of the informal tax collection and redistribution system were never followed. From the outset, the conditions and requirements mandated to receive monies from the tax-collecting governments were more detailed and controlling than was expected by the governments running programs. The proverbial "strings" attached to funding were more like heavy ropes. Rules and regulations, reporting requirements, and limits on actions based on unique circumstances were now common. As time went on, the assumptions and expectations that framed that informal system adjusted to reflect the realities of practice. The new assumptions by the end of the twentieth century were:

- Effective tax administration, tax capacity, and equity revenue collection are a by-product of economies of scale and of superior, professional management, having nothing to do with policy initiatives. "*They*" were collecting money for "*themselves*."
- The money collected "above" was returned/redistributed based on expectations that reflected the policy goals of the agency "writing the check." The sense was that this was their money, collected by *them* and given to others to serve *the grantors purposes*.
- Policy implementation represented narrow program policy goals that would be jeopardized if the recipients attempted to tailor the funding to reflect their needs.
- There was a growing reliance upon competitive grants, rather than simple transfers and formula allocations to fund projects. (Cox 2009)

As long as the money flowing was stable, then these new rules were manageable (that is different from saying that the funding recipients did not object to these changes in the rules of the game). There were always the inevitable political controversies over policy and program implementation, and, during those periods when the flow of funds shrank, there were complaints about "unfunded" mandates. In general, however, this new arrangement worked. As can be seen in Table 3.1, one of the reasons that the changed rules were less controversial than expected is that, for much of the 1980s and 1990s, state governments stepped in to provide a larger share of support, replacing federal dollars that were disappearing. This was a system in a tenuous equilibrium. The money flowed downward at increasing rates, though the conditions placed on receipt of those monies meant they were applied in different ways and put to different uses than if the recipient governments had been free to shape the programs themselves. This had become a highly regulated and inflexible system, but it worked from the standpoint that municipalities and states could not provide the same breadth of services and programs without these intergovernmental transfers and grants.

This steady-state arrangement is fragile. It is dependent on funding sources (the federal government and the states) to continue, jointly or independently, to maintain the funding stream. A sense that the *intergovernmental system* is meaningful for everyone is the glue that holds this complex set of relationships together. As long as those funding sources continue to feel an obligation to support the funding recipients, the system would not collapse (though neither was there any great outcry for change). With only minor setbacks, the period from 1980 to 2000 was one in which that commitment held.

Increasingly, funding is controlled by rules that are beyond the control of those who must deliver services. Administrative decisions and court rulings that mandate expenditures for programs rarely consider budgetary or tax constraints. The courts do not consider that a community may be "capped" in terms of its authority to increase taxes. Court rulings and administrative decisions are made sequentially and independently of all other actions. The consequences are not relevant to the decision maker.

The Fiscal Crisis of 2008–2012: Impact on the Intergovernmental System

When the National Conference on State Legislatures (Pound 2009) issued its report on the fiscal condition of the states in February 2009, few would have guessed how much worse conditions would be by the fall of that year. With national unemployment hovering around 10 percent, trending upward toward 14 percent in some states and nearly 20 percent in some metropolitan areas, it is little wonder that journalists called this the "Great Recession." The benchmark was no longer how bad things were in comparison to the recession of 1981–1983, but rather how bad things were in comparison to the Depression of the 1930s. While few public policy mechanisms and little political perspective existed to defend against the ill fiscal effects of the Depression, they were available to address the downturn in 1981 (and its regionally more devastating cousin in 1972–1974). Many of the policy mechanisms that helped address the fiscal crisis in cities and states in the 1970s and 1980s simply are no longer available, but more critically the public support for significant public action by state and local governments also is gone.

Ray Sheppach, the executive director of the National Governors Association (NGA), has argued that the public sector has entered an era of "perpetual fiscal crisis." He described the convergence of forces that are swelling to buffet public finance as "a perfect storm" (Osborne and Hutchinson 2004). We must keep in mind that Sheppach was describing the situation as the country was emerging from the economic downturn of 2001–2002, not the economic crisis of 2008–2012.

The current situation began against a backdrop that Osborne and Hutchinson (2004) describe as one of the ever-increasing cost of health care and public safety needs, an aging population, pension plans, continuing resistance to major tax increases, and an increasing demand and need for public assistance programs that have placed new stresses on state and local governments. They go on to note that state governments were passing their problems down to cities and counties, with deep cuts in local aid, while the federal government dug a fiscal hole so rapidly that future cuts and unfunded mandates for states and localities were inevitable. Even a much less severe economic downturn may have triggered the crisis.

With the nation in a technical recovery for more than three years, where are we now? The National League of Cities' survey of city finance officers in September 2009 reported that nearly nine of ten (88 percent) city finance officers report that their cities are less able to meet fiscal needs in 2009 than in the previous year (Hoene and Pagano 2009, 1). Economic issues such as decreasing revenues from sales tax, property tax, income tax, and state aid have plagued cities and their budgets in the past, but a new set of factors have come into play which has set the stage for a historical budget crisis.

According to the National Conference of State Legislatures (NCSL):

> 2009 will mark one of the most difficult years in history for state budgets. The fiscal challenges are enormous, widespread and, unfortunately, far from over.
>
> Lawmakers in virtually every state scrambled to keep their fiscal year (FY) 2009 budgets balanced while at the same time struggling to enact new ones for FY 2010. Hemorrhaging revenues drove the massive difficulties they faced. No matter how pessimistic revenue forecasts were, actual collections seemed to come in lower. This happened over and over and over again. Ultimately, states were not just faced with lower revenue growth rates, they confronted year-over-year declines in actual collections. (Pound 2009, 3)

How have the cities and states survived? Most states used American Recovery and Reinvestment Act (ARRA); stimulus funds to fill their budget gap. According to the NCSL, Texas addressed nearly 97 percent of its deficit by using stimulus funds (Pound 2009). It is somewhat more complicated for cities and counties. Harkness (2009) notes that most of the stimulus dollars were channeled through existing funding mechanisms. In some agencies, it was as though there was simply an extra round of grants and awards. It meant that the projects that could be funded were those closest to being ready for approval. Old projects had new, earlier starting dates. For example, road work still had to be approved by regional agencies and then the state before work could begin. For larger projects, there may be a 24- to 36-month internal approval process. Virtually any project that was not nearing final administrative approval and, thus ready to be funded, would not be part of the stimulus. "New" projects were not funded; only administratively approved projects that would meet the tight deadlines imposed by the law were undertaken.

This is a more complex administrative task than may be apparent. Changing the start date of one seemingly small project has a ripple effect across multiple projects. For example, an integrated economic development initiative that involves public and private funding for facilities, employment training, and complementary road work might be the highest priority for a local government, but the available ARRA funds may accelerate the wrong "piece" of the development puzzle. Road work needs to link to the new facilities, not to vacant land or to an existing property that must at some point be demolished. Similarly, job training to fill jobs in a facility that does not yet exist serves little purpose. To some extent, smaller, more distinct or discrete projects stood the best chance of being funded. For example, despite the hopes of city officials, the private sector, and the public, a major redevelopment effort in the City of Akron that was close to the "shovel ready" category was not materially affected by the ARRA. There were simply too many moving parts. The success of the project was in the fitting together of the various project elements. Finishing one part early did not affect the speed at which other parts of the project were finished and thus did not affect the end date for completion of the final project. Some of the work that might have speeded the overall project was not in the administrative pipeline. What could get done were some smaller projects that met the shovel-ready criteria (street improvements and bridge repairs). In the grand scheme, the city certainly would have preferred to accelerate the completion of the economic development project, with the resulting new employment, rather than smaller construction projects (road upgrades and related improvements) that were funded and thus completed earlier than anticipated. Obviously, the citizens who lived in the neighborhoods where the projects took place were pleased that "their" project moved forward and the stimulus effect of the jobs created (albeit temporary) served the purpose of the law. Nevertheless, given a choice the city would have opted for a different order of completion. ARRA met the goals given the funding available, but the goals accomplished were those of the federal government and only secondarily those of local governments.

This is a crisis that will not go away anytime soon. Unemployment rates have been slowly receding for three years, but in much of the country dropped to pre-recession levels only in the fall of 2012. Housing prices are rising to 2002–2006 levels. State and especially local government revenues trail economic indicators by 18 to 24 months, meaning that tax revenues would reach 2007 levels in 2012 or 2013 (Hoene and Pagano 2009) .

The fiscal crisis brought on by the Great Recession did not affect each state or each local government with equal severity. Just as in any economic downturn, some parts of the public and private sector were harmed more than others. The difference at the end of the first decade of the twenty-first century was that neither the state nor local governments were in a strong financial position going into the recession. The states were already pulling back from support of local governments and public schools before the recession. They would not, or could not, continue the historic arrangements of intergovernmental cooperation and funding transfers. In the depths of the recession, they could not respond except to continue the established pattern of cuts (or at best level funding in the face of rising costs).

State and local governments were caught in the trap caused in part by the elasticity (or inelasticity) of their dominant revenue sources. The relatively more elastic income taxes reacted quickly (initially downward), while less elastic taxes such as sales taxes, took slightly longer to drop, but then plummeted. Inelastic property tax revenues held briefly and then crashed under the weight of unemployment and foreclosure. This cascade effect, coupled with the broken chain of intergovernmental transfers, has trapped local governments and special districts. States that are the least reliant on property taxes were the first to recover (with income tax revenues outpacing sales tax revenue in the recovery). But there is little interest in the states to put more money into intergovernmental transfers, even as state revenues rebound. Ohio, hard hit by the recession in part because it never came out of the localized downturn in 2001 and 2002, now offers, at best, funding at 2007 levels to local governments, school districts, and post-secondary education. There is little indication that funding will grow, rather it is expected that level funding is a best-case scenario (Carroll and Chapman 2013).

More critical for the future of the intergovernmental system is that states are becoming more directive in how monies are spent. By this, we do not mean the decades-old complaint about "unfunded mandates," but the new strings attached to funding, which affect the structure of local government. For example, the State of Ohio adjusts funding to local governments (through its local government fund) based on the extent to which certain governments engage in service sharing and other partnership arrangements that the state believes will reduce the cost of managing and operating local governments. Even setting aside the reality that some local governments and all "special districts" are exempt from these requirements, these mandates impose a fairly narrow range of partnership arrangements for the "opportunity" to access a shrinking pool of funds. The local government fund, which at first would have been classified as a "revenue sharing" program or a "block grant," increasingly is a program in which the policy on use of the funds is controlled by the state.

Concluding Thoughts and Things to Ponder

Questions about the viability of the intergovernmental fiscal system abound, yet it is not clear whether there is any sense of peril. Yes, the states and local governments need federal support. On the other hand, the status quo still leaves us in the storm (at least in 2013). The spirit of partnership and shared fiscal policy perspectives that built the intergovernmental system is gone and has been gone for decades. Even though we do not do very well operating as semi-autonomous units, we cannot break the habit of such behavior.

The fragile equilibrium of the intergovernmental system has collapsed. The funding sources, which supported the system, have made radical cuts in, or simply stopped, funding programs. There is no longer a margin for error. Thirty years of doing more with less has left little capacity to keep up with the demand for services even though there is no tolerance for increasing resources to provide those services. The continuing problem of deficits again becomes one of, in the public's mind, mismanagement and waste.

The Depression spawned an entire new system of intergovernmental partnerships and a decades-long discourse on effectiveness and equity in tax policy. The last three decades have been a period of retrenchment. The informal understandings that brought federal dollars into urban areas and encouraged a shift away from traditional taxes such as the property tax and a collaborative arrangement across all levels of government were to change in the 1980s. Since that time there is much more of a "you are on your own" attitude about other governments, forcing governments to increase reliance upon regressive taxes such as the property tax, even as states cut income taxes.

In summary, the state and local government system in the United States has evolved specialized roles for states and their constituent local governments. State governments are the primary revenue generator for the system and they rely heavily on sales and income taxes. States deliver services, primarily in the areas of social services and higher education. States are the primary recipient of federal aid. States also provide significant funding in the form of aid to local governments. As such, states use local governments as administrators of some of their programs.

Local governments are the primary service providers, and they rely heavily on their own source revenues, primarily in the form of property taxes and user fees. Not only do local governments directly deliver more programs than states, those programs tend to be more diverse with a focus on education and property-related services. Local governments no longer receive substantial direct support from the federal government. They do receive significant contributions from state governments to support operations. This state aid serves two purposes; it can be used to administer state programs, or as general-purpose funds that help local governments administer locally defined programs.

Things to Ponder

1. Discuss the connection between policy implementation (interpretation of policy as well as delivery of services) and the way it is funded in regard to state and local taxation and revenue.

2. Intergovernmental transfers changed in the early 1980s and have resulted in lowered amounts of reliable federal aid to state and local governments. Describe the downward spiral of budget cuts and the effects on state and local government funding of implementation of federal mandated policies.

3. The disintegration of cooperation between the levels of government finances has led to many changes and experiments in state and local taxation policies. Discuss some of the fiscal issues resulting from the lack of social collective action in intergovernmental relations.

4. The demand for services has placed a high demand on state and local governments. How are they working to resolve these issues? How might regionalism help to solve some of the issues between state and local governments?

4

The Primary Types and Roles
of Local Governments

Local government is a term that covers not only the more easily recognized forms of government—municipalities and counties—but also the numerous other types of districts that the public often does not necessarily associate with government and certainly not with governance. These entities range from school districts to "special" districts that may represent the geographic boundaries of a service provider such as a public utility or a park system, or that of a limited-purpose organization such as an entity that provides water for the irrigation of agricultural land. The one distinguishing feature of these governments is their relatively direct and unfiltered access for and by citizens.

"School board, city council, and county commission meetings are literally and figuratively 'more accessible' to the public than those held by state and federal governments."

There is a sense that local elected officials are closer to the public, if only because the area or district they represent is smaller. Such an elected official often is a neighbor or a friend's neighbor. The expectation that the "county seat" should be no more than a day's buggy ride (20 miles) from any resident or that wards should subdivide cities harkens back to an era in which the opportunity to meet elected officials face to face was both a right and an expectation.

Local governments can be aggregated into five types that fall into three broad categories (Figure 4.1). In no particular order, the first category and type is the county. The second category is the municipality. We are taking some liberties with the latter term because of the many forms and nuances that are found within the American states. There are two primary types of municipality—the city and the township. The third category of local government is the district. As with municipalities there are two broad types. The special district is a unit of government that usually undertakes a single or a small set of purposes and the school district is a variant of that concept, simply applied to primary and secondary education.

The U.S. system of local government features many governments. In 2007, as demonstrated in Figure 4.2, there were 89,476 local governments in the

Figure 4.1   **The Major Types of Local Governments in the United States**

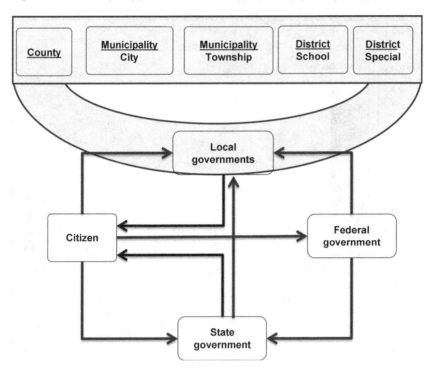

United States. Between 1952 and 2007 the overall number of local governments declined. That decline is misleading as consolidation and closing of "one-room" schools occurred, particularly in the 1950s and 1960s. At the same time small schools were closing or consolidating, the growth of special districts accelerated, representing one of the most significant trends in U.S. local government administration. Since 1952, more than 25,000 new special districts and 2,000 municipal governments have been created. To put those numbers in perspective, there have been approximately 500 new local governments created in the United States each year for the last 50 years.

Through most of the twentieth century, the number of county governments has remained virtually unchanged. Historically, state governments created county governments as a means by which to administer certain functions, primarily judicial. As a result, county governments were laid out at roughly the same time a state was formed. There were 3,062 county governments in 1932 and 3,033 in 2007. The decline is partially explained by the decision of the State of Connecticut to abolish county governments and a small number of city-county consolidations that effectively eliminated the county as a distinct government.

Figure 4.2 **Number of U.S. Local Governments by Type, 1952 to 2007**

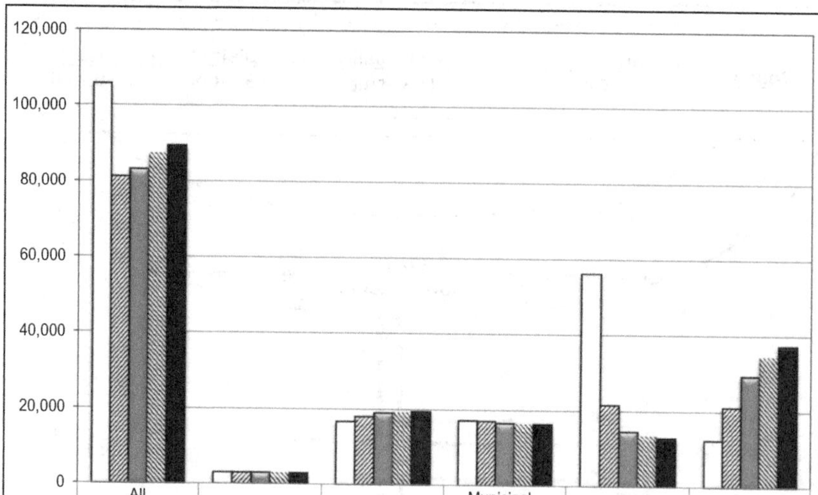

	All Governments	Counties	Municipal - City	Municipal - Town	District - School	District - Special
1952	105,694	3,049	16,778	17,202	56,346	12,319
1967	81,208	3,049	18,048	17,105	21,742	21,264
1987	83,186	3,042	19,200	16,691	14,721	29,532
1997	87,453	3,043	19,372	16,629	13,726	34,683
2007	89,476	3,033	19,492	16,519	13,051	37,381

In states with counties, all other forms of local government usually are nested geographically within the boundaries of a county. It is easy to presume that states are made up of counties that, in turn, are made up of municipalities. In such an arrangement, municipalities are presumed to report to counties that report to states. Though these local governments are typically located within a county, there is no hierarchical relationship between county government and local governments.

Under existing law, all counties, municipalities, and independent school districts are creatures of their respective states. Some special districts and dependent school districts are creatures of a respective county or municipal government that created the special district. By law, these districts are wholly owned subsidiaries of those local governments. Some dependent school districts are not even subsidiaries, but departments within the municipal or county government. Other special districts are separate and distinct from municipal or county governments and are truly independent governments.

As is the case with most pronouncements on the governance structure of America, there are exceptions to every rule. Such is the case with special districts. Just as state legislatures can create and abolish units of local government,

Figure 4.3 **Summary of 2007 Operating Expenditures and Revenues by Type of Local Government** (in billions of U.S. dollars)

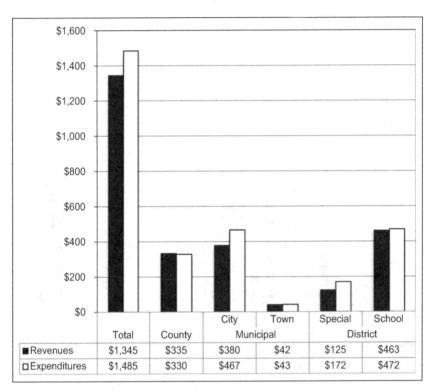

	Total	County	City Municipal	Town	Special District	School
■Revenues	$1,345	$335	$380	$42	$125	$463
□Expenditures	$1,485	$330	$467	$43	$172	$472

they can also create (or abolish) special districts. As a result, some special districts report directly to the state, circumventing local control. For instance, in Allegheny County, Pennsylvania, the state legislature created a special taxing body in 1995 called the Regional Asset District. It legislatively mandated the nature and structure of this organization. Similarly, the Metropolitan District Commission in Massachusetts is a state-funded regional agency that has been responsible for the provision of drinking water and some recreational activities for much of the greater Boston area for many decades.

In this chapter we provide a broad overview of the fiscal roles of each type of local government followed by a detailed look at each type of local government.

Financial Overview of Major Types of Local Governments

In Chapter 3, we discussed the distribution of responsibilities and financial resources between state and local governments. The piece of pie allocated to

Figure 4.4   **Summary of 2007 Operating Revenues by Type of Local Government** (in billions of U.S. dollars)

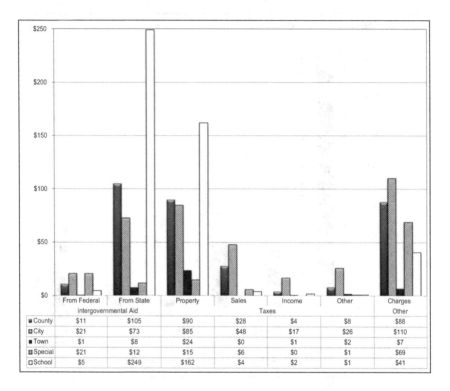

| | From Federal | From State | Property | Sales | Income | Other | Charges |
	Intergovernmental Aid			Taxes			Other
■ County	$11	$105	$90	$28	$4	$8	$88
▣ City	$21	$73	$85	$48	$17	$26	$110
■ Town	$1	$8	$24	$0	$1	$2	$7
▨ Special	$21	$12	$15	$6	$0	$1	$69
▢ School	$5	$249	$162	$4	$2	$1	$41

local government is further divided among the types of local government, as each type plays a different role in the system. In 2007, the largest portion of total local government revenues (34 percent, or $463 billion) was received by the nation's school districts (Figure 4.3). The fact that this allocation was greater than the total revenues received by cities (28 percent or $380 billion) is a reflection that the primary function of local government in the United States is education. County governments (25 percent or $330 billion), special districts (9 percent or $125 billion), and towns (3 percent or $43 billion) round out the list.

County governments have a revenue portfolio that differs from cities in two important ways. First, state and federal aid play a more important role (35 percent of total revenues, 90 percent of which comes from the state). Second, taxes as a percent of revenues are less (38 percent compared to 48 percent for cities) and, more important, the concentration of tax dollars derived from the property tax is greater (less than half for cities; 70 percent at the county level).

The sources of revenues also vary considerably by type of local government

Figure 4.5   **Summary of 2007 Operating Expenditures by Type of Local Government** (in billions of U.S. dollars)

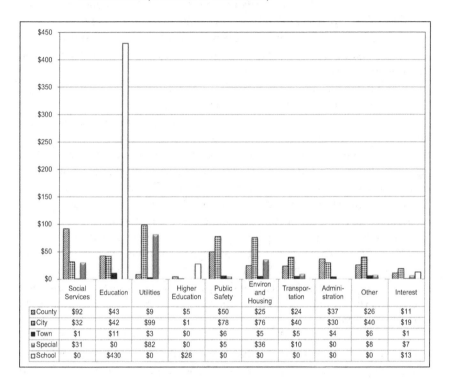

	Social Services	Education	Utilities	Higher Education	Public Safety	Environ and Housing	Transpor-tation	Admini-stration	Other	Interest
County	$92	$43	$9	$5	$50	$25	$24	$37	$26	$11
City	$32	$42	$99	$1	$78	$76	$40	$30	$40	$19
Town	$1	$11	$3	$0	$6	$5	$5	$4	$6	$1
Special	$31	$0	$82	$0	$5	$36	$10	$0	$8	$7
School	$0	$430	$0	$28	$0	$0	$0	$0	$0	$13

(see Figure 4.4). For school districts, 89 percent of funding is derived from either state aid (54 percent) or property tax (35 percent). Indeed, from the perspective of the state, the majority of its financial support for local government (56 percent) is allocated to elementary and secondary education. Further, 43 percent of all property taxes generated in the United States are raised by school districts to support primary and secondary education.

The type of local government with the most diverse revenue portfolio is the city. Less than half (46 percent) of city revenues come from taxation. Of the types of taxes for cities, the property tax is the most widely used but is still less than half (48 percent) of all taxes. Just under 29 percent of total city revenues are derived from charges and user fees. The final category, federal and state aid, accounts for less than 25 percent of total revenues. Of these intergovernmental transfers, an overwhelming majority (78 percent) come from the state government. But, to put it in perspective, federal aid to cities is a very small part of the financial picture at just 23 percent of state/federal aid and less than 6 percent of total city revenues.

Special districts are generally created to operate and deliver a particular public service. As such the majority of their revenues (55 percent) are derived from user fees. Towns, generally smaller units of local government, rely on local taxes for 64 percent of their revenues, and property tax constitutes 89 percent of taxes. It is in these types of local governments that dependence on the property tax is most acute.

Where the funds are spent also differs by type of local government (see Figure 4.5). In Chapter 3, it was noted that education is the single largest local government expenditure (35 percent of all local government expenditures) and is almost three times greater than the next highest expenditure category, utilities (12 percent). Of total educational expenses 82 percent are spent by school districts. The remaining 18 percent of school expenditures are made by counties, cities, and, to a lesser degree, towns. That said, for town governments, elementary and secondary education is the largest single category of expense, comprising 25 percent of total town expenditures.

Revenues for utilities (12 percent of local government expenditures) are almost exclusively provided by cities and special districts (94 percent). Dominated by water, sewer, and electrical authorities, these services often cover relatively large geographic areas and larger populations such that a city or a special district would constitute an appropriate type of local government to perform this function.

The third largest expenditure, constituting just over 10 percent of all local government expenditures, is that of social services. County governments provide approximately 60 percent of all funding in this category. Indeed, it has become the single largest expense of county governments, making up 28 percent of all expenditures. By comparison, city governments spend less than 7 percent on social services and cities allocate about 20 percent.

Local government spends just 9.6 percent on environmental and housing programs and 9.5 percent on public safety programs. In both categories, cities are the dominant local government, providing 53 percent of total spending in the former category and 56 percent of all spending in the latter.

County Government

Geographically, the largest units of local government are counties. The term "county" includes those entities called "boroughs" in Alaska and "parishes" in Louisiana. County governments exist in all states but Connecticut and Rhode Island.

Two distinct images of counties have emerged as part of the American political system. First, in New England and, to a lesser degree, the middle-Atlantic states, where towns and villages were the primary organizing unit, county government was seen as a subdivision of the state or colony. Shortly after independence, the newly formed states divided themselves into administrative units (counties) for purposes of delivering state-level services. The most extreme version of this is Massachusetts, where the boundaries of the counties are fixed in statute by listing the municipalities that fall within that geography. As a result, counties were not self-constituted governments and became, in the minds of local inhabitants, a more remote and less interesting form of local government. Similarly, the governing responsibilities of these counties are limited. Counties rarely provide direct citizen services. For example, county governments in Massachusetts have two functions: running a jail and keeping records (everything from birth certificates to deeds). When Connecticut abolished county governments in the 1960s, they were replaced by regional planning agencies.

Second, and generally associated with the South where larger-scale agricultural development was more prevalent, the county was more apt to be the primary unit of local government in all but the more highly developed urban centers (Adrian and Fine 1991). Although not formed from the bottom up, designation as a county seat represented a significant economic opportunity for a number of communities. County seats were trade centers; the preferred meeting place for local political elites; the site of the year's biggest event, the county fair; and the place of institutional memory for the local inhabitants through the record-keeping function (Adrian and Fine 1991). Particularly in rural areas, county government served as the access point for most citizens to governmental services and opportunities.

This stark contrast in the fundamental building blocks of local civil society in the United States can best be dramatized by comparing practices in Georgia and Massachusetts. Georgia is representative of a number of southern states that employed the "county unit system" (Marando and Thomas 1977). In this system, each county was entitled to at least one representative in the state legislature. This organizing principle elevated the importance of county government in the state political process and afforded rural constituencies a far greater role in state policy than they would have had otherwise. In Massachusetts, towns constituted the Colonial Congress. Zuckerman asserts that such an arrangement had the effect of reducing the [state] House of Representatives to a virtual congress of communities and establishing a town's "inalienable right to representation" (1970, 20). Such a relationship in Massachusetts led Tocqueville to comment, "It is important to remember that they [the townships of New England] have not been vested with privileges, but that they have, on the contrary, forfeited a portion of their independence to the state" (1953, 57). Indeed, early deputies to the state legislature were actually town employees and paid by those towns (Zuckerman 1970).

Municipal Governments

Municipal governments include townships and cities in most states. Pennsylvania also has municipalities called "boroughs." Ohio uses the term "village" to designate smaller municipalities (in this case under 5,000 population).

Generally, there are two images of municipal governments. The first is positive and views local governments as civic communities empowering their citizens to engage in the making of important decisions about the social world in which they live (Elazar 1966, 1971). The second is a more critical view. Burns (1994) argues that the formation of municipalities is an expensive and time-consuming process that is not always successful. Given these constraints, it takes a combination of citizen interest and business interests to mobilize the resources necessary to be successful. Consequently, business interests, particularly developers and manufacturers, more often have been the drivers of the process. These business interests are searching for favorable regulatory and tax climates and mechanisms that increase land value at minimal risk to developers. Middle- and upper-middle-class citizens share the interest in low taxes and desire the acquisition of services without having to address the poor. Together, these interests merge to form a coalition that has the staying power to see that the new government is formed.

Township Government

As defined by the Bureau of Census, "township government" includes towns in the six New England states, Minnesota, New York, and Wisconsin, and townships in 11 other states. However, this definition lacks practical meaning as township government defies easy categorization. On one hand, as is the case with the New England towns, they are the foundation from which many local governments in the United States sprang. On the other hand, as is the case in many midwestern states, they are mere shells of institutions, barely worth more than a footnote. Ohio and Indiana use the term "township" to designate a unit of government that has limited taxing and governing authority. Our discussion of townships does not include these "partial" governments.

Even though they are seen as important institutions, traditional textbooks follow the Census Bureau and consider the New England towns as different from cities, with substantially less power (Halloway 1951; Zimmerman 1984; Adrian and Fine 1991). For purposes of statistical presentation, we have retained that distinction. Nevertheless, it is recognized that New England towns often exercise more discretionary authority than most cities (Zimmerman 1983). One of the authors of this book started his working life as a town manager in a small community in Maine called Dover-Foxcroft. Upon entering the town, one is greeted with the sign that says "Incorporated, 1769." This town of 4,500 people owned and operated its own hospital, airport, and several industrial parks. Such a community embodies the notion of local government, whether its title is "city" or "town."

Perhaps a better way to distinguish between types of municipalities is to consider whether the community was created as an act by the local inhabitants to be a duly constituted civil society or whether the territory was created as a means of subdividing the state or colony. Such self-constituted communities can be officially cities, New England towns, or boroughs, as they are referred to in Pennsylvania.

Outside New England, townships generally fall into two groups (Blair 1986). Both groups originated as "congressional townships," six-mile-square subdivisions designated by congressional order under the Articles of Confederation, starting in 1787 (Adrian and Fine 1991). In eight states, the township governments are based on the principle of the New England town meeting in which the legislative body is any qualified voter who attends the duly called town meetings. However, this structure is mandated by the legislature, and the townships have far fewer powers than those of the New England towns on which they are based.

The townships in seven other states are more like miniature county governments (Blair 1986). The governing body, usually a board of supervisors or township commissioners, who are often town employees, serves both legislative and executive functions, operating the snowplows in the winter and tar trucks in the summer.

City Government

The second type of municipality is the city. Officially, city government includes cities, boroughs (except in Alaska), villages, and towns (except in the six New England states, Minnesota, New York, and Wisconsin), as well as composite city-county governments are also treated as city government.

Generally, city governments are considered corporate entities. The act of incorporation implies that some part of the community desired to empower itself to exercise local self-government. City governments are "bottom-up" institutions, which derive their power from an act of incorporation (often called a charter). They differ from county governments and the previously mentioned townships, which are "top-down" institutions; that is, they are subdivisions of the state, created by the state to undertake certain state functions.

Treating city governments in the United States as corporations is based on English tradition (Frug 1999). That said, at a practical level, American local governments have retained their cultural status as associations. Although an oversimplification, it is the local citizens, not the state government, who create a local government. Liberal incorporation laws in most states allow groups of citizens to declare self-government.

In addition to easy incorporation statutes, some states have granted de facto corporate status to their local governments. As a result, in a number of states, particularly in the Northeast and Midwest, all of the territory within the state has been incorporated. In these states, the creation of new local governments occurs when residents of one incorporated territory elect to create (or change) their own government. Two historical examples that illustrate this are the consolidations (or "metropolitanizations") of New York and Boston in the 1890s. New York City was initially the island of Manhattan, surrounded by other cities, most notably Brooklyn and Staten Island. By vote of the constituent citizens, New York City was reconfigured as five "boroughs," four of which had been independently incorporated cities. In the process, one of the four largest (by population) cities in the United States—Brooklyn—disappeared to reemerge as a part of New York City. On a much smaller scale Boston did the same thing. Twenty-one small, incorporated towns and cities were dissolved and then incorporated into the city of Boston (expanding that city from a minuscule two square miles to a still small 43+ square miles).

Not all states have all their territory incorporated into municipal governments. In a number of states, primarily in the South and West, much of the nondeveloped territory is unincorporated. County governments are responsible for providing services in those unincorporated areas. Depending on the particular state laws, when development of the unincorporated territory creates a more densely populated area, that area can become incorporated. This incorporation occurs in two primary forms. The territory can become incorporated as a new, separate local government, or the territory may be annexed to an existing incorporated municipality.

Generally, towns do not have corporate status and lack the discretionary authority of municipalities. The most notable exceptions to this rule are the towns of New England. Although they are referred to as "towns," they were incorporated and predate the American Revolution. As such, they have retained significant discretionary authority and operate much like cities in that regard.

Structures of Municipal Government

American municipalities are structured in hundreds of different ways. Voters often decide on issues from size of the legislature to management of the municipality. This authority might be subject to some state limitations, but not enough to withdraw the fact that Americans have a fundamental right to decide how they want to be governed at the local level. Although exceptions

Figure 4.6   **Two Primary Forms of Local Government Organization and the Major Policy Issues Facing Each Form in Adapting (Integrating) into a Hybrid Form**

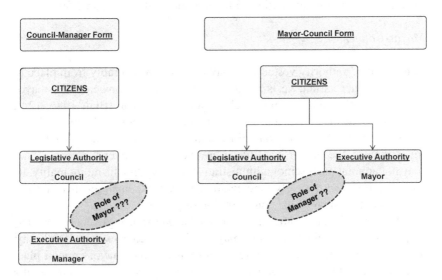

abound, there are five primary organizational designs found in municipal governments. All models have, at their core, different approaches to the nature of the relationship between executive and legislative authority. The five forms are mayor-council, council-manager, adapted city, commission, and town meeting.

The mayor-council form is based on the premise that an adversarial or political relationship exists between executive (mayor) and legislative (council) authority. The council-manager form is based on the premise that a unitary or collaborative relationship exists between legislative (council) and executive (manager) authority. The "adapted city" model is a hybrid of the first two, seeking to integrate the political leadership of the mayor and policy leadership of the manager in a way that complements both (Fredrickson, Wood, and Logan 2001).The other two forms, commission and town meeting, are perhaps more important for their historical value than as current forms of local government.

In Figure 4.6, we show the major issue facing the introduction of a mayor in a council-manager system, which is what legislative and/or executive authority the mayor will have. Conversely, the major issue facing the introduction of a manager in the mayor-council form is what executive authority, if any, the manager will have and what, if any, would be the nature of the relationship between the manager and the council? As we will discuss, efforts to balance the perspectives of a council, a mayor, and a manager often bring to mind the old adage, "two's company, three's a crowd." These three structures are the most common in municipalities with populations of more than 2,500.

Mayor-Council

The extent of authority vested in a mayor varies considerably from place to place. An older variant vests relatively little executive power in the mayor and is often referred to as the weak mayor-council plan (Blair 1986, 124). Often this status is affirmed by the fact that the selection of the mayor is the result of a vote of the city council from among the council membership. In this structure, the mayor has little if any veto power over the council and may not appoint most senior administrative posts within the municipality. Its roots are found in the early nineteenth-century Jacksonian ideals of citizen government and fear of the concentration of power.

Particularly in larger cities, the perceived need for strong executive leadership has served to help invest some mayors with far greater executive authority. This organizational form, often referred to as a strong mayor-council plan, is characterized by a clear separation of powers. The council serves as the legislature and the mayor serves as the executive, exercising full appointive powers and veto powers over legislative actions of the council. Again, it is the method of selection of the mayor that affirms this distinction. Traditionally, the strong mayor form provides for the direct election of the mayor by the citizens, who generally do not serve on the council.

Council-Manager

In the early part of the twentieth century, American local government faced two significant challenges. The first challenge was the need to build, quickly and economically, the public infrastructure of roads, water, and other utilities. The second was the need to address serious issues of graft, corruption, and a general inefficiency in service delivery (Stillman 1974; Nalbandian 1991). Reformers believed that there existed a clear distinction between the making of public policy and its implementation: In one domain, elected officials engage in a process of making policy through legislation. In the other domain, professional managers implement and administer those policies. They further believed that local government should be committed to principles of political neutrality. In the end, there really was no distinction between the "Political Party A" and the "Political Party B" snowplowing program. And finally, reformers believed that the best path to efficient and effective government was through employing experts who would lead.

The organizational answer to the needs of American local government was the council-manager plan. In its simplest form, the plan called for a small council responsible for making public policy and a council-appointed manager who was a member of a national association/network of experts specifically trained in the management of local governments. This manager would implement the policies of the council in an objective and politically neutral manner.

This form of local government originated in Staunton, Virginia, with the appointment in 1909 of a city administrator (Blair 1986; Cox 2004). The plan gained credibility and relevance for larger cities with its adoption in Dayton, Ohio, in 1912, and by 1921 was employed in 121 cities. By 1940, the number of communities using this form of government was about 400. The principles of the manager plan resonated well with the suburban communities of metropolitan America. It has experienced rapid expansion since World War II and is now the principal form of local government in communities with populations of more than 2,500 (3,302 communities comprising 75.5 million citizens) (Hansell 2000).

The manager plan was associated with three reforms. The first was the short ballot, a process wherein the voters elected only a few but important positions in the community. The long ballot included obscure and administrative positions that were unfamiliar to voters but conducive to providing patronage and favors to party loyalists in a corrupt government. The second reform was the at-large election of the council. The community as a whole was perceived as the most important consideration for an elected official. District elections would simply interfere with an official's pursuit of what was best for the community. The third reform called for nonpartisan elections, with no political party designation for candidates on the ballot. Such elections were seen as an important step toward ensuring that the community was "run like a business."

Many early city managers took on their new responsibilities with missionary zeal (Stillman 1974). Not only were they bringing management improvements to a community, they perceived themselves as reformists, enlightening the unenlightened. Although ethically committed to the particular community they were in at the moment, their ultimate responsibility was to spread this new form of government to other communities. That legacy still exists, as most managers will serve multiple communities during their careers.

On the positive side, the council-manager plan has created a national network of professionally trained managers whose career is service to local governments in a responsible and ethical fashion. The International City/County Management Association (ICMA), an association of managers in service to local governments, anchors this network. Education for this network is primarily through graduate schools of public administration and management, many of which offer master's degrees specifically focused on the management of local governments. By 1995, nearly 73 percent of managers in council-manager communities had a master's or professional degree (Hansell 2000, 18). Regulation of the network occurs primarily through adherence to an inviolate code of ethics outlined and enforced by the ICMA. This code of ethics has become deeply rooted in communities that have adopted the council-manager plan and is often informally adopted by nonparticipating communities informally (Cox 2004).

The ICMA membership originally adopted the code in 1924. It has been modified several times since then, most recently in May 1998, but still retains the original principles. The 12 tenets of the ICMA Code of Ethics are presented in the Figure 4.7.

The ICMA Code of Ethics

On the negative side, since its inception, the council-manager plan has suffered from the impractical notion that politics and administration can truly be separated. In theory, the manager is not supposed to be involved in the making of policy. In practice, managers are very much involved in the policy-making process (see, for example, Ammons and Newell 1988 and Protasel 1989). Nalbandian (1991) refers to the desired dichotomy between politics and administration as an important symbol that is sought after but never obtained. However, the idealized pursuit legitimizes the manager plan and guides the actions of the manager in minimizing the perceived role that the manager plays in the policy-making process.

The relative advantages and disadvantages of the mayor-council and council-manager plans have long been debated (Lineberry and Fowler 1967; Lyons 1978). These efforts at comparison are inconclusive. The council-manager plan seems to be more responsive to pressures in controlling overall costs while the mayor-council plan seems to be more responsive to individual constituent demands. In the end, the decision on the appropriate organizational approach is a local one and either plan appears to work satisfactorily. Local community citizens are provided with processes that allow their communities to switch from one form to another should their evaluation warrants such a change.

The Adapted City

While the two forms—mayor-council and council-manager—dominated the reform efforts at the beginning of the twentieth century, the reality is that in practice those forms of government are becoming blurred. Some have even

Figure 4.7   **ICMA Code of Ethics**

The mission of ICMA is to create excellence in local governance by developing and fostering professional local government management worldwide. To further this mission, certain principles, as enforced by the Rules of Procedure, shall govern the conduct of every member of ICMA, who shall:

1. Be dedicated to the concepts of effective and democratic local government by responsible elected officials and believe that professional general management is essential to the achievement of this objective.
2. Affirm the dignity and worth of the services rendered by government and maintain a constructive, creative, and practical attitude toward local government affairs and a deep sense of social responsibility as a trusted public servant.
3. Be dedicated to the highest ideals of honor and integrity in all public and personal relationships in order that the member may merit the respect and confidence of the elected officials, of other officials and employees, and of the public.
4. Recognize that the chief function of local government at all times is to serve the best interests of all of the people.
5. Submit policy proposals to elected officials; provide them with facts and advice on matters of policy as a basis for making decisions and setting community goals; and uphold and implement local government policies adopted by elected officials.
6. Recognize that elected representatives of the people are entitled to the credit for the establishment of local government policies; responsibility for policy execution rests with the members.
7. Refrain from all political activities which undermine public confidence in professional administrators. Refrain from participation in the election of the members of the employing legislative body.
8. Make it a duty continually to improve the member's professional ability and to develop the competence of associates in the use of management techniques.
9. Keep the community informed on local government affairs; encourage communication between the citizens and all local government officers; emphasize friendly and courteous service to the public; and seek to improve the quality and image of public service.
10. Resist any encroachment on professional responsibilities, believing the member should be free to carry out official policies without interference, and handle each problem without discrimination on the basis of principle and justice.
11. Handle all matters of personnel on the basis of merit so that fairness and impartiality govern a member's decisions pertaining to appointments, pay adjustments, promotions, and discipline.
12. Seek no favor; believe that personal aggrandizement or profit secured by confidential information or by misuse of public time is dishonest.

Source: ICMA.

suggested that the distinction may have lost relevance as a way of classifying forms of local governments (Svara 2001). A 1996 study found that in governments with either a mayor-council or council-manager plan only 3.7 percent were pure mayor-council cities, 17.5 percent were pure council-manager cities, and 78.8 percent were adaptations of the two forms (Fredrickson, Wood, and Logan 2001). Frederickson and Johnson (2001) suggest that cities tend to change their structures incrementally. Over time, cities with mayor-council statutory platforms will incrementally adapt many of the characteristics of the council-manager form to improve their management and productivity capabilities. The principal form of adaptation for the mayor-council form is the introduction of professional management positions within the government. One variation of this three-headed government is that the mayor, not the council, appoints the professional manager (generally referred to as city or town administrator). Under such arrangements the mayor is the CEO and the manager the chief administrative officer (CAO). Conversely, the primary adaptation of the council-manager form is the presence of a separately elected mayor who may have extensive power and authority within the government. Such cities now constitute a third form—the adapted city.

Special/School District Government

If one were to ask Americans about local government, they would likely describe cities, towns, and counties. Yet there are another 50,000 units of local government that have some type of taxing or expenditure authority. Equally important, these are predominantly units of government that provide direct services. These districts, as local government institutions, fall into two broad categories—special and school. Such districts are different in two ways. First, the idea of local special districts is essentially a twentieth-century concept. While a few parks, water, and mass transit districts were created around a few major cities at the end of the nineteenth century most special districts were created after World War II. Second, special districts typically have limited taxing authority, with revenues coming from service fees. School districts in one form or another go back to the very first public schools in seventeenth-century New England and become common by the beginning of the nineteenth century. Furthermore, the taxing authority of schools ranges from zero in New England to the authority to use multiple types of taxation (including income taxes) to raise revenues. Let us first focus on noneducational special district governments.

Special Districts

The variation in role, responsibility, and geographic reach of special districts makes them difficult to categorize. Nonetheless, there are a few general observations that can be made about them. First, they represent the largest group of local governments, with 37,381 such districts in 2007 (see Table 4.1). Second, they accounted for 90 percent of the growth in total new local governments between 1952 and 2007. Third, they tend to be narrowly focused,

Table 4.1

Change in the Number of Special and School Districts, 1967–2007

Districts	Year 1967	1997	2007	Change
Total				
School Districts	21,782	13,726	13,051	−37%
Special Districts	21,264	34,683	37,381	63%
Special				
Single Purpose Districts	20,811	31,965	—	54%
Multipurpose Districts	453	2,718	—	500%
Single Purpose Special				
Fire Protection	3,665	5,601	—	53%
Housing, Community Development	1,565	3,469	—	122%
Water Supply	2,140	3,409	—	59%
Drainage, Flood Control	2,855	3,369	—	18%
Soil and Water Conservation	2,571	2,449	—	−5%
Sewage	1,233	2,004	—	63%
Cemeteries	1,397	1,655	—	18%
Libraries	410	1,496	—	265%
Multipurpose Special				
Sewerage and Water	298	1,384	—	364%
Natural resources and water	45	117	—	160%
Other	110	1,217	—	1,006%

Source: U.S. Department of Commerce, Bureau of Census. Volume 1: Governmental Organization.

serving a single purpose. In 1997, 92 percent of special district governments were undertaking a specific function or responsibility. Fourth, their formation usually arises from the perceived need of participants to solve a particular problem rather than as the result of a desire to address a set of complex and interrelated problems or issues in a metropolitan area.

There are two broad types of special districts. The first is generally designed to have a service territory approximately coterminous with a particular city or town government or a part of that single jurisdiction. Occasionally, that service area includes parts of several communities. These special districts function as extensions of individual communities acting in a capacity that is isolated from the broader region of which they are a part. Examples of such districts would be a park district, a water and sewer district, or an irrigation district. The second type of special district reflects a more regionalized perspective. For instance, the county government may establish a special district to serve all of the county territory or a significant percentage of the municipalities within the county. Another example is when a group of municipalities create a special district to serve their collective needs. Such districts range from regional transportation districts to water districts. These forms of special districts will be treated in more detail in Chapter 9.

School Districts

Interestingly, the highest expense category of local governments is education. Yet, the discussion of school districts constitutes a relatively small part of most textbooks on the subject of local government. Further, most school districts are independent local governments. Of 15,834 school districts, 14,422 (91 percent) exist with an elected board and taxing powers. Of the dependent school districts, the majority are departments within a municipal government. These school departments are concentrated in the New England states of Connecticut, Maine, Massachusetts, and Rhode Island.

The reasons for this light treatment are not obvious, but several can be offered. Initially, the management form and structure of independent school districts is comparatively uniform across the United States. That form consists of a generally small elected board (5 to 11 members) that serves the legislative function and a school superintendent who serves the executive function. While school superintendents are elected in a few parts of the country, in general they are selected on the basis of professional training and background in school management. A loose comparison would be to view the organization of school districts as if all municipal governments had adopted the manager plan as their organizational design.

Secondly, although education policy and management is a highly complex field, the issues in school policy are not as divergent as those of municipal or county governments. The forms of "governance" of public school systems are few. Even in states where the superintendent is elected, candidates must meet basic qualifications. This is not to say that school district issues are not politically controversial, but the focus tends to be on the internal management of the schools.

Concluding Thoughts and Things to Ponder

It is all but impossible to adequately capture the variation and variety of local government forms and types. We will return to a more detailed discussion of each of these governments in relation to metropolitan governance in coming chapters. At this point, four observations are important:

- Regional and historic variations in the use of and approaches to local government dominate our understanding of these entities. As we begin to look at metropolitan and regional approaches to governance, these variations will mean that solutions that are politically and historically acceptable in one part of the country may be rejected elsewhere.

- While the relative independence from state controls through incorporation seems a minor topic, in reality state control of local governance structures is critical.
- The "city management" movement, with its emphasis on professional public management at the local level, is a mixed blessing; professional management of small and mid-size local governments is regarded by the general public as the best form, but for larger cities (and for counties) the public is less certain that professional management is the most appropriate form of governance. Managers are trained to first look inward to what is best for the community and second support rather than lead the policy process. Neither of these perspectives is likely to make city managers see regional solutions as the "best" alternative for urban areas.
- While "special districts" are different from the more familiar municipal and county governments, their role in metropolitan governance may be important.

Things to Ponder

1. This chapter begins by explaining the differences of expectations from the nineteenth century in comparison to current views of local government. Using the examples presented in this chapter, share thoughts about your current place of residence's local government. How is it set up? What are the special districts and/or school districts? How does it seem they set up within the local government—are they subsidiaries or departments within the government? Does your state have counties, for example?
2. Compare and contrast municipal, township, and city governments as described in this chapter.
3. Compare and contrast the five structures of municipal government, specifically mentioning the benefits and drawbacks of each.
4. Why was the ICMA created? Discuss its importance in local government.
5. Discuss the role of special districts within local governments. Be sure to include information on special district authority, types of special districts, fiscal resources, advantages and challenges they create.
6. How does regionalism bring these governments together to benefit the citizens of a particular area?

5

Fifty States, Fifty Different Systems

As presented in Chapter 2, there is a fundamental tension that exists between a state and the local governments within its borders. This tension has and is being played out in fifty different ways. Partially as a result of this, textbooks on intergovernmental relations devoted considerable attention to federal-state and federal-urban relations, but relatively little to state-local relations. Seemingly there was not enough going on in common to justify a more detailed examination of the relationships. Even if academics had ventured into this unexplored territory, they would have found that the rules of the game are as numerous as the states. Nevertheless it is our task to analyze state-local relations to determine the extent to which we can derive some common practices and potentially generalizable lessons about state-local intergovernmental relations.

To meet this challenge we present data on several aspects of intergovernmental relations, as viewed from the states. The first step is to examine who the players are in this relationship. As described below, the numbers of "local" governments vary in number and those numbers vary by region of the country. Four factors contribute to this variation: the frequency of special districts in states, the population within a geographic region, the scope of independent authority granted by states to local governments, and the historic evolution of local governments in different regions of the United States.

From a numbers perspective, the first part of this chapter explores the rich diversity of approaches to local government delivery in the state. That lays the foundation to better understand the legal and statutory constraints (or freedoms) that the states place upon their constituent local governments, which is our focus in the second part of this chapter. For example, is the capacity to cooperate or even consolidate local governments authorized through a general grant of statutory authority or can it be achieved only (or typically) by special legislation? Another example might be the extent to which the legislature is active in creating legal barriers to consolidation and cooperation through special or general laws limiting annexation or interagency service sharing. The reality is that the American intergovernmental "system" is neither systematic nor consistent. Instead our national system diffuses authority across and among regions.

The Relationship "By the Numbers"

Although the number of governments does not necessarily reflect the presence or absence of power, it dramatizes the different approaches that have been taken by American states to implement policy and deliver public services at the sub-state level. Figure 5.1 identifies the ten states with the largest number of local governments. A cursory review of the data suggests that geography and population size have a modest impact on a state's decision to create a few or many units of local government. The ten states with many local governments all have at least 3,000 units of local government. Utilization of school districts and special districts is also a common feature of those states. Except for Texas and California, these states generally have high instances of utilization of the town form of government and are generally located in the Northeast and Midwest.

The states on the other end of the continuum are far more heterogeneous (see Figure 5.2). Initially, it includes the smallest state, Rhode Island, and the largest state, Alaska. It includes states from New England, the South, and the West. Finally, it includes the first state (Delaware) to join the union as well as the last two (Alaska and Hawaii).

A number of states have the equivalent of a local government every 10,000 or so square miles. They fall into the categories of states with large numbers of local governments (Illinois and Pennsylvania) and states with fewer numbers of local governments (Connecticut and Delaware). It is also not uncommon for there to be the equivalent of a local government for relatively few people. In Kansas, there is a government for every 627 residents of the state. Only a few states exceed 10,000 residents per local government, with Hawaii being a true outlier with more than 58,000 residents per local government.

Table 5.1 (p. 76) compares the relative contribution of each state government and the local governments in that state in service provision by considering the direct expenditures made by each. Three broad approaches exist to the basic state-local relationship: state-dominant, balanced, and local-dominant. For classification purposes we designate a state as fiscally dominant when a state spends at least 20 percent more per capita than the sum of the local governments on the direct provision of services. While we do not want to read too much into this terminology, these governments also can be thought of service-dominant. Hawaii is the exemplar of a state-dominated arrangement. Services, which are typically delivered and *funded* by local governments, are funded and delivered by the state. While there are many factors that contribute to its distinctiveness, the facts that Hawaii is an island state and is dominated in population by a single city, Honolulu, the state capitol, contribute to the bias toward centralized power at the state level. Finally, this bias toward

74

Figure 5.1   Types of Local Governments in the Ten States with the Highest Number of Local Governments and Public School Systems, 2007

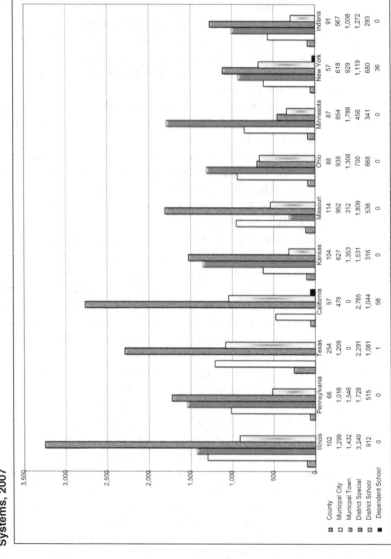

	Illinois	Pennsylvania	Texas	California	Kansas	Missouri	Ohio	Minnesota	New York	Indiana
County	102	66	254	57	104	114	88	87	57	91
Municipal City	1,299	1,016	1,209	478	627	952	938	854	618	567
Municipal Town	1,432	1,546	0	0	1,353	312	1,308	1,788	929	1,008
District Special	3,249	1,728	2,291	2,765	1,531	1,809	700	456	1,119	1,272
District School	912	515	1,081	1,044	316	536	668	341	680	293
Dependent School	0	0	1	58	0	0	0	0	36	0

Figure 5.2   **2007 Ratio of Direct Per Capita State Government Expenditures to Direct Per Capita Local Government Expenditures**

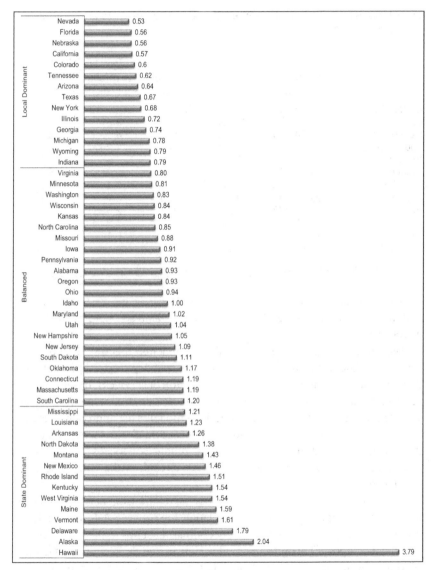

centralized service delivery makes more tightly controlled rules for service delivery possible, so that rule exceptions are less frequent.

In a number of states there is a balance between the state and the local government. This approach is most represented by Idaho where the direct expenditure levels are virtually identical. Idaho is unique in that it has a

Table 5.1

Ten States with the Lowest Number of Local Governments and Public School Systems, 2007

	2009 Population	Square Miles	Total Local Gov'ts	No. of Governments	
				Per 10,000 Population	Per 50 Square Miles
United States	306,406,893	3,536,217	89,476		
Utah	2,784,572	82,168	599	2.2	0.4
New Hampshire	1,324,575	8,969	545	4.1	3.0
Louisiana	4,492,076	43,566	526	1.2	0.6
Virginia	7,882,590	39,598	511	0.6	0.6
Delaware	885,122	1,955	338	3.8	8.6
Maryland	5,699,478	9,775	256	0.4	1.3
Nevada	2,643,085	109,806	198	0.7	0.1
Alaska	698,473	570,374	177	2.5	0.0
Rhode Island	1,053,209	1,045	134	1.3	6.4
Hawaii	1,295,178	6,423	19	0.1	0.1
% of U.S.	9%	25%	4%		

Source: U.S. Census Bureau, 2007 Census of Governments.

relatively widely dispersed population emphasizing its western, ranching culture, but it also has a significant portion of its land still held by the federal government (61.7 percent).

The third approach is for the local governments to act as the dominant service providers (i.e., the local governments spend at least 20 percent more than the state government for the direct provision of services). If only because of sheer numbers, it is reasonable to expect more variation in methods of service delivery under this more decentralized model. This approach is seen in Nevada, where in 2007 the local governments spent almost twice as much as the state government. In Nevada's case, the reliance on local service delivery exacerbated Nevada's financial condition as a result of the Great Recession (see Chapter 3).

It would be unwise to interpret the financial relationship between state and local governments as equal to a power relationship between state and local governments. This point is represented by comparing states in the state-delivery dominant category. This group includes Hawaii and the New England states of Maine, Vermont, and Rhode Island. In these states local government power and influence is far greater than the fiscal relationship suggests. In each of these states the intermediate local governments such as counties and special districts are relative weak. The historic developments in the New England states has meant that there have been in effect only two governments with the resources and authority to deliver public services—the state governments and the municipal governments. The dominant intergovernmental decision has been who will deliver (and fund) public services. This is a critical political choice that reflects the considerable political influence of local governments in the debate, even as the choice is for state delivery of the service.

States also vary considerably in the role played by the various types of local governments in each state. Some states prefer greater utilization of county government, while other states rely heavily on special districts, and others place greater emphasis on cities and towns (see also the discussion in Chapter 2). We frame this discussion around the conceptual and methodological work of Stephens and Wikstrom (1999). In their analysis, per capita direct expenditures are utilized as a measure of effort. The use of direct expenditures is key to understanding this relationship. Some programs, most typically social service programs, are funded by the states (and the federal government), but nominally the service is delivered by local government employees. The extent to which a local government uses its own resources is a more accurate depiction of its role in service delivery.

Computationally, all governments of a particular type (for instance, county governments) within a state are averaged and then each state is ranked by expenditure effort. In the above example, counties in Oregon represent the average of all counties in the United States. County governments in Oregon are assigned a value of 100 and average scores in other states are indexed against that value. New Jersey's county governments spend about 13 percent more than Oregon counties and New Jersey is assigned an index value of 113. Conversely, Pennsylvania's county governments spend about 22 percent less than Oregon's and Pennsylvania is assigned an index value of 78. This process is repeated for each type of local government (city, town, special district, and school district). Finally, an overall index value for all local governments within a state is developed.

Scores were calculated for each state. We present a summary of average state scores by region of the United States in Figure 5.3. As with the previous discussion, we use variation of 20 percent to distinguish between the scores. Therefore, one would interpret a score above 120 to indicate that a local government is considerably more active than the same type of local government in other states. For purposes of this analysis, scores between 80 and 120 represent states where the different types of local government are consistent with national averages. Scores below 80 represent states where that type of local government is significantly underutilized.

States in the Northeast are highlighted by the general dominance of their municipalities, both cities and towns. Conversely, it is also the region of the United States where county government is utilized the least. Indeed, towns in Connecticut scored 456, Massachusetts 314, Rhode Island 300, and Maine

Figure 5.3   **Relative Activity of a Particular Type of Local Government Compared to That Type of Local Government in Other States**

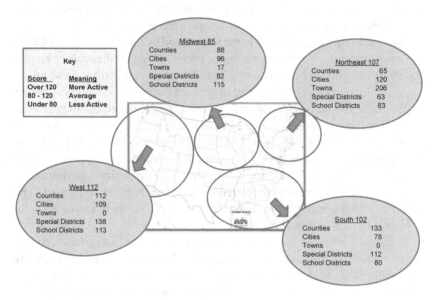

240. Towns in the Northeast, particularly in New England, have no counterparts in any other part of the country. As a companion to the dominant role of municipalities is the virtual absence of a role for county government in New England. The overall score for county government for the Northeast (the lowest in the United States) is higher by virtue of New York (114) and New Jersey (113).

Cities in the Northeast also scored highest of all regions. New York (360) leads the list, followed by Rhode Island (182), Massachusetts (166), and Connecticut (148). In terms of power and authority, cities and towns in the Northeast are virtually the same.

The role of special districts is generally limited in this region. Pennsylvania is the only state where special districts scored above 120 (129). The next highest score for special districts was 81 in New York. Generally, school districts in New England break into a pattern of underutilization, with Vermont (140) the exception, and a pattern of significant utilization in other parts of the Northeast typified by New Jersey (135), Pennsylvania (129), and Delaware (122).

School districts are the most active type of local government in the Midwest. Eight of the 13 states in the Midwest have school districts with scores above 120. With the exception of Illinois (179) and Nebraska (159), special districts, unlike school districts, are underutilized.

City governments, although utilized in all states, play, at best, a modest role, as do county governments. It also appears that there is little trade-off between the relative role of county government and city government. In five of the states (Kansas, Kentucky, Minnesota, Nebraska, and North Dakota) the relative role of city and county government is the same. In Illinois, South Dakota, and Missouri, county government is less utilized and city government is more utilized. In the other states, the situation is reversed; lower utilization of city government corresponds to a higher utilization of county government (a fuller discussion of the role of counties is presented in Chapter 9).

Common to the South is the absence of the township form of government. Apart from that similarity, this region is difficult to categorize. It has the most active county governments (Maryland, North Carolina, Tennessee, and Virginia). Yet county governments are underutilized in some states. The role of city government ranges from negligible in Maryland to above average in Tennessee.

The utilization of special districts also varies widely. Negligible utilization in Arkansas, Mississippi, and Oklahoma is offset by significant utilization in Alabama and Georgia. School district utilization follows a similar pattern; from significant use in West Virginia to negligible use in Maryland, Tennessee, and Virginia, where schools are administered through the county government.

In the West, like the South, the township form of government is nonexistent. Unlike the South, this region is much more homogeneous in the distribution of power among its local government institutions. It is highlighted by the hyperactive utilization of special districts in 7 of the 11 states. It is the area of the United States that relies most heavily on special districts. The outliers are Nevada's utilization of county government and New Mexico's underutilization of special districts.

Unique Situations, Systems of Local Authority, and Cultures

Comparing states by region is one lens that provides useful insights into the dynamics of U.S. state and local government. Another point of comparison is the discretionary authority granted to local governments by their respective state legislatures. Zimmerman's (1983) definition of discretionary authority presents a useful framework and includes four characteristics:

- The degree to which a local government can raise revenues necessary to support the functions it has decided to undertake (finance)
- The ability of a local government to choose activities or functions it wishes to undertake (function)
- The ability of a local government to regulate and determine the makeup and responsibilities of its workforce (personnel)
- The degree to which a local government can define its own organizational structure (structure)

Although Zimmerman treated all four factors equally, they have been weighted for this analysis. Adequate finances and the flexibility to raise revenues are fundamental to governments. Without resources, all other discussions are academic. The finance factor, therefore, is given the greatest weight. Selection of the activities that the government will engage in based on local initiative and interest constitutes the next most important element of discretionary authority (function). Many local governments throughout the world are constrained by legislative prohibitions on the activities in which a local government can engage.

Next in importance is control over personnel. State legislatures have often created specific conditions protective of local government employees that are mandated for the local government. Until recently, it was state law to set a minimum staffing rate of 150 for the city of Scranton, Pennsylvania Fire Department. That law was only changed after the city went through a financial collapse and subsequent restructuring.

The least important criterion is structure. Structure is clearly important, but most local government structures are standardized either as council-manager or mayor-council organizations.

Discretionary authority appears to be related to a number a factors. First, the greater the number of units of local government in a state, the more likely states will grant increased discretionary authority. More governments create more complexity for state officials and, as a result, local governments are afforded a greater opportunity to exercise their own initiatives.

Second, population serves a similar function. As states become more populated, there is greater local discretion. This observation is consistent with the findings of Berman and Martin (1988). However, population density works in the opposite direction. As density increases, discretionary authority decreases. It is likely that greater density creates pressures on the state system to regulate the interplay of local government actors. That said, states that have both significant urbanized (greater density) and significant rural areas (lesser density) grant greater discretionary authority. In states where both exist, the rural and urban areas require autonomy to address their unique issues.

Another dimension is political culture. Elazar (1966, 1975, 1984) has classified three dynamically interactive political subcultures embedded within American society. These cultural perspectives establish frames of reference by which the debate over the role and nature of local government is processed in each state. Political culture can best be described as "an enduring set of beliefs, values, and traditions about politics which constitutes a general framework of plans, recipes, rules, and instructions for the conduct of political life, especially who gets what, when, and how" (Kincaid 1980, 91). Tracing historical settlement and migration patterns, Elazar (1966) has classified the types of political culture as moralistic, individualistic, and traditionalistic. Although each type shares common values of the American culture, each has distinct interpretations of those values and has synthesized and manifested them into different political systems.

There are several major themes underlying Elazar's work. The first relates to contrasting views of the fundamental nature of government in society. One view is that of a commonwealth, while a second is that of a marketplace. In a commonwealth, there tends to be a collective or communal pursuit of a "good society," which, although often a vague abstraction, becomes an end unto itself. With such an orientation, issues of substantive justice prevail. Conversely, in a marketplace, government is an arena in which individuals and groups bargain out of enlightened self-interest. The notion of a "good society" is seldom an end unto itself. As a result, concerns over procedural justice prevail.

A second theme involves how space and territory are defined. To Elazar, there are two principal views. The first view originated in New England and sees territory as the domain of a particular group. A group is free to pursue its own vision of society. New England towns of the eighteenth century were primarily built as religious communities wherein each of the inhabitants shared a common belief about the relationship between Man and God (Zuckerman 1970). When community members' beliefs differed from those of their fellow townspeople, their option was often to move and create another community in which their beliefs became dominant. Indeed, much of the early growth in New England occurred in this fashion. The second view of territory is much more heterogeneous. It presumes that many groups will occupy the same territory. Control and power over that territory is a constant competitive battle among groups for dominance.

The moralistic cultural perspective tends to view the world as a commonwealth and territory as the domain of a particular group. Its primary roots are in the covenanted communities of New England and the Puritan/Calvinist religious movements. It is represented by an activist orientation that may or may not involve governments in the search for the "good society." Individuals are expected to engage in that search, making government everyone's responsibility and duty. Government structures become forums in which the issue is the center of debate.

The individualistic cultural perspective is that of the marketplace and a more heterogeneous view of territory. The primary role of government is to provide the process that keeps the economic sphere in order. Government is a business, often organized through a hierarchical party apparatus, that tends to be the arena for professionals and perceives a more limited role for the citizen. Although government exists to maximize the preferences of constituents, it also allows for the accumulation of personal gain on the part of actors.

The traditionalistic cultural perspective manifests ambivalence toward the marketplace and an elitist concept of the commonwealth. Its primary roots, historically, are in the South. The fundamental role of government is the maintenance of the existing social order. As such, it is predicated on a hierarchical-ordered class system in which government is under the control of elites, who in turn use the tools of government to address (some) of the needs of the lower classes.

As was the case with discretionary authority, political culture plays a significant role in defining state and local government systems in the United States. States with a dominant moralistic or traditionalistic culture tend to assume a greater share of fiscal responsibility whereas states with a dominant individualistic culture are more apt to place a greater fiscal role on the shoulders of local governments.

The Institution of Home Rule

In Chapter 2 we noted the considerable influence of the state in the organization and structure of all local governments. Partially in response to Dillon's rule, county governments sought approval for general legislative authority to shape municipal and county governments to fit the political and societal demands placed on them. For example, Pennsylvania's home rule law, enacted in 1972, establishes the procedure by which municipal and county governments may adopt a home rule charter:

- The voters of a local jurisdiction first decide whether to form a government study commission.
- The voters then elect nonpartisan commission members, who are charged with studying the existing form of government, exploring alternatives, and deciding whether to recommend change.
- The election of a government study commission can be proposed through petition or by the current county commission.
- If the government study commission decides to recommend home rule, it drafts a proposed charter that is then presented to the voters.
- The new home rule charter becomes effective only after the approval of majority voting in a referendum.

This process was successfully applied in the reform of the Luzerne County (Pennsylvania) government in 2010 (Sanford, Hudson, O'Looney, and Gordon 2012).

The primary direction in the reform of county government structure has been to move toward creating a single executive officer, either elected or appointed (Blair 1986). The elected executive plan was first adopted in 1893 in

Cook County, Illinois, and now describes more than 60 of the larger county governments. Overall, it is estimated that 480 county governments are organized in this manner (Hansell 2000). It is most prevalent in New York (where it is referred to as the supervisor form), Maryland, and Wisconsin. The only two home-rule counties in Ohio adopted the elected executive model: Summit County in 1979 and Cuyahoga County in 2009.

Blair (1986) suggests the advantages of the elected executive include a more visible policy-making process for voters to see, the potential for strong political leadership to unite diverse segments of the county, an ability to focus responsibility and accountability for the voters, the potential for increased prestige within the intergovernmental hierarchy, and a more understandable system of checks and balances between the executive and legislative branches. Its critics, particularly in light of a historical culture of patronage in many counties, see the concentration of power in the executive as too great an opportunity for bossism.

The appointed executive plan was first introduced in Iredell County, North Carolina, in 1927. In this form of government, either the board of commissioners or a county council holds the legislative powers, while the executive authority is vested in a single individual appointed by the legislative body. In effect, this is a council-manager form of government applied to a county. This has become a relatively popular form of government. The Luzerne County, Pennsylvania, charter change created just such a form of government. Currently, more than 300 counties have positions that are recognized by the ICMA as generally meeting the requirements of the single executive, and thus making the executive eligible for membership in that organization. Not surprisingly, given our earlier commentary on importance of counties in the South, more than 60 percent of counties "recognized" by the ICMA are located in the South. In addition, there are a number of counties that have chief administrative officers who probably meet some parts of the definitional requirements for single executive structure. Blair (1986) estimates the total number of county governments with this form of county government at about 500. A later estimate is 1,151 (Hansell 2000). Nonetheless, approximately 2,200 county governments, or about 66 percent, retain the traditional structure of county government (the commission) as their organizational design (Hansell 2000).

State Approaches for "Managing" Local Relationships

We began this chapter with the assertion that state-local relations would be hard to capture or categorize. Not only are state-municipal, state-county, and state-special district relationships different substantively, politically, and fiscally, their political culture and history differ as well. It is easier to express the relationship by describing policies and practices rather than by using structural terms. Most states depend on local governments to a greater or lesser degree to deliver services, and in particular social services. There is a growing perception that all local governments, especially cities, are becoming more constrained in the exercise of discretion and thus control over "local" affairs (Bowman and Kearney 2012). The loss of local control may extend to the reality that the state not only defines the policy parameters within which the local government employees work, but even the revenues for their paycheck. It is difficult to think in "partnership" or relational terms for such activities. In all but name, these are state employees, performing tasks through regional offices that happen to be cities or, more likely, counties. In other settings, such as law enforcement, transportation and most regulatory settings, there is a dominant partner, who carries most of the burden of financing the endeavor. In transportation and higher education the dominant partner is the state. In law enforcement, as well as in water and sewer distribution and mitigation, the primary partner is local government. There is a third category of programs for which the dominant partner may no longer be the primary funder of the activity, but for political and historic reasons the public continues to see them as the dominant partners. Americans persist in defining primary and secondary education as "local" even though most states provide somewhere between 50 and 70 percent of the funding.

The other side of this equation concerns the "structure" of local government. In Chapter 4 we described the structural and organizational aspects of local government, with particular emphasis on municipal governments. In preparation for the discussion about regional governance models in Chapter 6, we turn to the role of the state in fostering the development of local government partnerships through the authorization of a variety of service-sharing approaches such as interlocal agreements, cross-jurisdictional arrangements, cross-jurisdictional reorganization, two-tiered governments, multijurisdiction organizations, annexation, and the consolidation of services through the merger of departments or governments. These partnerships may involve relatively simple service agreements, such as mutual aid agreements, or extend to the merger of governments on multiple "levels." While some service-sharing practices are possible without the consent or involvement of state governments, even at the agency level, the state may have a role, and inevitably schemes for consolidation of governments require the active concurrence of the state.

States employ two broad strategies: (1) those that foster cooperation and (2) those that foster consolidation. Such strategies can also vary depending on the service or services around which cooperation or consolidation is occurring. On one hand, it could involve departments within several governments,

Figure 5.4   **Broad Strategies for States to Organize Intergovernmental Activities in Metropolitan Regions**

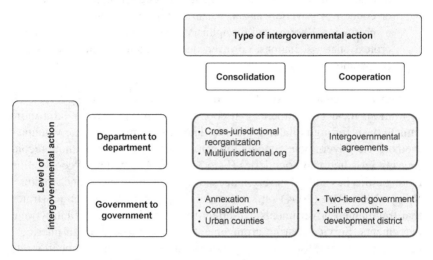

which we refer to as department-to-department cooperation, or consolidation. On the other hand, it could involve the governments themselves, again either through cooperation or consolidation. These strategies are summarized in Figure 5.4.

Interlocal Service Agreements

Town and township governments are often challenged by policy problems that extend beyond their boundaries. "Jurisdictional fragmentation complicates the management of boundary-spanning public infrastructure, environmental pollution, crime, regional economies, and other problems that spill over the borders of one city to the next" (LeRoux, Brandenburger, and Pandey 2010, 268). These problems are complex and require a multijurisdictional approach to their solution. Because of the breadth of reach of these jurisdictions, it becomes necessary to have a collective action to "effectively manage regional problems, minimize negative externalities, and maximize economies of scale" (ibid.).

Recent studies have shown that municipalities with scale economies benefit from shared service delivery. The National Administrative Studies Project IV (NASP-IV) from 2008–9 is a multivariate analysis examining a range of topics, including that of interlocal service among 919 municipal managers and department heads in the United States. According to LeRoux, Brandenburger and Pandey:

The findings indicate that interlocal service cooperation increases when jurisdictional actors network frequently through a regional association or council of government and when they are united by a common set of professional norms and disciplinary values. Manager participation in professional associations, however, does not increase interjurisdictional cooperation. (ibid.)

Rather than creating a single-purpose government, or forming a regional institution, local governments can cooperate with one another on a more limited basis through bilateral and multilateral agreements. These voluntary methods for government cooperation can be successful even without reconfiguring jurisdictional boundaries (Feiock 2004). The nature of cooperation among cities has shifted in recent decades toward this governance structure. Research by Post (2004) on service delivery, for instance, demonstrates that fragmented governments can effectively establish new voluntary joint agreements. Service-sharing arrangements can be made through interlocal agreements (ILAs), for example, parks, libraries, water management, waste management, law enforcement, fire departments, and land management. The flexibility of the ILA makes it a widely used tool "with more than half of cities and counties in the United States using them for at least one function" (LeRoux et al., 268).

As Reynolds (2003) notes, joint service agreements are rarely used as substitutes or alternatives to a regional approach. Compared to regional partnerships, they tend to be narrowly defined and limited in scope, but they also offer a way to complement preexisting local government policy. Wood (2005) classified intergovernmental agreements for service delivery as joint initiatives, contracts, transfer of services, city-county consolidation, and partnerships with regional institutions.

The key conclusion from the NASP-IV survey of local government practitioners searching for ways to increase collaboration was that "networks that afford opportunities for more face-to-face interaction yield better results" (LeRoux et al., 268). Zeemering and Delabbio (2013) found that counties and other local governments enter into "service-sharing" agreements for a variety of reasons. Among these are:

- Economic reasons
- Budget savings
- New revenue streams
- Stimulating innovation
- Improving decision making
- Building on complementary strengths

- Transferring knowledge and skills
- Increased levels or quality of service
- Improving work relationships

Cross-jurisdictional Reorganization

A second category of service sharing involves merging of departments and agencies across governmental boundaries or the transfer of a service to another government (whether another township, the county, or a regional organization). Such efforts do not necessarily require state approval via general or special statutory authority. This has been an increasingly popular strategy across the country. For many of the same reasons that agency-to-agency interlocal agreements make both organizational and financial sense, service responsibility transfers and cross-jurisdictional transfers work for local governments. For example, the City of Akron merged its building inspection division with that of Summit County and consolidated its public health department with that of the City of Barberton and Summit County, creating a single, countywide department. As noted in Chapter 3, the state legislature in Ohio has made alterations to the local government fund that creates incentives for such mergers and consolidation and disincentives for failure to do so.

Two-Tiered Government Agreements

A still more sophisticated version of service sharing involves agreements whereby services are allocated to both the municipal and county governments. The origin of this model dates to the "counties" of the United Kingdom before the founding of this country. The original idea was to assign tasks to specific governments. As this practice evolved in the United States it became more common for the two governments to perform the same tasks and functions, but typically in different geographic areas. Even though the goal of the two-tiered government was to separate functions, operationally the capacity to perform the function existed at both levels. To facilitate that distribution, government-to-government contracting of services is required. These agreements do not necessarily require any state authorization. Two examples of this arrangement are found in neighboring counties in Florida—Miami-Dade and Broward. In the case of Miami-Dade County, the two-tiered system was embedded in the 1957 "home-rule" charter. The county government essentially offered the same services in the unincorporated areas as the municipalities did in their individual communities. The vision was that as the unincorporated areas organized into new municipal governments, services (public safety, sanitation, etc.) might well remain under the control of county government

through contract-for-services agreements. While the number of new municipalities was fewer than expected, with upwards of 40 percent of the land in
the county still "unincorporated" as late as 2000, there was a new push for
the development of new communities at the start of the decade. Use of county
services via contracts remains a popular choice in these newly incorporated
municipalities. By 2002, Broward County had achieved what Miami-Dade
had not: the incorporation of all land in the county into the 29 municipalities
of the county. There is a strongly competitive process of contract-for-service
agreements so that incorporating all the land did not mean ending the service
role of many county employees.

Multijurisdictional Organizations

This is the one form of service sharing that requires the active involvement of
state government. While a number of states have approved of such arrangements through special legislation, another group permits such efforts through
a grant of general statutory authority. A multijurisdictional organization is
any government agency or district with the capacity to levy taxes in support
of a specific function or a range of functions. The most important of these
organizations are regional governing organizations, which will be discussed
in more detail in Chapter 10.

Annexation

The most traditional of all methods of boundary expansion is annexation. Most
states authorize such an enterprise but with varying degrees of regulation.
Typically, annexation is directed at two types of land: unincorporated land
and parts (or the entirety) of a township. In looking at the statutes governing
annexation it is quickly apparent that they are directed to facilitate the transfer
of small and even isolated parcels of land into a neighboring municipality.
The basic formulation is as follows:

- Either the city or the landowners in the unincorporated area initiate a
  petition process for annexation.
- The land must in some way be adjacent to (contiguous with) the city
  annexing the land.
- The state reviews the petition for compliance with state law.
- There is a public hearing on the petition.
- There is a "vote" of some kind (for example the vote may be of the city
  council in the annexing community and the property owners in the area
  to be annexed).

An important aspect of this general framework is the assumption that small parcels being annexed make annexation of larger areas and especially townships more difficult. Small communities view annexation as a threat. Legislatures have responded by making it difficult for the central city (or even the larger suburb) to easily annex property. For example the State of Arizona requires that "[t]he governing body shall have approved a plan, policy or procedure to provide the annexed territory with appropriate levels of infrastructure and services to serve anticipated new development within ten years after the date when the annexation becomes final pursuant" (Arizona Revised Statutes 2005).

The State of New York offers a prototypical law for municipal annexation. The General Municipal Law, Article 17, stipulates the following:

Petition for Annexation (§703)

Territory in one or more local governments adjoining one or more other local governments may be annexed to the latter pursuant to the provisions of this article. A petition for such annexation, describing the territory, stating the approximate number of inhabitants thereof, and signed (1) by at least twenty per cent of the qualified persons residing therein, or (2) by the owners of a majority in assessed valuation of the real property in such territory assessed upon the last preceding assessment roll of, or utilized by, the local government or governments in which it is situated, may be presented to the governing board or boards of the affected local government or governments in which such territory is situated and a certified copy or copies thereof to the governing board or boards of the local government or governments to which it is proposed to annex such territory. A petition for annexation must describe the territory, state the approximate number of inhabitants, and be signed by at least twenty percent of the residents or by the owners of a majority in assessed valuation of the real property in such territory.

Resolution Initiating Annexation (§703-A)

Within ninety days after the hearing, the governing board of each affected local government shall determine by a majority vote whether the petition complies with the provisions of Article 17 and whether it is in the overall public interest to approve such annexation. At such time, each governing board shall adopt a resolution that includes findings with respect to compliance of the petition with the provisions of Article 17 and with respect to the effect of such proposed annexation on the overall public interest. Each board shall then make and sign a written order containing its determination and file copies together with copies of an agreement, if any, the petition, the notice, the written objections, if any, and testimony and minutes of proceedings taken and kept on the hearing, in the offices of the clerks of all the affected local governments. If a governing board does not make, sign, and file a written order, then the governing board shall be deemed to have approved the proposed annexation at the expiration of the ninety day period.

Notice of Petition Hearing (§704)

In the event it is proposed to annex territory, the governing board or boards of the local government or governments to which it is proposed to annex such territory and the governing board or boards of the affected local government or governments in which such territory is situated shall within twenty days after the receipt of a petition for annexation, the governing board(s) of the local government(s) that would annex such territory and the governing board(s) of the affected local government(s) in which such territory is situated must publish notice in their official newspaper(s) or newspaper(s) in the county having general circulation within such area. The governing board(s) of the local government(s) in which such territory is situated shall mail notice to each person or corporation owning real property in such territory. Notice shall state that a petition for the annexation of territory has been received, and that a joint hearing will be had upon such petition at a specified place and date not less than twenty nor more than forty days after the publication and mailing of such notice.

Petition Hearing (§705)

Such governing boards shall meet at the time and place specified in such notice. The governing boards shall hear testimony and receive any evidence and information regarding the validity of the petition and whether the annexation is in the overall public interest. Whether the annexation is in the overall public interest must be determined by weighing the benefit or detriment to the annexing municipality and the area to be annexed. Annexations may be in the overall public interest where, for instance, the annexation would enhance municipal services such as police and fire protection, subsidized sewer and water services, and other public facilities. However, proposed annexations may not be in the overall public interest where, for instance, the proposed annexation would place a heavy tax burden on the local government losing the land, or would not result in an improvement to either municipality involved but only benefit an individual private property owner.

Adjudication and Determination in the Supreme Court (§712)

In the event that a governing board of an affected local government determines that it is not in the overall public interest to approve the proposed annexation, the governing board of any other affected local government may apply to the Appellate Division of the Supreme Court for adjudication and determination of the issue.

Election (§713)

Within ninety days after the entry of a final judgment of a court or the filing of orders of the governing boards of such affected local governments approving a proposed annexation, the governing board of each municipality in which such territory is situated shall call a special election to be conducted to determine whether the proposed annexation should be approved. If such proposition is approved by a majority of the qualified voters, then the petition and a certificate of election shall be filed by the governing board(s), within twenty days after such election, in the office of the clerk of such local government(s) and in the office of the clerk of the local government(s) in which such territory is to be annexed.

Annexation After Election Approving Proposition (§714)

Upon the filing of the certificate or certificates of election approving the proposition together with the notice of entry of a final judgment of a court or of the approving orders of the governing boards of the affected local governments, the governing board(s) of the local government(s) to which such territory is to be annexed shall by local law, and without any hearing, annex to such local government the territory described in the petition. In the case of a municipality consisting of wards, council districts or other subdivisions from which representation on any elective board or body is selected, such local law shall designate the wards, council districts or other such subdivisions within which the territory annexed shall be included, which local law shall be adopted without referendum. A local law annexing territory to a local government pursuant to this section shall specify the date on which such annexation shall become effective, giving due regard to the taxable status dates of all the local governments to which and from which such territory is annexed and to the fiscal years of such local governments for which taxes, special ad valorem levies or special assessments are imposed. Such date shall be no earlier than the date of filing such local law in the office of the secretary of state.

Metropolitan Consolidation

The states are most directly involved in the rules controlling annexation and metropolitanization of government. The rules controlling these processes vary considerably, but generally share the features of a new charter and then a referendum in which distinct majorities in every jurisdiction involved must approve the charter. We discussed earlier the attempts at metropolitan consolidation that began in the nineteenth century and the city-county consolidation that was successful in the middle of the twentieth century. The political conditions for approval of such efforts seemingly were most favorable in the period from 1947 to 1997 when 24 such consolidations were approved (Hall 2009, 64). Presumably, because of the unique circumstance of the existence of independent cities in Virginia, 6 of those 24 city-county mergers occurred in Virginia. Relative to the process in other states, the merger of a county with an independent city (in a sense reuniting them) or of two independent cities is relatively straightforward, requiring a charter for the proposed new city and then a voter referendum. Compared to other places, such as Florida, where consolidation has been discussed but rarely succeeded, the fact that Virginia's independent cities are essentially on the level means that it represents the partnership of near equals has greatly facilitated the process.

The Virginia Approach: The Path Less Trod

Virginia has 95 counties, covering all of the territory not within the independent cities. As with virtually all other states, under Virginia law counties are an arm of the state itself and exist at the will of the state government, and their populations vary widely. Although Virginia has a long history of placing county government at the heart of local governance, the population changes in the state presented the general assembly with a problem, particularly with the densely populated northern Virginia area (metropolitan Washington, D.C.). Prior to creating the category of independent cities (see below) with authority equivalent to that of a county, the state had relatively few towns of any size (geographically or in population), and with small parcels of unincorporated land scattered across both rural and urban counties, the county was the de facto municipal government for much of the state. In a unique effort to address the needs of urban areas, the state created a new type of county government—the urban county.

Independent Cities

Typically, cities and towns are linked to the counties within which they are found. Counties, which are "creatures" of state constitutions and laws, historically were the primary local government across the southern United States. In the classic two-tiered model of governance, the county provides services that are not available through the cities or towns. The Commonwealth of Virginia is unique among the states in the legal construct of independent cities. Virginia's towns exercise limited functions of self-government and are subordinate, in most respects, to the counties in which they are located. The independent cities have the same authority as counties. Thus they may have their own court system, and with a few exceptions, their own record depositories. There are 41 independent cities in Virginia. Not only may independent cities comprise areas that are located in more than one county (a distinction they share with all Ohio cities), in some cases the independent city may constitute an entire county, as is the case with Suffolk, for example (The Pettit Company 2011).

Virginia's independent cities were classified by the Virginia General Assembly in 1871 as cities of the first class and cities of the second class. The Virginia Constitution of 1902 defined first-class cities as those having a population of 10,000 or more based upon the last census, while second-class cities were those that had a population of less than 10,000. Since 1871, all incorporated cities in Virginia have been independent of their surrounding counties (Wikipedia 2013b). Independent cities in Virginia are thus similar to unitary authorities in some states. In fact, the U.S. Census Bureau treats all cities in Virginia as county equivalents.

The distinction between first- and second-class cities was ended with the Virginia Constitution of 1971. However, cities that were classified as second class at the time of its adoption were authorized to continue sharing their court systems and three constitutional officers with the adjacent county. As of 2003 14 of Virginia's independent cities retain these features.

An independent city in Virginia may serve as the county seat of an adjacent county, even though the city by definition is not part of that county. Fairfax, for example, is an independent city as well as the seat of Fairfax County. An area within a county, which may or may not have been a town previously, incorporates as a city and thus becomes independent (Wikipedia 2013a).

A Tale of Three Cities: Suffolk, Virginia Beach,
and Norfolk, Virginia

The cities of Suffolk, Virginia Beach, and Norfolk in Virginia represent three paths to metropolitan consolidation. All were designated as independent cities and, like all independent cities in Virginia, have authority akin to that of a county. One result of this grant of authority was a series of consolidations in which independent cities merged with counties to create new, larger independent cities. Initially, Suffolk had close ties to its county because it served as Nansemond County seat. This relationship continued even after it gained status as an independent city. Then the county changed its form from county to independent city, but within a short period the two reconnected by merging as the expanded City of Suffolk, creating a very large (430 square miles) independent city.

The Virginia Beach path was somewhat different. It was not the county seat and was a very small independent city at a mere two square miles. On the other hand Virginia Beach was a thriving resort community. In the late 1950s the City of Norfolk gained independent status from first Norfolk County (1953) and then Princess Anne County (1959). Almost immediately the remainder of Princess Anne County merged with Virginia Beach, becoming the new independent City of Virginia Beach. Together, the City of Norfolk and the City of Virginia Beach constitute a land area larger than the original Princess Anne County. Of the two independent cities, Virginia Beach is the larger of the two, though both have relatively large land areas and populations.

Concluding Thoughts and Things to Ponder

At a certain level there are two sets of relationships between the states and their constituent local governments. In Chapter 2 we discussed the historical evolution of townships in New England and counties in the southeastern United States. There is also the historic development of a partitioned government whereby the states (and initially the federal government) were most likely to partner with county governments for the provision of public programs and, especially, social services. Well into the middle of the twentieth century, municipal government, especially in New England and across the northern half of the United States, provided services that were distinct from those offered by county government. Even in the southern United States where the primary government was the county, the practice of separating government functions between municipal and county governments was common. As early as the middle of the nineteenth century the municipal level began to dominate service delivery such as streetlights, water and sewer, and sanitation. Yet when the social welfare programs of the New Deal were created, the partner for the delivery of these new programs was the county. In the post–World War II era, Congress (belatedly and only briefly) and the state legislatures had an active "urban" agenda. During this period urban municipalities were the beneficiaries of urban-specific funding. Social service and other programs, such as highway construction, often began in the states and then migrated to the federal government. Federal funding followed the typical state path through the state and county governments to the municipal governments. However, when the federal government began developing urban-specific programs, they did so before most states. The funding pattern was more direct; from federal agency to city government, bypassing the states, making them primarily a conduit. While the states would follow with their own programs, the practice begun by the federal government of direct funding at the municipal level continued. Even without the variations in local governments, the funding flow and the emergence of urban-specific funding would increase the variability in the state-local relationship.

It remains to be seen whether or not the state is a help or a hindrance to metropolitan governance. The dynamics of state-local relations are influenced by the patterns of relationships that in some instances go back centuries, yet it can also be said that the increases in federal dollars that left the states as the least important partner also influences where we are today. There is nothing in the general approach to governance that makes the state a threat to metropolitan governance. Certainly and most notably, Virginia, Tennessee, and Florida in the last 50 years have facilitated metropolitan governance. On the other hand, some of the most "urban" states—Massachusetts, New York, Michigan, California, Minnesota, and the northeastern United States in general—are the places most reliant on municipal government for service delivery and the most reluctant to experiment with regional and metropolitan governments as an urban initiative. We will return to this topic in Chapter 11 when we examine the extent to which the states are a hindrance to the implementation of metropolitan "solutions" to urban issues.

Things to Ponder

1. Compare and contrast the three approaches to the basic state-local relationship.
2. Finance, Function, Personnel, and Structure are four factors that affect discretionary authority granted to local governments by states. Discuss how discretionary authority is affected by outdated legislation, number of local governments, and population.
3. Discuss the political, moralistic, individualistic, and traditionalistic cultural perspectives through themes of commonwealth/marketplace, space/territory, and the expectations of individuals.
4. What are the benefits of home rule law? Compare the advantages of elected and appointed executives.
5. Compare and contrast the strategies of cooperation and consolidation. How do these strategies support the formation of metropolitan regions?

6

The New Kid on the Block

The Metropolitan Region

State and local governments in the United States are political entities; metropolitan regions are not. Often, as a result, the definition of a region depends on who is thinking and what is being thought about. Recognizing that, at least for data collection, a standard definition is essential, the federal government has developed a set of definitions and terminology that can serve as a starting point. The federal government had to be careful when it created a nationwide definition for metropolitan regions. As with many federal-state issues, such a definition had to be nuanced in a way that would not be viewed by the states as federal meddling in the internal organizational affairs of the states. This was accomplished by defining these regions as "statistical areas," with a warning that these regions were designed for statistical purposes only.

The Federal Office of Management and Budget (OMB), designated as the agency to establish the boundaries of the regions, is explicit in capturing this perspective:

> MAs (metropolitan areas) are federal statistical standards designed solely for the preparation, presentation, and comparison of data. Before the MA concept was introduced in 1949 with Standard Metropolitan Areas (SMAs), inconsistencies between statistical area boundaries and units made comparisons of data from federal agencies difficult. Thus, MAs are defined according to specific, quantitative criteria (standards) to help government agencies, researchers, and others achieve uniform use and comparability of data on a national scale.
>
> OMB recognizes that some federal and state agencies are required by statute to use MAs for allocating program funds, setting program standards, and implementing other aspects of their programs. In defining MAs, however, OMB does not take into account or attempt to anticipate any of these nonstatistical uses that may be made of MAs or their associated data. Agencies that elect to use MAs for such nonstatistical purposes are advised that the standards are designed for statistical purposes only and that any changes to the standards may affect the implementation of programs. (OMB Bulletin 99–04)

Figure 6.1   **Distribution of U.S. Population by Metropolitan-Micropolitan Area, 2000 and 2009**

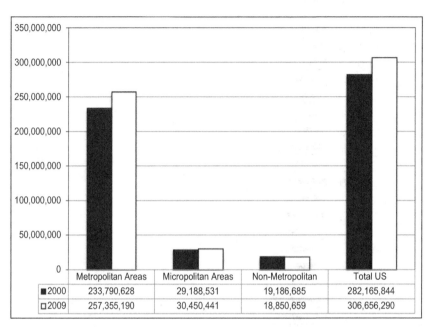

	Metropolitan Areas	Micropolitan Areas	Non-Metropolitan	Total US
■2000	233,790,628	29,188,531	19,186,685	282,165,844
□2009	257,355,190	30,450,441	18,850,659	306,656,290

Over time, these "statistical" regions have come to take on more than a data collection role. More often than not, individuals, groups, and organizations in these regions are beginning to think and act as citizens. As such, federal policy has encouraged the formation of embryonic regional institutions around those statistical boundaries. Regions are becoming political, as well as data collection, entities. Conceptually, the transformation of metropolitan regions from artificial data collection areas to political bodies is not unlike the transformation of county governments (see Chapter 4) over the last two centuries.

Part of the explanation for these "statistical" regions transforming into quasipolitical regions lies in the basis on which the statistical region is drawn. OMB defines a region as a core area containing a large population nucleus together with adjacent communities that are economically and socially integrated with that core. As a result, a metro area is built outward from an urban core (either city or county) to encompass outlying areas that have a significant interrelationship and interdependency with that urban core. When an outlying area no longer meets the test of social and economic connection to the core, the outer boundary is drawn and the metropolitan region defined. As such, these metropolitan regions are statistical in one sense but political in another as they define a community connected by virtue of social and economic ties. It is not that much of a reach for citizens with such interdependency to find

Figure 6.2   **Change in Population of Major U.S. Metropolitan Regions Between July 2000 and July 2009**

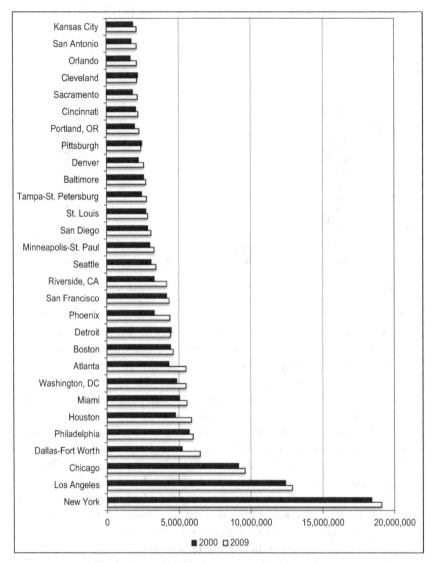

common political and policy reasons to work together to advance their collective and economic well-being.

OMB uses the county as the building block in constructing metro areas. A county and all the local governments within the county are either in or out of a metro area. OMB does not, as a rule, subdivide a county into multiple metro areas. Metropolitan regions are classified as Core Based Statistical Areas (CBSA). A region is further defined as "metro" if it contains a core urban area population of 50,000 or more, or "micro" if it contains an urban core population of at least 10,000 but less than 50,000. A portion of the largest metro areas are further divided into "divisions."

The United States has become an urban nation with just under 94 percent of its population living in an officially designated metropolitan area or CBSA (see Figure 6.1). Moreover, about 84 percent live in one of 366 metro areas while just under 10 percent live in one of 574 micro areas. Nonmetro areas comprise a relatively small percentage of the country, and those areas saw a population decline of almost 2 percent between 2000 and 2009. Conversely, population in metro areas increased by 10 percent during the same period.

Twenty-nine metro areas have populations in excess of 2 million (Figure 6.2). Even the largest metropolitan regions are comparatively small on a global basis. Globally, only 2 of 23 metropolitan regions with more 10 million population are located in the United States (New York City is ranked fourth and Los Angeles twelfth). Of the 100 largest metropolitan regions in the world, only 9 are located in the United States. That said, 136 million, or 44 percent of the American population, live in these 29 metro areas. Overall, this group grew by 10 percent in the last decade, but the growth was not evenly distributed in these regions. Even though all but 3 grew in population, 7 grew by more than 20 percent, headed by Phoenix (33 percent) and Atlanta (28 percent). The three large regions that lost population included the former manufacturing centers of the Northeast and Midwest (Pittsburgh, Cleveland, and Detroit). In these three regions, the population decline in their respective center city was so great that even growth in the outlying areas was unable to compensate for the losses.

The 942 metro and micro areas vary in size and geography. For purposes of this discussion, metro and micro areas were first grouped into population categories: large (more than 2 million); medium large (1–2 million); medium (500,000–999,999); medium small (250,000–499,999); small (fewer than 250,000). Areas are further defined by location (Figure 6.3).

A look at Figure 6.3 leads to a general assessment that U.S. metropolitan regions are relatively small. Indeed, more than 80 percent have populations under 250,000 and only 51, or just over 5 percent, have populations over 1 million. A geographic look reveals a concentration of regions. Indeed, more than 60 percent of all regions and 67 percent of regions over 1 million are located in the South and West. These areas have experienced a rapid population growth partially attributable to relocation from the Northeast and Midwest.

That 20 of the 29 largest metro regions (those with more than 2 million population) are located in the South or West dramatically captures the changing

Figure 6.3   **Distribution of U.S. Metro and Micro Regions by Location and Population Size, 2010**

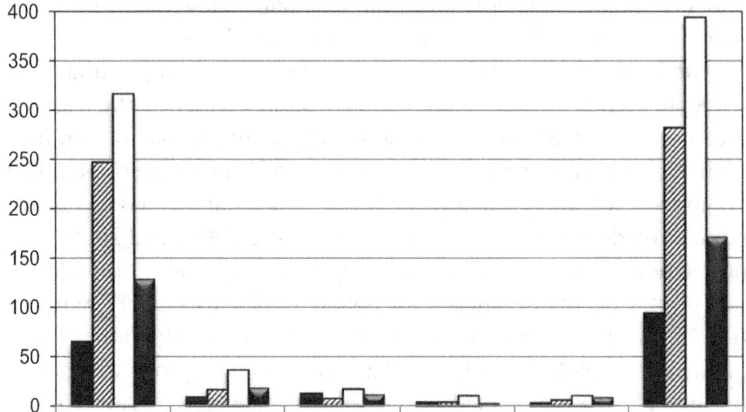

	Small	Medium Small	Medium	Medium Large	Large	Total
■ Northeast	65	9	13	4	3	94
▨ Midwest	247	17	8	4	6	282
▢ South	317	37	18	11	11	394
▨ West	129	19	12	3	9	172

American political geography. In 1950, close to 70 percent of the population who lived in U.S. cities were located in the Northeast and Midwest. In 2010, 54 percent of city dwellers lived in the South and West. The population of those South and West cities grew by 155 percent during that period while the population of the Northeast and Midwest cities declined by 6.5 percent.

Structural Characteristics of Metropolitan Areas

The number and mix of local governments in metropolitan region varies considerably across the United States. Arguably, the average of 57 units of local government in southern metropolitan regions could be classified as decentralized by international standards. However, the South is highly centralized by U.S. standards (see Figure 6.4). A typical metropolitan area in the Northeast contains more than 169 units of local government. The Midwest and the West fall between the Northeast and the South with 129 and 103 respectively.

This structural complexity of metropolitan regions, regardless of location in the United States, makes cross-boundary relationships both difficult to develop and hard to manage. Consider the Northeast wherein a typical metropolitan region is made up of more than 2 county governments, 75

Figure 6.4   **Average Number of Local Governments in a Metropolitan Region by Type of Local Government**

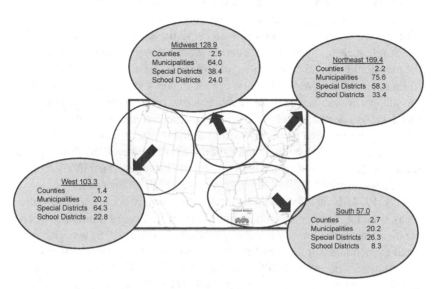

municipal governments, 58 special districts, and 33 school districts. Without collaborative arrangements that establish clear institutional frameworks for the management, arbitration, and resolution of disagreements among those actors, and short of formal legal remedies in the courts, there is little impetus to resolve the problems and issues from a metropolitan perspective. These issues are particularly acute in the Northeast and Midwest.

Utilization of types of local governments also varies across the United States. Municipalities are the primary organizing units in the Northeast and Midwest, making up 45 percent and 50 percent respectively of local governments in a typical metropolitan region. At the other end, municipalities constitute only 14 percent of a typical metropolitan region in the West. Conversely, more than 62 percent of a typical western metropolitan area is composed of special districts.

The Metropolitan Power Diffusion Index

Theory

In an effort to better understand the structured relationships that exist within local governments in a metropolitan area, a useful measure developed by Miller (2002) is called the Metropolitan Power Diffusion Index (MPDI).

Prior to the introduction of the MPDI, efforts to provide some comparative analysis of the structure of relationships of governments in metropolitan areas in the United States fell broadly into one of two methodological approaches. Miller's work represented an effort to bring these two approaches together in a single measure. Much of the earlier works characterized the structure of the metropolitan local government relationships question as one of degrees of fragmentation. As a result, the first approach was a simple process of counting the governments, either in absolute terms or on some per capita basis. Dolan (1990) defined local government fragmentation as the proliferation of government units that may exist within a given region. This work was built on the earlier work by Goodman (1980), who had identified four types of fragmentation—two of which were counts of (1) incorporated municipalities and (2) special districts, public authorities, and school districts.

Hill (1974), in an effort to assess inequality among residents of metropolitan areas, used the number of municipalities and the number of municipalities per capita as measures for comparative purposes. Bollens (1986) was also interested in inequality in metropolitan areas and used the number of non-center city municipalities over 10,000 population for every 100,000 population in the center city as a measure. Zeigler and Stanley (1980) used the number of local governments per 100,000 in their effort to distinguish geopolitical patterns of the frost-belt regions (Northeast and Midwest) from the sun-belt regions (South and West). Hawkins (1971) developed a measure of fragmentation as total governments per 100,000 population in an effort to determine the impact of that fragmentation on the cost of government. Oakerson and Parks (1988) used governments per 10,000 as a "fragmentation score."

The idea that the more governments there are, either in absolute or per capita terms, the more power is diffused in the region has merit. Creating a government puts in play another actor with political power and rights of entry into the decision-making process. However, one significant problem with the numbers game is that it fails to provide a measure of the role each government plays in or contributes to the region. As suggested in our discussion of special districts, many such districts have close ties to one, or a group of, government(s). They are essentially instruments of service provision. As such, having a significant number of governments that exist "on paper" can inflate that statistic as a meaningful indicator.

Indeed, several of the works cited above attempted to address this weakness. Dolan (1990) compensated by introducing the concept of fiscal dispersion fragmentation that is simply the standard deviation of the per capita expenditures of all the governments in the region. Bollens (1986) added the percentage of non-central city population that lives in incorporated municipalities with over 10,000 population as a measure. Zeigler and Stanley (1980) attempted to reduce several dimensions into a single index by using the number of governments as a direct proportion and the percentage of the population living in the center city as an inverse proportion.

Regardless of the efforts of these authors to add a political dimension, none of the studies added a time dimension. This generally can be understood in that the authors were using their measures to explain some other condition in metropolitan areas of the United States. As such, they fail to assess how power has changed over time.

The second approach applies a methodology from the business sector as it relates to market share of firms in a competitive arena and is often referred to as the Hirshmann-Herfindahl Index (HHI). This approach also has a simple premise—power is market share. If one firm has 90 percent of the market, whether 50 players or 5 players share the remaining 10 percent is of marginal interest. These small players have little "political power." Indeed, Scherer and Ross (1990, 72) observe: "The HHI weights more heavily the value for large firms than for small" (see also, Shepherd 1985). The methodology employed is to use the squared percentage of each player's share of the market. As that applies to local governments in a metropolitan area, some measure of expenditures on some array of public services usually substitutes for sales by the firm.

Lewis (1996) employs a variation of this approach in his political fragmentation index. Using the sum of the squared percentages of total expenditures in relation to the degree of expenditures, this index creates a single number that is more sensitive to the total level of expenditures than to the distribution of those expenditures within the metropolitan area.

Although both methodologies capture important principles—the first a measure of political power and the second a measure of economic power—they need to be combined so that both make a contribution to the resulting scale. As such, the problem can be viewed mathematically on a single scale. A colleague of ours (a mathematician) suggested that the square root of the squared contributions could be substituted for the square of the contributions. Whereas the square of the percentage contributions has the impact of exaggerating the contribution of the larger players, the square root of the percentage contribution has the impact of giving greater mathematical value to the smaller units. Basing the scale on the percent contribution of each player serves to reflect the economic dimension while using the square root of that contribution to reflect the political dimension of power derived from the relative autonomy of political jurisdictions in a metropolitan environment.

In the process of using the squared-percentage approach (HHI), the resulting scale ranges from 0 to 1. As the scale approaches 1, the greater is the concentration of market power. Hence, a low score represents a more diffused system. By switching to the square root, the scale starts at 1 and goes, theoretically, to infinity. Like the first scale, 1 represents pure concentration or one player with 100 percent of the market. Higher numbers, however, represent diffusion. Figure 6.5 illustrates this point.

Suppose there are two regions. One is called Region Six and the other Region Twelve. Region Six has 6 governments and Region Twelve has 12. Total local government expenditures in both regions are $1 million, of which $900,000 (or 90 percent) is spent by the largest government in each region. In Region Six, there are 5 smaller governments that each spend $20,000 while in Region Twelve there are 11 smaller governments that each spend $9,091.

If we compare three common measures of diffusion, we can reach three different conclusions about the distribution of power within these regions. Method 1 is to simply count heads (Region Six has 6 and Region Twelve has 12). However, to conclude that Region Twelve is twice as diffuse as Region Six would be erroneous. In both regions, one government makes 90 percent of the expenditures.

Method 2 is the Herfindahl approach (HHI); that is, the square of the percentage contribution of each government. That computation generates an index score of .812 for Region Six and .811 for Region Twelve—a virtual tie. However, to conclude that Region Twelve and Region Six are equivalent would also be erroneous. One region has twice as many governments as the other.

Method 3 is the MPDI; that is, the square root of the percentage contribution of each government. That computation generates an index score of 1.656 for Region Six and 1.997 for Region Twelve—a 21 percent difference. Because Region Six's score is closer to 1, it can be said to have a greater concentration of power and, because Region Twelve's score is higher, it can be said to be more diffuse than Region Six.

Applied

Expenditures serve as an excellent surrogate for political power in a metropolitan region, and we use them to develop the MPDI. The act of making particular expenditures by particular units of governments represents an individual choice about the expenditures being made and a collective choice on which types and levels of government will make those expenditures. The MPDI is a single score that measures how many separate local, county, and special-district governments provide 11 common public services and how much each of those governments spends in providing those services. The services measured include fire, central staff services, public buildings, highways, housing and community development, libraries, police, sewerage, solid waste

Figure 6.5 **Three Different Measures of the Governmental Structure of a Metropolitan Region**

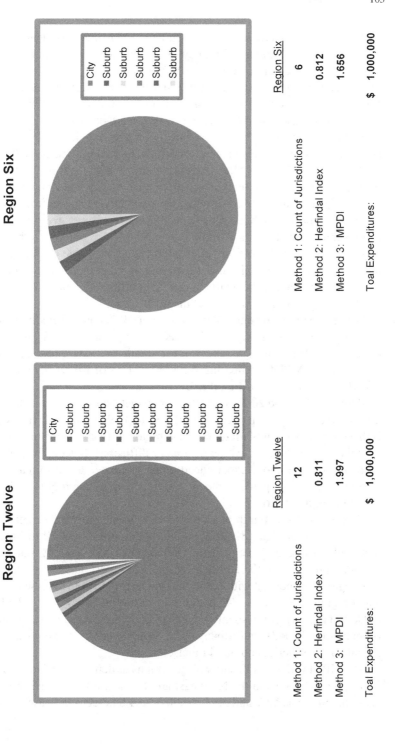

Region Twelve

Region Six

	Region Twelve
Method 1: Count of Jurisdictions	12
Method 2: Herfindal Index	0.811
Method 3: MPDI	1.997
Toal Expenditures:	$ 1,000,000

	Region Six
Method 1: Count of Jurisdictions	6
Method 2: Herfindal Index	0.812
Method 3: MPDI	1.656
Toal Expenditures:	$ 1,000,000

management, and water utilities. The more individual governments there are spending greater amounts of money on the services, the higher the MPDI score. The data used to compute the MPDI are from individual government financial reports compiled and distributed by the U.S. Census Bureau's Census of Governments program. For the analysis and discussion that follows we have used the metro and micro boundaries as they were defined in 2007.

There are several important caveats on interpreting the MPDI over time and comparing current results to prior results. First, the boundaries of Metropolitan Statistical Areas (MSAs), as previously noted, are forever changing. As the OMB warned, boundaries will change (sometimes dramatically) as new urban cores are created or counties are added/deleted to/from an MSA based on criteria (which itself has gone through revisions over time). As an example, the 2007 boundary of the Pittsburgh MSA is unlikely to be what it was in 1987, or 1972 for that matter. To compensate, we have defined metropolitan regions as they existed at a particular point in time. Change the point in time and it is likely the analysis will yield different numbers at the micro level but be generally consistent at the macro level.

Second, the most recent OMB iteration of MSAs puts virtually the entire U.S. population into a single region. As a result, many smaller jurisdictions have been added to the analysis. Because smaller regions tend to have lower scores on the MPDI, comparing the presentation of MPDI herein to prior MPDI versions may be difficult to do.

Between 1987 and 2007, the MPDI for all metropolitan areas in the United States increased by 6.5 percent—from 3.37 to 3.59. A more relevant statistic is that over 75 percent of all regions had higher diffusion scores in 2007 than they did in 1987 (an indication of greater diffusion). Indeed, 21 percent of all metropolitan regions experienced a rate of change toward greater diffusion in excess of 10 percent. Steadily and inexorably metropolitan America is becoming more diffuse.

Chicago and Pittsburgh head the list as the most diffused metropolitan regions with scores of 18 and 17. Table 6.1 compares the 10 most diffuse metropolitan areas by location in the United States. As expected, higher scores are more prevalent in the Northeast and the Midwest, and the six most diffuse regions are housed with them. It is interesting to note that the relatively small region of Scranton, PA (population 76,089) is as diffuse as the Dallas or Detroit regions while Allentown, PA (population 118,032), Providence, RI (population 178,042), and Albany, NY (population 97,856) are as diffuse as Atlanta, Los Angeles, and San Francisco.

The MPDI varies significantly by geography as demonstrated in Figure 6.6. Metropolitan regions in the Northeast are the most diffuse. Their collective score in 1987 was 5.69 and 5.95 in 2007—a 4.6 percent increase. Although

Table 6.1

Most Diffused Metropolitan Areas in Each Region of the United States, 2007

| MPDI Score | Region of the United States | | | |
	Northeast	Midwest	South	West
18		Chicago		
17	Pittsburgh			
16				
15	New York, Philadelphia	St. Louis		
14	Boston			
13				
12		Minneapolis	Houston	
11		Cincinnati		Denver
10	Scranton PA	Detroit, Kansas City	Dallas	
9	Allentown PA, Providence RI, Albany NY	Cleveland	Atlanta	Los Angeles, San Francisco, Seattle
8	Portland ME, Harrisburg PA	Columbus, Omaha NE, Indianapolis	Louisville, Miami	Riverside CA
7			Birmingham AL	Portland, Sacramento
6			Nashville, Little Rock AR, Austin TX, Tulsa OK	Ogden UT, Salt Lake City
5				San Diego

the most diffuse, the Northeast also experienced the smallest change over the 20 years. The Midwest is slightly less diffuse than the Northeast and its diffusion score increased by slightly more (5.4 percent). Conversely, the metropolitan areas of the South and West are the least diffuse but they experienced the highest rates of diffusion between 1987 and 2007—6.4 percent and 10.3 percent respectively. It seems reasonable to speculate that, as the U.S. population has shifted from the Northeast and Midwest to the West and South, the latter regions would experience greater diffusion power as they became more complex. Perhaps discouraging is the fact that the MPDI in the Northeast and Midwest grew by as much as it did given the overall lack of growth relative to the South and the West. The hollowing out of urban cores in the Northeast and Midwest had two beneficiaries—metro areas in the south and west and outlying areas in the metro areas of the Northeast and Midwest.

The size of a metropolitan region affects both the MPDI and its rate of change (see Figure 6.7). Generally, larger metropolitan regions have higher MPDIs, and the MPDIs move more quickly toward greater diffusion. The average MPDI

Figure 6.6   **Average Metropolitan Power Diffusion Index Scores Across the United States, 1987 and 2007**

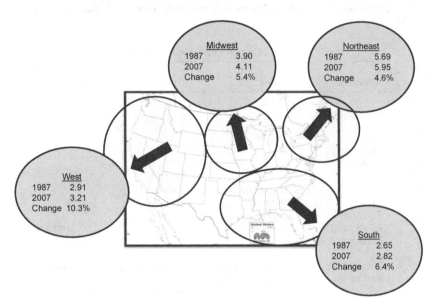

for the 29 largest metropolitan regions grew from 8.78 to 9.69 between 1987 and 2007—a 10.4 percent increase. Conversely, the average MPDI for the 758 smallest regions (under 250,000) grew by 5.1 percent—from 2.96 to 3.11. This data would suggest that, as regions grow in population, there is a point at which that growth accelerates the rate of diffusion. That acceleration, however, is anchored by the relative degree of diffusion that a particular region has. As such, the newer regions of the South and West might experience accelerated rates of change in the MPDI but this acceleration is unlikely to create MPDIs as high as the most diffuse regions of the Northeast and Midwest.

Grouping the 942 metropolitan areas into six categories of diffusion provides some insight into the changes that have occurred between 1987 and 2007. For purposes of this analysis, the regions have been divided as follows: a score between 1 and 2 is classified as "highly centralized"; a score between 2 and 3 "moderately centralized"; a score between 3 and 4 "slightly centralized"; a score between 4 and 5 "slightly decentralized"; a score between 5 and 7.5 "moderately decentralized"; and a score over 7.5 as "highly decentralized." We recognize the subjective nature of these classifications but think they are reasonable translation of arithmetically derived numbers and their relative meaning.

Using those categories, in 1987 62 percent of American metropolitan regions fell into one of the three centralized categories (see Figure 6.8). By 2007,

Figure 6.7 **Change in Metropolitan Power Diffusion Index Score for U.S. Metropolitan Areas by Size of the Metropolitan Area, 1987 to 2007**

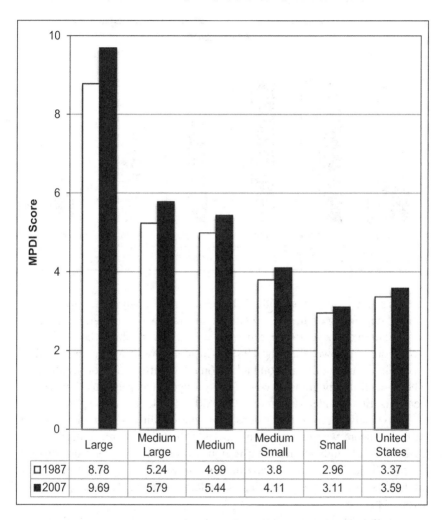

	Large	Medium Large	Medium	Medium Small	Small	United States
□1987	8.78	5.24	4.99	3.8	2.96	3.37
■2007	9.69	5.79	5.44	4.11	3.11	3.59

that percentage had dropped to 57 percent. Indeed, all categories of centralized regions decreased while all categories of decentralized regions increased. The "highly decentralized" group grew the fastest (17 percent)—increasing from 53 to 62 members. Conversely, the ranks of the "highly centralized" shrunk the fastest (13 percent)—decreasing from 68 to 59 members.

This broad analysis over time captures overall trends, but it is not particularly effective in identifying variance within particular regions. Grouping metropolitan regions by their rate of diffusion change between 1987 and 2007

Figure 6.8   **Distribution of Metropolitan Regions on the Metropolitan Power Diffusion Index, 1987 and 2007**

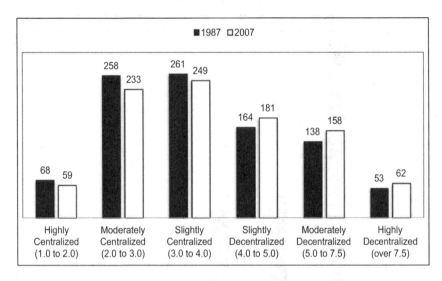

creates a better view of individual changes. For this analysis, six groups were created depending on the rate of change in a metropolitan region's diffusion score. Three of those groups represent conditions in which the 2007 diffusion score was lower than the 1987 diffusion score. A lower score in 2007 would indicate that that region had become less diffuse or more centralized. Those centralizing regions were then grouped according to their rate of centralization—under 10 percent, 10 to 20 percent, or over 20 percent.

Conversely, three of the groups represent conditions in which the 2007 diffusion score was greater than the 1987 diffusion score. A higher score in 2007 would indicate that that region had become more diffuse or more decentralized. Those decentralizing regions were then grouped according to their rate of centralization; that is, under 10 percent, 10 to 20 percent, or over 20 percent.

The most striking result of this analysis is that 75 percent of all U.S. metropolitan areas are decentralizing, and this trend is most prevalent in the West, where 87 percent of all regions are decentralizing. Furthermore, 33 percent of the West's regions are decentralizing by more than 10 percent (see Table 6.2).

The MPDI is a useful tool in both understanding and conducting research on U.S. metropolitan regions. It offers a commonly defined representation of the power distribution within a region by simultaneously capturing the number of governmental service providers and their relative contributions to

Table 6.2

Rate of Centralization-Decentralization as Measured by the Metropolitan Power Diffusion Index Between 1987 and 2007 for Regions in the United States

	Area of the United States					% change
	Northeast	Midwest	South	West	Total	
Centralizing						
More than 20%	0	0	2	0	2	0.20
10 to 20%	1	7	10	6	24	2.50
Less than 10%	31	64	102	17	214	22.70
Decentralizing						
Less than 10%	51	164	197	92	504	53.50
10 to 20%	11	40	63	40	154	16.30
More than 20%	0	7	20	17	44	4.70
Total	94	282	394	172	942	—

those public services. As a description of regions over time it demonstrates a broad trend toward decentralization and the markedly different approaches to power diffusion across the geography of the United States.

Role in Research

The MPDI is also an open source measure that can be used in researching and analyzing a broad range of policy issues affecting U.S. metropolitan areas. Researchers are encouraged to use the MPDI (University of Pittsburgh 2012). Researchers have explored a number of policy questions using earlier versions of the MPDI (e.g., Miller 2002).

Rusk (2003a, 2011) employs the MPDI to assess how more diffused metropolitan regions have made economic growth and equity more difficult. Lewis and Hamilton (2011) explored the issue of segregation and concluded, similar to Rusk, that there is a positive correlation between segregation and the MPDI "in general and for the poor." Lewis and Hamilton, however, concluded that the analysis did not suggest that changes in regional government structure were likely to have a significant impact on income disparities.

Hendrick, Jimenez, and Lal (2011) addressed the same issue using the MPDI as a measure of fragmentation, and concluded that their analysis supports a positive relationship between vertical fragmentation and dispersion and total government spending.

Miller-Adams (2006, 2009) employs the MPDI in her discussion of school policy and the adverse role diffusion plays in maintaining social and economic diversity in city schools. Edwards (2008) uses the MPDI in her discussion of the politics of annexation, a highly controversial issue for many metropolitan areas in the United States. Giuliano (2007) examined the changing structure of decision making in public transportation using the MPDI as an indicator of fragmentation and suggested that decentralized and fragmented decision making gives veto power to local interest groups.

Metropolitan economic development performance is a common policy issue assessed using the MPDI. Hamilton, Miller, and Paytas (2004) concluded that there is a relationship between diffusion of power within a metropolitan area and the amount of local authority the state has granted governments within their boundaries. The metropolitan regions that maximized the economic growth opportunities afforded to them were those that were less diffused (more centralized regional systems) and were located where the state granted more autonomy (more decentralized state systems). Using the MPDI as well as other indicators for metropolitan areas, Wolman and Levy (2011) reached a similar but more nuanced conclusion in that any efficiencies that may be inherent in decentralization are probably offset by the adverse impact of decentralization on equity. Grassmueck and Shields (2010) found a positive correlation between levels of decentralization and higher rates of employment growth and per capita income (see also Grassmueck, Goetz, and Shields 2008). Aurand (2007) shows that greater fragmentation is associated with a greater relative supply of affordable housing for extremely low and very low income households, but does not affect its distribution.

Other Measures of Metropolitan Regions: Resiliency

Through the lens of resiliency, a recent effort, sponsored in part by the Mac-Arthur Foundation, has attempted to answer several important questions. The first is, "What makes for a region that has a better chance to deal with the issues confronting it?" The second is, "What is regional governance?" (Barnes and Foster 2012).

On the first question, the answer relates to a region's overall capacity as measured by the following:

- Underlying economic strength of the region
- Characteristics of the citizens that constitute the region
- The civic culture and institutions that are present within the region

Economic capacity is measured by

- the degree to which a region's citizens have relatively equal incomes such that income disparity is minimized;

- the degree to which the region's economy contains a healthy mix of jobs across the goods-producing firms, the service-producing firms, and the governments;
- whether more citizens in the region are able to pay less than 35 percent of their incomes for mortgage or rent payments; and
- whether a region's economy is featured by a high proportion of small business, a high level of business start-ups, high percentage of residential high-speed internet connections, and ample venture capital.

The capacity of the citizenry in the region is measured by

- the measure of which a region's citizens have obtained at least a college degree;
- the degree the citizenry is not constituted by citizens who have not obtained at least a high school diploma or general education degree;
- the degree to which a region's population does not contain high numbers of citizens who report no sensory, mobility, self-care, or cognitive disabilities;
- the degree to which a region's citizens are not in poverty;
- and the degree to which the citizens of the region have access to health insurance coverage.

The extent of the civic culture of the region is measured by

- the degree to which the region contains a high number of civic organizations such as voluntary health organizations, social advocacy organizations, social organizations, business associations, professional organizations, labor unions, and political groups;
- the degree to which the citizens of a region have remained in the metropolitan region and, as such, are more anchored in that region;
- the degree to which the region's housing stock is made of owner-occupied units;
- and the extent of voter participation in general elections.

These measures are aggregated to create a measure referred to as "regional resiliency." This measure is not one of economic performance, but rather the underlying institutions that determine how a region might cope with adversity. When applied to U.S. metropolitan regions, the five most resilient regions among those over 1 million in population turn out to be fairly diverse. Minneapolis-St. Paul heads the list followed by Washington, DC, Raleigh, NC, Seattle, and Boston. Other resilient regions include Baltimore, Hartford,

CT, Pittsburgh, Philadelphia, Salt Lake City, St. Louis, Kansas City, MO, Rochester, NY, and Denver.

At the other end are regions that lack the underlying structure to cope with adversity. Heading that list is Miami followed by Riverside, CA, Los Angeles, Las Vegas, and Houston. Other less resilient regions include San Antonio, Tucson, AZ, Memphis, TN, Orlando, FL, New Orleans, and Dallas-Fort Worth.

On the second question, regional governance is not about legal government or even the act of formal governing. (Foster and Barnes 2012). Unlike the premise of this book that local governments are the building block of regions, this approach defines regional governance as "deliberate efforts by multiple actors to achieve goals in multi-jurisdiction environments" wherein regional governance is "not an end in itself; it is a means by which an end is sought" (Barnes and Foster 2012, 2). As such, the focus shifts to the capacity of a region to mobilize to identify, organize, determine, and implement regional policies.

Concluding Thoughts and Things to Ponder

An image of a metropolitan region is beginning to emerge. When the federal government used criteria that included social and economic connectedness to create statistical areas, they, in effect, captured the coming together of urbanizing areas into metropolitan regions. As a result, when local governments and others began working together (mostly out of necessity), it was often convenient to use those federally drawn boundaries. As such, the federal government did not create regions but captured a reasonable approximation of what local officials could use.

When we dig deeper into those regions, the complexity and diversity of local government systems emerges. Some regions, particularly in the South, have relatively few local governments. Some, particularly in the Northeast and Midwest, have many. That said, they share two important features. First, they are all built by and around local governments. Every square inch of every metropolitan region is under the jurisdiction of at least one local government. It might be a county or a municipality (city or town), but it is a local government nonetheless. To pretend that local governments are superfluous or dismiss them as an irritating nuisance to metropolitan region building is to defy practical reality and to miss an opportunity to work with the tools at hand.

Second, virtually all regions are decentralizing (at least as measured by the MPDI). The implications of this observation seem to run counter to our proposition that decentralizing local governments can serve as building blocks for a centralizing initiative to creative regional decision making. Our response is that because regions are becoming more diffuse, it is now imperative that we empower mediating institutions that serve as a means for those local governments to engage in regional decision making. It isn't a question of "how many blocks?" but rather, "how do the blocks fit together?"

Things to Ponder

1. Discuss how metropolitan regions are developing politically as well as the challenges of defining metropolitan regions in this way.
2. One challenge with metropolitan areas as defined by the OMB is that the boundaries change. How do these changes affect the relevance of the statistical information that might be obtained about MSAs?
3. The MPDI was developed to help ascertain the diffusion of power in metropolitan areas. Explain what this index measures, what entity compiles and distributes the data, and how it is utilized and applied in research.
4. What does regional resiliency mean? What three measures are used to determine regional resiliency? How does this assist metropolitan governance?

7

The Urban Core as Outward Region Building

A City and Its Contiguous Municipalities

A century-long conundrum facing many center cities, particularly those in the Northeast and Midwest, has been and continues to be their inability to capture or hold onto a fair share of the economic growth that is occurring in the metropolitan region of which they are a part. The primary explanation for this dilemma is the relative permanent fixing of their boundaries. A period of aggressive and rapid expansion in the latter half of the nineteenth and early twentieth centuries by center cities, characterized as "imperial" by historian Jon Teaford (1986), was followed by an equally aggressive suburban reaction that politically and legally closed the door to further expansion. The geographic size of cities such as New York, Boston, Pittsburgh, Detroit, Chicago, and St. Louis in 2012 is remarkably similar that of 1912.

The static nature of city boundaries and post–World War II urban expansion has led to an unprecedented realigning of the location and dynamics of U.S. cities (Figure 7.1). In 1950, the cities of the Northeast housed 19.8 million people and covered 2,205 square miles. In 2010, those same cities covered 2,277 square miles and had a collective population of almost 2 million *fewer* (17.9 million). Conversely, the cities of the South covered 1,833 square miles and had a combined population of 7.5 million in 1950. By 2010, they covered 9,530 square miles with a combined population of 17.4 million. In similar fashion, the cities of the West grew from 1,796 square miles to 6,031 and from 8.4 million people to 23.1 million. Put in perspective, in 1950, 70 percent of all city dwellers in the United States lived in the cities of the Northeast and Midwest. In addition, 54 percent of all city land area was in the Northeast and Midwest. In 2010, less than half (46 percent) of U.S. city dwellers lived in the Northeast and Midwest and less than a third (32 percent) of city land area was in the Northeast and Midwest.

This analysis highlights a fundamental difference among cities in the United States. Indeed, the ability (or inability) of a city to change its boundaries to grow with the post–World War II economic boom constitutes a great divide in American cities. Rusk (2003a) measures this divide by employing the concept

Figure 7.1 **Change in Population and Land Area of U.S. Central Cities by Geographic Regions, 1950 to 2010**

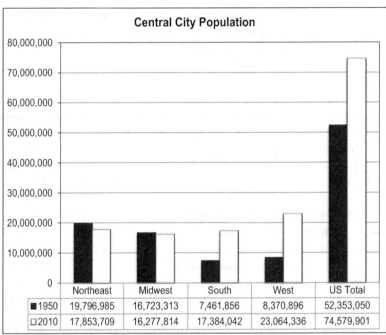

Central City Population	Northeast	Midwest	South	West	US Total
■1950	19,796,985	16,723,313	7,461,856	8,370,896	52,353,050
□2010	17,853,709	16,277,814	17,384,042	23,064,336	74,579,901

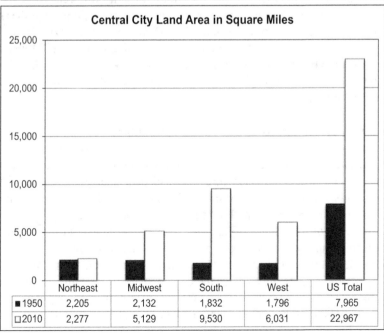

Central City Land Area in Square Miles	Northeast	Midwest	South	West	US Total
■1950	2,205	2,132	1,832	1,796	7,965
□2010	2,277	5,129	9,530	6,031	22,967

of elasticity. Northeast and Midwest cities are generally inelastic (boundaries are hard to change) while cities in the South and West are elastic (boundaries are expandable). The southern and western cities, primarily through annexation of territory, have been able to expand and capture more of the growth of their region than their inelastic counterparts. This expansionist strategy was very similar to that employed by the Northeast and Midwest central cities in the nineteenth century.

Often, reform efforts for cities in the Northeast and Midwest call for center cities to take over existing local governments. Such efforts invariably run up against unfriendly state laws and unfriendlier citizens in those existing local governments. Indeed, such boundary-changing solutions seldom are implemented and serve to further the often contentious gap between city and suburb. Today's urban America often seems to have an iron curtain between city and suburb 5 feet wide and 100 feet high.

Center cities have simultaneously become isolationist and isolated from the region of which they are a part. The isolated center city is cut off from engagement with the other municipalities of the region as it is easier for suburbs to "talk to" other suburbs. Common ground between suburbs as opposed to between city and suburb seems more self-evident and practical. Indeed, growth in intersuburb transactions characterizes most metropolitan areas, with the center city isolated from the relationship. The isolationist city perceives the problems of the city as so fundamentally different from the suburbs that city-suburb transactions are just not important. Current policies of the U.S. Department of Housing and Urban Development (HUD) reinforce the separation of the center city from the region of which it is a part while its rhetoric seeks to break down the wall. The result has been to over-inflate the relevance and importance of this century-old geopolitical boundary separating city and suburb.

From a City Boundary to an Urban Core Boundary

Efforts to address urban issues that work within the confines of existing local governments are often seen as less threatening to those local governments, but have had only limited success, especially in integrating the central city into those efforts. Finding a new path to a partnership between city and suburb starts with revisiting the issue through Rusk's lens of elasticity. Certainly, cities like Pittsburgh and St. Louis are geographically inelastic and unlikely to ever be as elastic as cities of the South (Houston, Charlotte) and West (Phoenix, Las Vegas) or growing cities outside the United States. A fundamental reform question is "how do we make inelastic cities less inelastic or more elastic?" If inelasticity is a product of an immoveable political-legal boundary, often

Figure 7.2   **The Traditional Model of the Metropolitan Region Built on a Clear Boundary Separating City and Suburb**

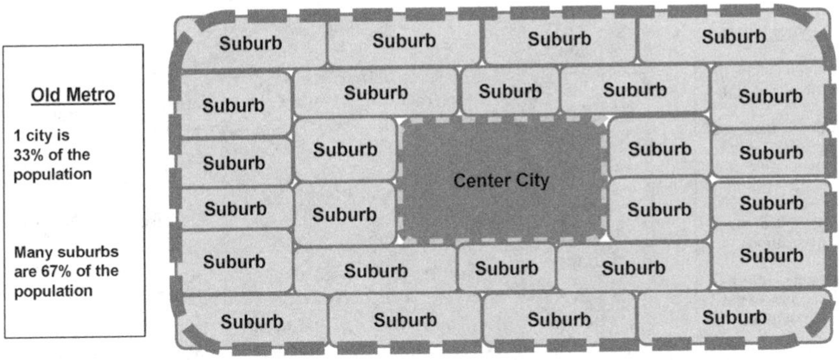

laid out in the nineteenth century, then looking closer at a street-level view of the boundary might be revealing.

The center city as the "hole in the doughnut" of a metropolitan region is a counter-productive metaphor and does a genuine disservice to conceptualizing urban America. It leads to equating the urban or "city" boundary to an outdated, century-old political-legal boundary of the center city. On the immediate other side of a city boundary is a municipality or a set of municipalities. What is the reality of those communities that are close to the border? The likelihood is that over time those outside the city have come to resemble city neighborhoods and those within resemble the neighboring municipality. Neighborhoods are likely to not stop at the boundary, but rather to transition with high degrees of economic and social interactions crossing back and forth over that border. Indeed, if travelers miss the little sign that marks the city/suburb boundary, they are seldom aware they are in a different municipality.

It is further likely that bordering municipalities have a very different view of the center city than other, more remote municipalities. Sharing a common border with someone or something creates a unique relationship unlike that of noncontiguous neighbors. To contiguous municipalities the city is more relevant than to municipalities further removed.

Rethinking the city border suggests two fundamentally different models of the structured relationship of a metropolitan region. Figure 7.2 depicts the standard image of a metropolitan region. It is constituted by a center city surrounded by a large number of suburban municipalities. For the sake of the example, the population of the center city is presumed to be 33 percent. The other municipalities are usually thought to be "outside" the city as suburbs. Suburbs that share a common border with the city are not considered to be significantly different from the other suburbs. Collectively, the suburbs

Figure 7.3   **The Emerging Model of the Metropolitan Region Built on a Transitioning Boundary (AlsoUrbs) Separating City and Suburb**

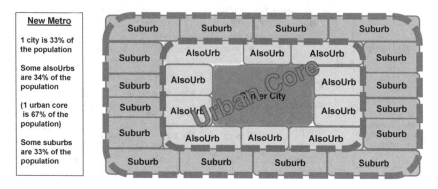

constitute 67 percent of the region's population. In this traditional model, suburbs interact with suburbs almost to the exclusion of the city and, hence, the metaphor of the doughnut. Intergovernmental activity starts at the city border and moves outward away from the city.

Figure 7.3 is a new conceptualization of the same metropolitan region. It assumes that the border between a contiguous municipality and the central city is at least as important as the border between that municipality and the rest of the region. In this example, we have presumed that municipalities with a common border are roughly half of the total suburban population, or 34 percent of the total region's population. As such, combining that population with the city's creates a connected urban core of 67 percent of the region's population. In this model, the city boundary, although still a significant artifact of the system, is no longer a wall. Intergovernmental activity moves into the city through its connection to its neighboring contiguous municipalities and out from the city through the same connection.

The potential of dynamically realigning intermunicipal relations in a metropolitan region should not be underestimated. Indeed, separating out those municipalities that share a common border with a center city from those that do not creates a new definition or type of suburb. For lack of a better term, municipalities that share a common border are referred to as "alsoUrbs." This term captures the idea that these regions are urban and share many characteristics of the city but they are also separate and distinct from the city and, in that sense, suburbs.

Reconceptualizing the meaning of the city border leads to some interesting observations. It minimizes the historically negative role that a center city boundary plays in defining metropolitan politics. An urban core defined as a center city and the municipalities with which it shares a common border moves that which is urban out beyond the antiquated city border in a way that creates the need for active discussion between city and suburb. Beyond the urban core lie the suburbs and rural areas that constitute the metropolitan region. Intergovernmental relations now has two dimensions. The first is within the urban core and alsoUrb. The second is between the urban core and the suburbs.

Such a realignment is hardly trivial or unique to places like Pittsburgh. In a typical metropolitan region in the Northeast and Midwest, there are about as many people who live in the alsoUrbs as live in the center city. The city of Pittsburgh has a population of 305,704; the 35 municipalities with which it shares a common border have a total population of 384,169. The ten older core cities in Pennsylvania (Allentown, Bethlehem, Easton, Erie, Harrisburg, Lancaster, Pittsburgh, Reading, Scranton, and York) have a combined population of 922,941. Collectively, they are surrounded by 97 municipalities with a combined population of 997,691. In Ohio, similar urban dynamics are in play. The core cities of Akron, Canton, Cincinnati, Cleveland, Columbus, Dayton, Toledo, and Youngstown have a combined population of 2,380,862. They are contiguous to 110 municipalities with a combined population of 1,857,826. Cincinnati's profile looks strikingly like Pittsburgh's with a population of 331,000 surrounded by 379,000 residents in 24 municipalities. In New York, the cities of Albany/Schenectady, Binghamton, Buffalo, Rochester, Syracuse, and Utica have a combined population of 925,000 surrounded by 1,112,705 people residing in 33 municipalities.

Although alsoUrbs are economically, politically, and socially diverse, that they share a common urban reality with each other may bring them together under the exigency of first being a part of that urban core and only secondarily as a richer or poorer suburb. The popular presumption of suburbs as uniformly constituted by single-family homes nestled among trees and green lawns on quiet streets belies the diversity of communities outside the center city. One challenge has always been how to engage the more affluent suburbs (the haves) with the less affluent ones (the have nots) in a way that more effectively addresses the social problems of the latter. Pitting the have nots against the haves has proved to be counterproductive. Coalition building in which the haves *and* the have nots work together toward a common goal is possible if their geography and urbaness are seen to trump their economic dissimilarity. As such, alsoUrbs have the potential to cross the chasm that separates rich and poor suburb in a way that enhances both types of suburb.

It is easier to think of an urban core as not necessarily made up of municipalities, but of neighborhoods. Indeed, the structure of local government in the United States, particularly in metropolitan regions with many governmental institutions, defies comprehension by all but scholars of local government. People don't think in local government terms as much as they think in neighborhood terms. In a poll conducted by Temple University in the summer of 2010, 1,462 randomly selected residents of Pennsylvania were asked their opinions on the quality of local public services they receive from their local, state, county, and regional governments (McLaughlin 2010). As part of the survey, respondents were also asked to identify their "most important sense of community." Options included their neighborhood, their local government, their county government, their metropolitan region, or the State of Pennsylvania. The most frequent response (38 percent) was neighborhood. The second most frequent response was their local government (24 percent). The state (23 percent), county (8 percent), and the region (7 percent) complete the list.

The meaning of neighborhood is more easily understood by its residents than that of the formal local government that serves that neighborhood. As such, neighborhoods are similar to each other and they simply have different relationships with their formal local government. Some neighborhoods are completely within a center city or alsoUrb; some are more or less contiguous to one municipality; and some span several municipalities. From a citizen's perspective, it is highly likely that any neighborhood in an alsoUrb has a counterpart in a neighborhood in the city. As such, the idea of common neighborhoods with similar problems and issues can unite rather than divide.

Rethinking the nature of the border between city and suburb leads to a unique and critical role for the alsoUrbs. They are the glue that holds some regions together. They can translate urban issues to the suburbs and communicate suburban issues to the city. AlsoUrbs perceive many urban issues (public transit, infrastructure investment, abandoned/blighted properties, emergency medical services) as more in tune with the city's perspective than with the more distant suburbs. When the alsoUrbs voice urban/city interests as *their* interests to the suburbs, suburbs are more willing to listen than had that same message come directly from the City. Conversely, because alsoUrbs have deep suburban roots, they are able to voice suburban interests to the city in a way the city is more apt to listen and adapt.

Rethinking the city border creates more weight for that which is urban within broader metropolitan discussions. Consider the change in the core's percentage of the metropolitan statistical area (MSA) from that of just the city's share. In the case of Pittsburgh, the city represents only 13 percent of the MSA, but, with the contiguous municipalities, that percentage increases to 28 percent. Cleveland's urban core increases from 20 to 37 percent; St. Louis's from 12 to 28 percent; Cincinnati's from 15 to 33 percent; Buffalo's from 25 to 58 percent; Dayton's from 20 to 50 percent; and Rochester's

Figure 7.4   **Two Types of Metropolitan Regions Based on the Relative Presence of the Center City, the AlsoUrbs, and the Suburbs**

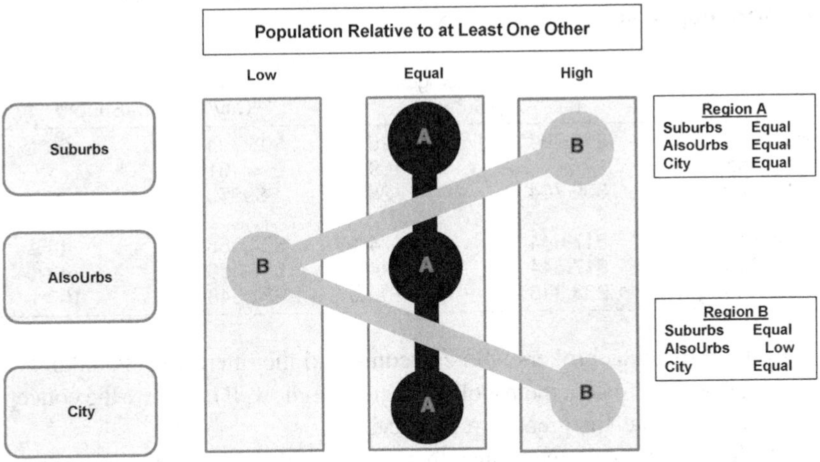

from 21 to 50 percent. In each case, the influence of the urban core is nearly doubled or more. The old adage of "there's power in numbers" is especially relevant in this context.

Different Degrees of Importance of AlsoUrbs

The potential influence of alsoUrbs in a particular metropolitan region depends on a number of factors but, most importantly, on the number of people in the alsoUrbs relative to the number of people in the city and the number in the rest of metropolitan region. Although a number of different relationships are possible, two important and common ones are presented in Figure 7.4.

As depicted in Figure 7.4, the population of the city could be "high," "equal" to, or "low" relative to either the alsoUrbs or the suburbs that exist on the other side of the alsoUrbs. The same "high," "equal," or "low" population relativity for the alsoUrbs and suburbs is also presented in the figure. A metropolitan region is represented by three circles connected by heavy lines.

In Case A, the populations of the city, the alsoUrbs, and the suburbs are about equal. Pittsburgh would be an example of a metropolitan region in this category. In such a metropolitan region, the alsoUrbs would have both power and leverage. Partnering with the suburbs they could significantly influence issues that are suburban focused. Partnering with the city, the alsoUrbs could significantly influence urban issues in which the city has generally exercised near monopoly decision making. The relative population of the alsoUrbs al-

Table 7.1

Pittsburgh as an Example of a Metropolitan Region with a Significant AlsoUrb Population

	Traditional Region City/Suburb		Urban Core Region City/AlsoUrb/Suburb	
Pittsburgh	305,704	25%	305,704	25%
AlsoUrbs	—	384,169		31%
Total Urban	305,704	25%	689873	56%
Suburbs	917,644	74%	534,358	43%
Total Suburban	917,644	74%	534,358	43%
Total County	1,233,348	100%	1,233,348	100%

lows them to act as brokers who can command the interest of the other two relatively easily. Such a metropolitan region might well be where the concept of the alsoUrb has the greatest relevance.

We have previously mentioned that more people live in the municipalities with which the city shares a common border than live in the city. Table 7.1 shows how connecting the common border municipalities to Pittsburgh and the urban core as opposed to connecting all the suburbs together changes the dynamics of intergovernmental relations in the Pittsburgh region. That which is urban increases from 25 percent to 56 percent of total population and that which is suburban decreases from 74 percent to 43 percent.

In Case B, the population of the city and the suburbs is high relative to the population of the alsoUrbs. Philadelphia is an example of this type of metropolitan area. The city's population is almost 1.5 million and the suburbs are multiple layers of municipalities that sprawl into three states. Those municipalities that physically touch the city (alsoUrbs) are dwarfed by the city on one side and the multitude of suburbs on their other side. In such a region it would be hard to imagine policy issues for which the alsoUrbs could play a particularly significant role. Indeed, this type of region might well be where the concept of the alsoUrb has the least relevance.

The Demographics of the AlsoUrbs

Bernadette Hanlon (2009) has undertaken a comprehensive study into the nature and distinguishing characteristics of inner ring suburbs or alsoUrbs. Analyzing 1,742 approximately contiguous (to their respective central city) local governments in the 100 largest metropolitan areas in the United States, Hanlon's research paints a portrait of economically and demographically diverse communities of people. The broad brush shows a primarily struggling set of local governments dealing with a host of urban issues from aging infrastructure to blighted, abandoned housing, to public safety concerns. They have been pushed to the edge. But, in the details, it also shows a resiliency in lower-, middle-, and upper-class communities seeking to maintain an attractive urban environment for the individuals and families within their borders. Collectively, using 2000 census data, these local governments housed 30.1 million citizens. Geographically they are concentrated in the older, first-industrialized part of the country. Both the overwhelming majority of local governments (76 percent) and people (65 percent) were located in the Northeast and Midwest.

Hanlon identified five broad types of inner-ring suburbs (see Figure 7.5). The largest category, representing 43 percent of all such communities, is "vulnerable." These communities usually experienced both population loss and a general decline in socioeconomic indicators between 1980 and 2000. Over 91 percent of vulnerable suburbs were located in the Northeast or Midwest where they constituted 48 percent and 57 percent respectively of all such suburbs.

The second most common type, representing 31 percent of inner-ring suburbs, are "middle class." These communities reflect socioeconomic conditions typical of all suburbs in the region of which they are a part. They are generally evenly distributed throughout the United States with the exception of the Midwest. They constitute 35 percent of the inner-ring suburbs in the Northeast, 42 percent in the South, and 31 percent in the West. They constitute only 16 percent of the suburbs in the Midwest. This relatively low frequency appears to be related to the Midwest having comparably more vulnerable communities than other parts of the United States.

The third category, representing 12 percent of all inner-ring suburbs, is "old," which refers to the age of the housing stock (pre-1939) and not necessarily the inhabitants. It is also the most diverse category with two very distinct variants, (1) "old and wealthy" and (2) "old and much poorer." In the former case, the average home value was $760,000. Even though the housing stock is old, it has been well-maintained. These communities are urban retreats of the upper- and upper-middle-income classes. Comparatively, the average housing value in the second category was $22,000. These communities are most prevalent around the cities of Pittsburgh, Philadelphia, Chicago, and St. Louis.

The fourth most frequent type of inner-ring suburb is the ethnic enclave, which constituted 11 percent of the suburbs studied. Of the 7.7 million Americans living in ethnic inner-ring suburbs, 5.3 million (69 percent) live in the West. Indeed, 50 percent of all inner-ring suburbs in the West are classified as ethnic and primarily Hispanic in make-up.

The final category, which covers 3 percent of all inner-ring suburbs are

Figure 7.5   **Number of U.S. AlsoUrbs by Type of Community Based on Hanlon's Categories**

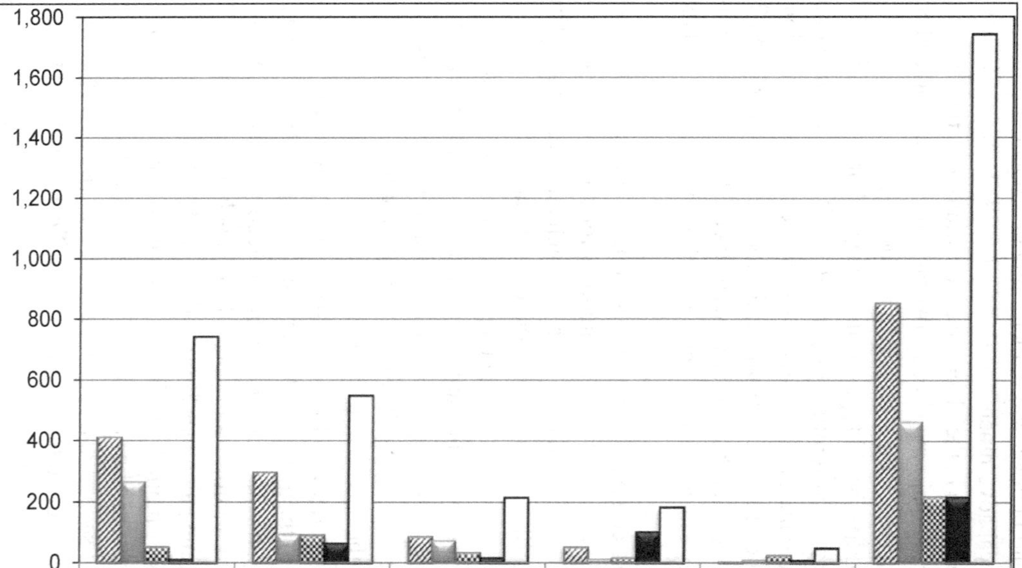

	Vulnerable	Middle Class	Old	Ethnic	Lower Income	Total
Northeast	411	297	88	52	4	852
Midwest	268	96	76	14	12	466
South	52	91	34	16	25	218
West	12	65	17	103	9	216
Total	743	549	215	185	50	1742

those classified as "lower income and mixed." Over half of this category is located in the South and Hanlon includes this separate category to distinguish poor predominantly Hispanic suburbs of the West from poor predominantly black suburbs of the South and Midwest.

Current Initiatives to Organize the AlsoUrbs

Efforts to organize the advocacy of interests of more densely built suburbs are being undertaken in a number of metropolitan areas employing a wide variety of organizational structures. What each of these organizations lacks is the pivotal role played by their respective dominant center cities, which can mobilize political capital and economies of scale for the betterment of all parties. The role of the center city in these regions ranges from outright hostility at worst to passionate indifference as norm to marginal importance at best.

Ohio First Suburbs Consortium

This is a statewide organization of inner-ring suburban areas in four metropolitan regions in Ohio. Altogether, there are 64 municipalities represented with a population of one million people, roughly 10 percent of Ohioans. There are four metropolitan areas represented: the Northeast Ohio First Suburbs Consortium (Cleveland area), the Central Ohio First Suburbs Consortium (Columbus area), the Southwest Ohio First Suburbs Consortium (Cincinnati area), and the Dayton Metro Area First Suburbs Consortium.

The four consortiums have slightly different missions. However, each faces the same problems, such as "aging infrastructure; deteriorating business and industrial bases; and an aging and sometimes dated housing stock," as well as the economic and social problems that stem from outmigration (Ohio First Suburbs Consortium 2013b).

The most active of the four is the Cincinnati area consortium, which is an office of the Hamilton County government. The office, in partnership with local elected officials and citizens, has developed a comprehensive economic development plan for first-ring suburbs within the county. The Community Revitalization Initiative Strategic Plan (Hamilton County Regional Planning Commission 2004) advocated for:

- public policies that do not create disposable communities;
- balanced investments in new and existing infrastructure;
- maintenance and enhancement of the tax base; and
- creation of redevelopment opportunities.

The Northeastern (Cleveland area, est. 1996) runs a much smaller operation with one half-time staff person based out of the suburb of Cleveland Heights that advocates for appropriate housing policies that remediate blight and encourage investment in urban areas and improved energy efficiency. Their economic development functions split into a separate not-for-profit organization (First Suburbs Consortium Development Council) in 2002. Given their limited staff resources, this organization makes tremendous headway, but lacks the infrastructure and city support to move to the next level. Finally, the Dayton Metro consortium and Central Ohio (Columbus) consortium are both much younger, smaller organizations that advocate on policy issues but provide little in the way of resources for their member communities.

The statewide coalition of consortia is largely an advocacy organization. The consortium seeks funding to maintain the public infrastructure, including parkland, roads, schools, and water and sewer facilities in addition to advocating policies providing equal support for mature communities. The consortium also promotes tax and other incentives that encourage regional cooperation and redevelopment of mature communities (Ohio First Suburbs Consortium 2013a). They meet periodically to deal with these issues and recently saw some success in defeating unfriendly tax policy in their legislature (Miller 2013).

MARC First Suburbs Coalition

The First Suburbs Coalition is a division of the Mid-America Regional Council (MARC), the Metropolitan Planning Organization of the Kansas City Region. The Coalition was formed in 2002 and is made up of local government staff, private sector partners, and elected officials from 18 older suburbs in Kansas and Missouri, as well as officials from Kansas City, Missouri. The coalition operates through working groups that include elected officials, local government staff, and private sector partners. The coalition is co-chaired by mayors from two of these cities and the director is a MARC employee who can call upon its resources for data and staff support. This coalition provides a crucial advisory role to the Metropolitan Planning Organization (MPO) on development and planning in the region.

Nineteen inner-ring communities approached MARC in 2002 with the common issues of development in old communities in hopes that they would benefit from working together. The main goal of the coalition is to improve housing infrastructure in these older suburbs. They provide loans and resources to homeowners to renovate their homes to be more eco-efficient in an effort to prevent more out-migration from these communities, help maintain the tax base, prevent sprawl, and build more sustainable communities.

The coalition also tries to attract businesses to these older suburbs. Its retail working group researches the new trends in retail development, new players in retail development, and particular opportunities for struggling strip malls. In addition, the working group jointly identifies and attracts new retailers to first suburbs and studies examples of successful redevelopment of underperforming strip centers.

Southeastern Pennsylvania First Suburbs Group

The Southeastern Pennsylvania First Suburbs Group is a grassroots, nonprofit organization of municipal, faith, and community leaders from the older, developed suburbs of the four suburban Philadelphia counties (Bucks, Chester, Delaware, and Montgomery). The organization addresses problems many older suburbs face, such as high taxes, crumbling infrastructure, declining schools, changing demographics, and inadequate aging housing stock.

The organization primarily acts as an advocate for these older municipalities by petitioning the state and federal government on the issues most affecting these communities. The group has also built a relationship with the MPO in the region, Delaware Valley Regional Planning Commission, and encourages the commission to address the needs of older suburbs.

The Southeastern Pennsylvania First Suburbs Group receives federal grants and has issued reports about the fiscal health and infrastructure of their region. The group also regularly organizes rallies and training sessions to get local citizens involved in smart growth issues.

Michigan Suburbs Alliance

The Michigan Suburbs Alliance is a nonprofit coalition of Southeast Michigan's mature suburbs. In June 2002, representatives from 14 metro Detroit suburbs unanimously agreed to form the Michigan Suburbs Alliance. Together, they sought to harness their collective power to demand an end to the systematic disinvestment in older suburbs. The mayors and city managers saw that cooperation among similar communities across the region would benefit them with finding solutions together for shared problems—a deficient state finance system, losing residents, old infrastructure, and so on.

Among other initiatives, the Redevelopment Ready Communities program helps built-out cities to adopt innovative redeveloping strategies through an efficient process. This program gives a scoring system, evaluation, technical assistance, and certificate to mature communities. The Michigan Suburbs Alliance also advocates and promotes policy agenda in five areas: regional collaboration, municipal finance, social equity, sustainable land use, and high-quality infrastructure.

The alliance has since grown to encompass 31 of the region's mature, inner-ring suburbs, representing more than 1 million residents. Through diverse innovation and initiatives, the alliance fosters and supports cooperative approaches to the challenges facing Michigan's metropolitan areas.

Chicago Metropolitan Mayors Caucus

In December 1997, a meeting of mayors led by Chicago Mayor Richard Daley created the Metropolitan Mayors Caucus, a forum for discussion and cooperation. The Metropolitan Mayors Caucus is made up of 272 mayors currently and jointly addresses issues in areas such as economic development, affordable housing, and energy and environment. The caucus has 10 committees/task forces, 5 executive board members (including the executive director), and 10 directors representing regions in the Chicago region (the City of Chicago and nine suburban municipal groups). These 10 members each appoint one director and one alternate to serve on the executive board, which meets every other month and is in charge of overseeing general operations of the caucus.

Since its establishment in 1997, the caucus has served as a voice for regional cooperation on policy agenda of school funding, tax reform, transportation, housing, infrastructure, as well as emergency preparedness. The caucus reached an agreement in supporting electric service reliability, funding for cleaner air, the creation of a statewide economic development plan, investment in the region's roads and other public infrastructure, plans to protect the region's critical utilities, including electricity, natural gas and water, plus the adoption of a housing agenda. It is unclear how this organization will shift now that Rahm Emanuel has taken over as Chicago's mayor.

Congress of Neighboring Communities

Another example of an effort to integrate urban governments (both city and suburb) is the Congress of Neighboring Communities (CONNECT). This organization was created in 2009 to coordinate the activities of the City of Pittsburgh and the 36 neighboring municipalities that make up the region's urban core. Earlier we described the governmental structure of Allegheny County and the City of Pittsburgh as one in which the city is only 25 percent of the county's population, but if the municipalities that share a border with it are added that number jumps to 56 percent—a potential game-changer.

When the city and its immediate neighbors are combined, a profile emerges of an urban core that happens to be comprised of a number of separate municipalities. It is a profile of considerable demographic, economic, and political strength:

- Economic power: two-thirds of all jobs in Allegheny County are located in CONNECT municipalities.
- Demographic power: 56 percent of the county population reside within CONNECT.
- Political power: Within Allegheny County CONNECT municipalities are all or part of
  - All 3 U.S. congressional districts
  - 14 of 15 Allegheny County Council seats
  - 17 of 23 Pennsylvania State House districts
  - 4 of 6 Pennsylvania State Senate districts.

CONNECT was created to enhance the connection of the city to its neighbors and neighbors of the city to each other and to the city. This notion is captured in its mission statement:

> CONNECT works through advocating for and voicing the collective interests of the urban core and its residents; developing and enhancing ways the 37 municipalities work together to deliver important public services; and maintaining a forum for the discussion, deliberation, and implementation of new ways to maximize economic prosperity for western Pennsylvania.

CONNECT is housed at the University of Pittsburgh's Center for Metropolitan Studies. In 2008, the Center invited the city and the neighboring municipalities to come together to discuss common issues and the potential of collaborating more closely. The city showed initial encouragement and support from the mayor, the elected city controller, and the active participation of Pittsburgh City Council. Close to 75 percent of contiguous municipalities sent representatives who overwhelmingly voiced their interest in working with the city and others on issues common to the urban core. In addition, key civic organizations, local and regional foundations, various associations of local governments, Allegheny County, and the Commonwealth of Pennsylvania engaged in shaping the first and subsequent meetings of CONNECT.

In addition to the active participation of the city, CONNECT's municipal membership reflects a coalition of richer and poorer communities. Using a statistical model more fully explained in Miller (2002), the 128 municipalities in Allegheny County (excluding Pittsburgh) can be ranked on the basis of relative fiscal health. Miller then grouped the municipalities into the 32 most affluent ("stately"); the 32 with relatively good fiscal health ("stable"); the 32 with moderate fiscal problems ("strapped"); and the 32 with severe fiscal and social challenges ("stressed"). Updating the rankings for 2009 shows that CONNECT draws relatively equal participation from the fiscally strong and the fiscally challenged. Just under 70 percent of the population live in municipalities in the "stressed" category that are actively engaged in CONNECT. This group of municipalities has:

- a per capita real estate value of $31,000;
- 48 percent of its residents living in renter-occupied housing;
- 11 percent of the households headed by single mothers; and
- 37 percent nonwhite population.

Just over 66 percent of the population live in municipalities in the "stately" category that are actively engaged in CONNECT. This group of municipalities has:

- a per capita real estate value of $90,128;
- 17 percent of its residents living in renter-occupied housing;
- 3 percent of the households headed by single mothers; and
- 6 percent nonwhite population.

Original membership rules required that municipalities share a common border with the city of Pittsburgh. This original definition was proposed for the sake of simplicity, and also because all of the communities within this urban core boundary share logical and intuitive practical connections. That said, an interesting development occurred in 2011 when two municipalities that did not meet this border condition petitioned for membership. In one case, the border that separated the municipality from the city was less than a football field long and, in the other case, the municipality was wholly within the municipality that bordered the city. As a result, noncontiguous municipalities may now join CONNECT if they are contiguous to a current member, petition to join by resolution of their council, and are approved by a majority of the CONNECT membership.

CONNECT's organizational structure is built on the basis that a member is a municipality. All municipalities designate three representatives to CONNECT (two elected and one appointed). Every municipality is a member of the executive committee and can cast one vote on issues before the body. For the city, the rules are slightly different. The mayor appoints the three representatives and has the voting power to represent the city. In addition, Pittsburgh City Council and the separately elected city controller also have seats on the executive committee of CONNECT. The rules for the officers of CONNECT require that a city representative always holds at least one of those positions. This elevated representation for the city serves a practical function in that it engages the three arms of city government (executive, legislative, oversight) while creating an egalitarian flavor to the organization desired by the smaller municipalities.

Policy issues and responses are developed by policy working groups comprised of any interested representatives and civic and governmental partners. In addition, a Citizens' Advisory Council is being developed that would help identify issues of concern to the urban core as seen by citizens.

Policy making for CONNECT starts with an annual congress. The congress is attended by a large percentage of the CONNECT representatives and they normally sit as a delegation from their respective municipalities. Each municipality is allowed to cast one vote on the items before them. As of 2012, four congresses have been held. In 2009, the congress approved 24 strategic resolutions designed to guide the organization in achieving its mission, to steer improvements in the region's waste collection and treatment system toward environmental justice and green infrastructure, and to call for solutions to public transit to recognize the importance of transit as an urban core issue. The congress also elected the mayor of the city as its first chair. At the second congress in 2010, CONNECT representatives passed 18 resolutions that addressed mutual public policy concerns including emergency medical services funding and energy efficiency. The third annual congress in 2011 adopted 25 resolutions that spanned a variety of policy issues including blighted properties, consistent data collection across municipal boundaries, and the development of a community and economic development forum for the economic development entities operating within in the jurisdiction of CONNECT.

The annual congress in 2012 featured an address by the newly elected Allegheny County executive delivering an important policy message on public transportation funding. That the top elected official in Allegheny County would select this forum to make that speech reflects a growing recognition that this urban core partnership has value. In addition, the congress passed 14 resolutions, including one that focused on the development of an Integrated Community and Economic Development plan for the urban core, another that adopted an intergovernmental agreement template that will be used by the member communities. Resolutions also continued to focus on blight issues as statewide land banking legislation.

Much of CONNECT's early efforts have been focused on building relationships and creating a stronger sense of trust between the city and the alsoUrbs. Trust building has been difficult as the traditional fears and hostilities that had divided the municipalities from the city were and continue to be significant. Further, there were few formal channels of communication and the informal ones were scattered throughout the various operating departments of the city. Official written agreements were invariably between the city and only one municipality with few, if any, of the officials who participated in the original agreements still available to provide context to those agreements.

Concluding Thoughts and Things to Ponder

Organizing the urban core around center cities and contiguous municipalities (the alsoUrbs) can be classified as an experiment in urban governance reform. In this chapter we have laid out the potential, particularly for the Midwest and the Northeast, to realign the border of that which is clearly urban. The most important border for a suburb is the one it shares with a center city. Urban policy has traditionally made this border a dividing wall. Indeed, the historically negative role played by city boundaries in defining metropolitan politics is perhaps our greatest obstacle to building modern metropolitan regions.

For the twenty-first century we need an urban core defined as a center city and those municipalities with which it shares a common border. This minimizes the antiquated view of the city border. Intergovernmental relations now have two dimensions: the interaction within each urban core-city and each alsoUrb and the interaction between the urban core and the suburbs. In this second dimension, a new role and responsibility is created for the alsoUrbs. They can be the common element or glue that holds a region together. Who better to translate urban issues to the suburbs and communicate suburban issues to the city? AlsoUrbs perceive many urban issues (public transit, infrastructure investment, abandoned/blighted properties, emergency medical services) as more in tune with the city's perspective than with the more distant suburbs. When the alsoUrbs describe urban/city interests as *their* interests, suburbs are more willing to listen than if that same message comes directly from the city. Conversely, because alsoUrbs have deep suburban roots, they are able to voice suburban interests to the city in a way the city is more apt to listen and adapt.

Things to Ponder

1. How does the action of the urban core affect the alsoUrbs? How does that then affect the suburbs?
2. A formal "first suburbs" (what we call the alsoUrbs) group has developed around a number of core urban cities. What are the sociopolitical and economic reasons for the formation of these groups?
3. Given their influence in population and adaptability to both sides, what role do you see alsoUrbs playing in the relationship between cities and suburbs?
4. What kind of political influence does a regional coordinating body hold versus individual municipalities?
5. What might other urban cities learn from the experiences of CONNECT in Pittsburgh?

8

Sharing Wealth and Responsibility

Fiscal Regionalism

Metropolitan regions in the United States have adopted or are considering adopting policies that share resources across jurisdictions. The common term used to describe these strategies is "sharing." Examples include tax-base sharing in Minneapolis and revenue sharing in Pittsburgh. Although the word "sharing" is seldom used in the official name of the various strategies, their policy purpose is invariably directed toward activities that the region considers to be common resources or needs of that region. Examples include the Cultural Asset Districts in Denver and Pittsburgh that fund zoos, libraries, symphonies, arts organizations, and other similar amenities toward which rural, suburban, and urban residents feel a common affinity. Sometimes sharing occurs out of mutual self-interest when cities, towns, and counties facing potentially crippling annexation wars agree to share and win a little rather than fight and risk losing a lot. A number of cities and counties in Virginia have entered into such agreements.

These approaches fall under a broad category referred to as "fiscal regionalism." They address the issue of equity across the region in a manner that does not overly threaten the existing structure of local government. As such, the question of "who pays" is separated from the controversial and confrontational question of whether a region has too many governments. These sharing mechanisms create the capacity or the authority to distribute benefits from economic growth or to more effectively have recipients of services pay a greater share of the costs of that service.

Fiscal regionalism approaches are distinguishable from each other on two important dimensions. The first is the source of the revenue. Overwhelmingly the source is either the property tax or the sales tax. The second is the method that authorized the sharing plan. Some plans such as in those in Denver and Kansas City were approved by voters through referendum while others were implemented through state legislation. The Minnesota tax-base sharing plan and the Pittsburgh regional asset district and revenue-sharing plan are examples of the latter. These strategies are presented in Figure 8.1. Another common approach, particularly for peaceful coexistence strategies, is a negotiated agreement between the affected governments that allocates resources and responsibilities between those governments.

Figure 8.1   **Fiscal Regionalism Strategies Adopted Based on Revenue Source and Legal Action That Created the Strategy**

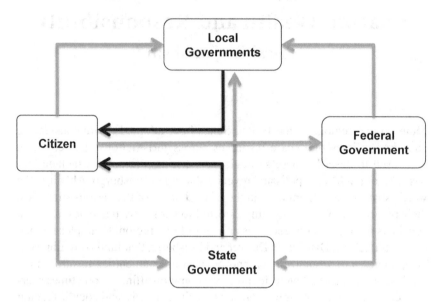

Tax-Base /Revenue Sharing

The first form of fiscal regionalism is tax- or revenue-base sharing. Base sharing is a simple idea—take a regional tax source, such as the property tax or sales tax, and distribute the proceeds to constituent local governments on objective criteria that reflect the needs of the region, taken as a whole. Its asserted benefits are its more effective and equitable impact on economic development and growth. To the degree that the fragmentation of government services and decision making in an urban area prevent any rational approach to the distribution of the gains and benefits from development and growth policies, tax-base sharing helps to mitigate the adverse effects of that fragmentation.

Tax-base sharing, particularly when the revenue source is the property tax, can potentially minimize the worst effects of fiscal mercantilism. Local government reliance on property tax revenues requires those governments to engage in competitive fiscal mercantilism—encouraging the location of net revenue-producing developments within their boundaries. Such practices exacerbate the difficulties associated with the location of undesirable or marginally desirable land uses within a metropolitan region.

Unfortunately, the costs for economic development are not always borne by the government within whose boundaries the growth has occurred. Although every government would like to derive economic benefit without cost, the

Figure 8.2   **The Minnesota Model of Tax-Base Sharing**

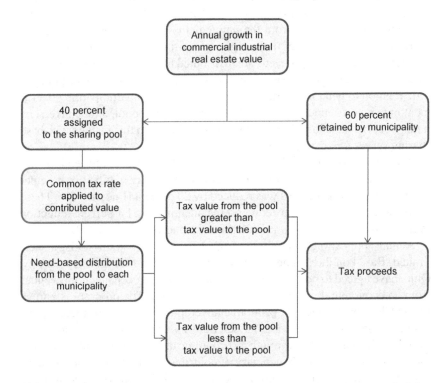

opportunity itself is dysfunctional because a government is rewarded for "free-riding." Few, if any, means exist whereby governments in a metropolitan region can share in the region's growth, as the only determinant of benefits is location within a particular jurisdiction.

Annexation laws create a "win-lose" outcome for governments—the government getting the new territory wins, but at a significant cost to the government losing the territory. Fiscal regionalism allows for the development of "win-win" outcomes.

Finally, wealthier jurisdictions are able to provide services with lower tax rates than less affluent jurisdictions. This disparity results in a vicious cycle as wealth gravitates to wealth and the poorer jurisdictions become even less competitive. Over time, the gap between rich and poor communities in a region grows wider. Fiscal regionalism aids in leveling the playing field.

The largest and perhaps best known tax-base sharing plan is in the Twin Cities of Minnesota. The Minnesota model of tax-base sharing has been in place for 40 years. Today, the program covers 2.5 million people, 7 counties, and 200 local jurisdictions, and involves $200 million in tax proceeds.

The program is graphically presented in Figure 8.2 and works as follows: 40 percent of a municipality's growth in commercial and industrial real estate valuation is diverted from the municipality's direct control to a "pool" shared by all municipalities in the region. A uniform tax rate is applied to this "pooled" value and the proceeds are distributed back to the municipalities on a needs-based formula. The amount a government contributes to the pool has little relation to what it will receive in distributions—a participating government may receive much less than it contributes to the pool, and, conversely, it may receive substantially more than it contributes. In this fashion, tax-base sharing serves a redistributive function.

Since its inception, the plan has reduced fiscal disparities between jurisdictions. For the period 1987 to 1995, measured inequality in total tax-base per capita between jurisdictions was reduced by 20 percent (Luce 1998b). These results were similar to an earlier report that identified a 21.1 percent reduction in fiscal disparities between jurisdictions (Minnesota House 1987).

Actual application of tax-base sharing in other jurisdictions is, at best limited. Based on the Minnesota plan, jurisdictions in Montgomery County, Ohio, have agreed to pool a portion of future growth in exchange for revenues from an economic development fund (Hollis 1998). The program is known as ED/GE, which stands for economic development and government equity. Unlike Minnesota, where some jurisdictions lose more than they contribute, the Ohio plan guarantees, through an economic development fund, that every jurisdiction will be a net beneficiary. If contributions to the tax-base sharing pool exceed distributions from the pool, the jurisdiction will receive more from the economic development fund to compensate.

Monroe County, New York, altered the way it shared revenues with the City of Rochester and other municipalities in Monroe County to assist the city in responding to a declining tax base and increasing service needs. Rochester, once a thriving city in upstate New York that housed the giant photo innovator Eastman-Kodak, fell on hard times starting in the late 1970s and early 1980s. In 1985, as a result of the Morin-Ryan Act, a program which had distributed county sales tax revenues to municipalities solely on the basis of population, was amended to weigh the city's portion more heavily. Basically, the city received 50 percent of the growth in receipts over the prior year. As a result, no municipality received less than they had been receiving. They simply received less of an increase from the growth in the sales tax.

The Meadowlands Area in New Jersey represents a planned commercial and economic development area that spans 14 separate jurisdictions. In 1972, the State of New Jersey established a commission to develop a master plan for the region. Recognizing that not all jurisdictions would benefit equally from the development, particularly if open and public spaces were to be incorporated, a property tax sharing program was developed for the affected jurisdictions. The Meadowlands region of northeast New Jersey had become a wasteland, an unattractive result of decades of environmental disregard. It had also become a strategic location for economic development. It made more sense for the region's 14 jurisdictions to work together on its development. Some communities had large portions of land set aside as natural wetland resources or parks while others were better suited to industrial or commercial development. The goal was to create a plan that all communities "would equitably share in the new financial benefits and new costs resulting from the development of the Meadowlands District as a whole," thus reducing competition among municipalities and allowing the region to develop in a fair, sensible manner (New Jersey Meadowlands Commission 2013).

Under the tax-sharing program, each municipality either contributes to or receives directly from an intermunicipal tax pool. Pre-1970 developments within each municipality are not subject to tax sharing while 40 percent of all post-1970 development is (similar to Minnesota's plan). The 40 percent creates a tax pool from which each jurisdiction receives credits for the elementary and secondary education costs of students located within the Meadowlands District and credits proportional to the percentage of property each jurisdiction comprises in the region. Based on this formula, some municipalities' credits equal more than the amount of revenue they have subject to the plan. They receive payments from the pool. Others municipalities' credits total less than the amount of money they have subject to the plan. They make contributions to the pool. In 2012, six municipalities received $7.4 million above their costs of education and proportional share, with the municipality of Kearny at $3.8 million the largest net recipient. Conversely, seven municipalities contributed a total of $7.4 million to the pool, with Secaucus at $2.7 million the largest net contributor.

A 1995 program adopted in Allegheny County, Pennsylvania, created a redistributive revenue-base sharing plan designed to reduce the fiscal disparity between the 130 local governments located with the county. There were a number of issues confronting Allegheny County and the City of Pittsburgh in the early 1990s. With the restructuring of, in particular, the steel industry, the Pittsburgh region saw a significant disruption of its economy in the 1980s. Over 100,000 manufacturing jobs were lost in a relatively short period and many citizens simply packed up and moved to regions where jobs were more plentiful. This disruption was especially acute for a large number of small industrial towns that had formed around the steel plants. One result was a growing fiscal disparity between the county's richer and poorer communities (Miller, Miranda, Roque, and Wilf 1995). More importantly, this research demonstrated that the gap was accelerating at an alarming rate. The City of

Pittsburgh was also adversely affected and faced a deteriorating fiscal condition that would lead to financial insolvency by the early 2000s.

To address the financial problems of the city and other municipalities adversely impacted by the economic downturn, a revenue-sharing program was adopted at the same time as the formation of a new cultural asset district This revenue sharing program, publicly less visible than the asset district, has been referred to as the "other half" of a two-pronged fiscal regionalism initiative (Jensen and Turner 2000). This less publicly visible reform, utilizing an additional 0.5 percent of the county sales tax, provides $100 million to all municipalities in Allegheny County annually. The distribution is as follows: 50 percent is allocated to the Allegheny County government, and 50 percent is shared among the participating municipalities in the county. The reason for the large share to the county government stems primarily from Pennsylvania counties' legislatively almost exclusive reliance on the property tax, which is state mandated. As a result, the county government's financial condition was adversely affected by the overall economic downturn as property tax receipts fell.

Although all municipalities in the county have a right to participate, the formula used for this distribution targets the less affluent. Per capita distribution under this program ranges from $9.81 in the county's wealthier communities to $18.86 in the most fiscally distressed (Miller 1999).

Cultural Asset Districts

A second form of fiscal regionalism is the cultural asset district. This financial arrangement has emerged in the last several years as a direct result of the deconcentration of population. Even after World War II, the majority of Americans lived and worked in center cities. Cultural and civic activities were usually, and appropriately, financed by the center city. For instance, in 1948, 73 percent of business activity in Allegheny County, Pennsylvania, took place within the City of Pittsburgh. For the City of Pittsburgh to be the sole public financial supporter of the zoo, as an example, was consistent with its economic base and fiscal capacity. However, by the late 1980s, only 38 percent of business activity conducted within Allegheny County occurred within the City of Pittsburgh. Less than 15 percent of attendees at Pittsburgh Pirates baseball games were city residents, even though the city was the sole public underwriter of the stadium.

As citizens and businesses dispersed to the suburbs, however, they continued to utilize the civic facilities financed by the center city. The city no longer had the fiscal base to support those services and noncity residents were becoming their primary users. Cultural asset districts, as a form of fiscal regionalism, represent a way for metropolitan regions to finance civic institutions used by the regional public.

Pittsburgh, Denver, and Kansas City are representative of metropolitan regions that have adopted cultural asset districts. The Allegheny County Regional Asset District (Pittsburgh) was created in 1995 and funded through an additional 0.5 percent on the sales tax. This revenue stream generates more than $100 million annually to provide funding to the region's shared assets. Facilities like the zoo, aviary, conservatory, libraries, parks, and stadiums are now the fiscal responsibility of the region. Two important regional funding issues were addressed through the program. First, more total financial support to the regional assets was made possible. Sales tax receipts were greater than the previous public financial support provided by the financially strapped City of Pittsburgh and the limited funding available from the county. By switching from inelastic property tax revenues to, at the time, more elastic sales taxes served to increase the available pool. Second, this transfer of funding responsibility away from the City of Pittsburgh and Allegheny County (the estimated impact is $18 million) helped to make those governments more fiscally sound and competitive than they would be otherwise.

The Allegheny County case is interesting in that a single piece of legislation created both a revenue-sharing program and a cultural asset district. The two programs were complementary and sold as a package. The Allegheny County program is graphically represented in Figure 8.3. As previously mentioned, 50 percent went to the revenue-sharing program, in addition to the 50 percent that went to the asset district. The revenue-sharing proceeds were allocated based on need and the asset district proceeds created a new organization to finance regional assets. Among those were assets formerly underwritten by the city and county. As such, the city and county received relief from having to continue financing those activities even though they might have continued to operate those activities. For instance, the county retained responsibility for county parks even though they were now financed by the asset district.

In 1988, the Denver region approved a Scientific and Cultural Facilities District. Approved with a 75 percent positive vote at a referendum, the district is financed by a one-tenth of 1 percent increase in the sales tax. The district supports institutions such as the zoo, museums, and large performing arts institutions (symphony) as well as a wide variety of local and community cultural groups (Hansberry 2000).

The Kansas City region enacted (again by referendum and through the use of a sales tax increase) a Bi-State Cultural District in 1997, to finance the capital and operating costs associated with historic Union Station (Hollis 1998). Union Station served as the nineteenth-century gateway to the American West

Figure 8.3 **The Allegheny County Revenue Sharing/ Regional Asset District Model**

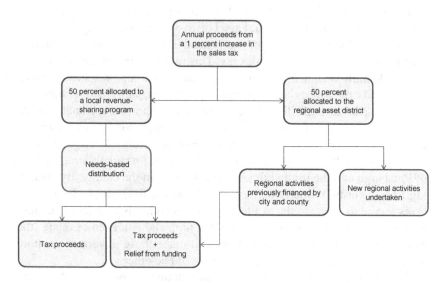

and was the pride of the two-state region. Unlike Denver, this district was to end when the financing of the station was complete. In 2004 voters rejected efforts to make the cultural district a permanent institution.

Peaceful Coexistence Strategies

No municipal boundaries are permanent. Some states, like Pennsylvania, come close to permanency in that only the voters, through a referendum, can agree to have their boundary changed. In a majority of states, however, boundaries can be changed through a process often referred to as annexation. In annexation, territory in one jurisdiction is transferred to another jurisdiction, sometimes in a friendly manner, more often contentiously.

American jurisprudence followed English practice and law by classifying municipalities as corporations. Citizens or businesses in a state can petition for the grant of self-government with all the rights and privileges afforded a municipality (Burns 1994). Virtually all modern cities and many towns can point to a particular moment in which they were incorporated or "came into legal existence." Often, these charters date back to the eighteenth and early nineteenth centuries.

Particularly in the eastern states, virtually all territory became incorporated into one municipality or another. Every square inch of Pennsylvania is located within a municipality that is considered to be vested with incorporated rights.

However, in a number of states, citizens have not elected to become incorporated. But unincorporated does not mean unoccupied. Indeed, significant populations, particularly in the more rural hinterlands of major metropolitan areas, reside in unincorporated territory. These populations require traditional local government services (elementary and secondary education, police, fire, public works, recreation, and leisure). In these instances, it is the county government that has become the local government service provider. The county provides the services and imposes property taxes to support them.

Particularly in states where territory is divided into incorporated areas that are usually run by cities and unincorporated areas that are usually run by counties or townships, fiscal equity arrangements have emerged. The core of the agreements addresses the problems surrounding the economic loss of one governmental jurisdiction when territory transfers from one government to another. The city of Louisville and Jefferson County, Kentucky, entered into a 12-year agreement in 1986, subsequently renewed in 1998, that has become known as the Louisville Compact. As a center city, Louisville was faced with severe fiscal problems and repeated attempts to consolidate the city and county had been rejected by voters. Although a difficult legal process, the city was poised to engage in a significant annexation campaign that would have serious financial implications for the county. Rather than engage in an adversarial battle, both parties agreed to negotiate a plan for the delivery of services and the funding of those services. Predicated on the assumption that there would be a moratorium on annexation, the parties divided service delivery between them. Services like air pollution control, public health, and planning were assigned to the county. Services like the zoo, museums, and emergency services were assigned to the city. The glue that held the compact together was an agreement to share in tax revenues. In 2003, the two governments made the final step and merged into a single government.

Citizens have the right to decide how they want to be governed. Sometimes, annexations can occur between municipalities and annexation wars can develop from the competing interests of the municipalities. Virginia represents another example of governments working together to avoid adversarial battles over territory (Hollis 1998). Agreements entered into by the City of Franklin with Southampton and Isle of Wright counties are representative. In areas of the counties that are experiencing significant commercial and industrial growth, the city has agreed to no annexation in perpetuity, but has agreed to deliver essential utility services in exchange for a percentage of all local tax revenues collected in the designated areas.

In Michigan, several peaceful coexistence strategies have been developed that create win-win outcomes for the state's cities and townships (Beach 2000). One in particular is Michigan's Land Transfer Act. Rather than annexing land, the township conditionally transfers land that would have been the subject of annexation to the city in exchange for a share of the tax revenues and state aid. Typically, the agreements are for a 50-year period at which point the land is scheduled to revert back to the township.

Assessing the Minnesota Tax-Base Sharing Program

What do we know about the success of fiscal regionalism? Luce's (1998a) analysis of the Minnesota plan found that the program significantly reduces property tax-base inequality but was not effective in reducing economic competition between municipalities. A possible explanation for the more limited impact on competition between jurisdictions is the relatively low percentage (40 percent) of commercial-industrial growth that is pooled. That 60 percent of commercial-industrial growth is retained by the municipality is still a significantly large enough "plum" for a municipality to be willing to compete with a neighbor. Notwithstanding the above caveat, Luce is not suggesting that the existing formula does not reduce competition. Rather, the impact on minimizing competition, although beneficial, is not as apparent as the more obvious fiscal property tax disparity reduction.

The Minnesota experience has also demonstrated that the formula as a redistributive tool works adequately, but is not perfect. The correlation between jurisdictional fiscal need and net distributions from the pool and the correlation between revenue-raising capacities and net distributions are statistically significant but modest (Luce 1998b). A possible explanation for the less than perfect match between fiscal need and actual distributions from the pool is the criterion that is used to assess fiscal need. A jurisdiction's need is determined by the ratio of its per capita assessed market valuation to the average per capita market valuation of all the other jurisdictions in the pool. The size of the gap between the jurisdiction's average assessed value and that of the pool affects the proportion of proceeds received. A community with 50 percent of the average assessed value of the pool would receive twice its population weight. Conversely, a community with 200 percent of the average assessed value of the pool would receive only half of its population weight. Per capita market valuation is only one of a number of measures that can determine fiscal stress or fiscal need. For instance, large cities may have comparatively high per capita market valuations but need far greater resources to address legitimate community needs. Minneapolis and St. Paul, using a more sophisticated formula for determining fiscal need, were identified as having relatively high need-capacity gaps. However, in 1989, Minneapolis contributed more in pooled value than it received in net tax benefits and St. Paul received only 23 percent of its estimated gap (Luce 1998b).

Several efforts have been undertaken to assess the replicability of the Minnesota plan in other states. In 1992, an effort was made to assess the application of the Minnesota tax-base sharing model to the state of Pennsylvania (McQuaid, Bok, Miller, and James 1992). The state as a whole was selected because uniformity provisions in the state's constitution precluded its application at a substate level. Methodologically, the study presumed that the state and adopted tax-base sharing plan were virtually identical to Minnesota's in 1975, and assessed its impact in 1990. What emerged from that analysis supports the notion that the program does serve a redistributive purpose. Hypothetically, in 1990 dollars, communities in the lowest quartile of fiscal capacity received $7.02 per capita in net proceeds from the pool while those communities in the most affluent quartile contributed, on average, $2.27. Such a distribution led to the conclusion that "the impact would be at a level that would be beneficial to those communities that would be net recipients from the pool, but not catastrophic to those communities that would be net contributors to the pool" (McQuaid et al. 1992, i).

This study also found that the overall effect of the program would be to slightly increase taxes on businesses. However, this effect would be more pronounced in the more affluent communities, making the business tax package more attractive in those communities in greater need (McQuaid et al. 1992, 36).

Finally, the study concluded the population size had little effect on a community's contribution to or distribution from the pool. Smaller, less affluent communities received the same general benefits as their larger counterparts while smaller, more affluent communities were not as adversely affected as their larger counterparts. Interestingly, business taxes in smaller communities, regardless of need, were adversely affected by the program (McQuaid et al. 1992). An argument could be made that such an impact has a long-term effect on a metropolitan region in channeling business growth to larger areas already equipped with the infrastructure to support that growth. The trade-off for the smaller jurisdictions is the net benefit in tax proceeds from the pool.

In an effort to assess the impact of tax-base sharing on other metropolitan regions, Luce (1998a) simulated the program in the metropolitan areas of Chicago, Philadelphia, Portland, and Seattle. Although each region has unique political characteristics, they shared a beneficial impact of tax-base sharing on enhancing the efficiency and equity of the existing property tax system. Interestingly, the Portland region, which had the least inequality in tax base across the region before tax-base sharing was introduced, showed the least beneficial impact of any of the regions analyzed. These findings suggest that the more diffused a metropolitan region, the greater net benefit tax-base sharing would have on that region.

As in the McQuaid, Bok, Miller, and James study, Luce's results confirmed that the wealthier communities tended to lose a little while the poorer communities gained a lot. On reflection, such an observation makes intuitive sense. If the average yield from the wealthier communities before tax-base sharing was $100 and that of poorer communities $50, a 10 percent reduction for the wealthy communities would result in a 20 percent increase for the poorer communities. Indeed, from a political perspective, Luce (1998a) found that the total population of the net winners (governments whose distributions from the pool exceeded contributions) outnumbered the total population of the net losers (governments whose contributions to the pool exceeded distributions) in three of the five regions analyzed.

Assessing the Allegheny County Revenue-Sharing Program

Assessment of the Allegheny County Revenue-Sharing program demonstrates a nuanced impact of the program. For this assessment, we employ a methodology that is useful in identifying the fiscal stress (or health) of a municipality relative to other municipalities in the same geographic area.

Think for a moment about the world of an elected official. First, she is concerned about her property tax rates relative to her neighbors. In American political culture, the principle of limited government has always placed an important premium on low rates of taxation. Higher rates of taxation are, in today's political milieu, impossible to propose or to defend to the public in their role as "voters." "Voters" expect her to lower the tax rate or, at least, not to raise it. Second, she is aware of the tax resources generated from the rates of taxation. In this regard, it is desirable to have that low or lower rate of taxation generate a significant amount of taxes. Indeed, those dollars enable her to address demands for services requested by the public in their role as "consumer." Voters want lower taxes and consumers want more services.

Such a push and pull suggests that our elected official could be in a community that falls into one of four general situations relative to her community's rate of taxation and the tax resources that rate generates. In the first, her community's rate of taxation is low relative to most other taxing jurisdictions but, even with those low rates, her community's yield relative to her neighbors is much higher. In this situation, she would be the envy, or "Ideal," as categorized in Figure 8.4, of all the other governments. With minimal tax rates, voters would applaud her "doing her job." She would also be envied, as the yield from that minimal tax rate would generate substantial dollars and consumers would applaud her for "doing her other job."

A second situation would be one in which her community had higher rates of taxation, but those rates of taxation generate relatively high amounts of

Figure 8.4 **Two-Dimensional Model of How Citizens of the Community View Taxation and Services Delivered**

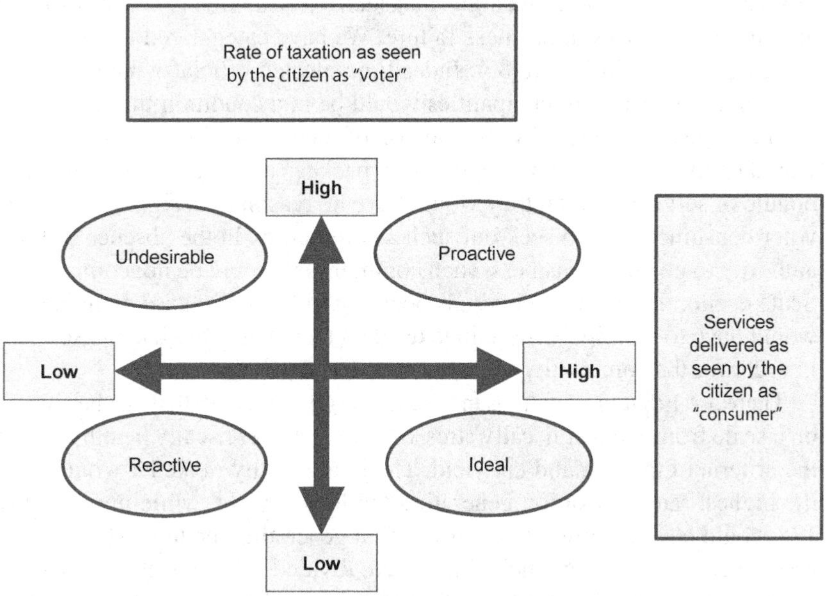

tax resources. We have labeled this situation as "Proactive" in Figure 8.4. Generally, as an elected official she probably could lower rates of taxation, but service levels appear to be acceptable to her voter-consumers. Older, more affluent suburbs are representative of this situation.

The third situation she could find herself in is one where the community has a relatively low rate of taxation and that rate generates relatively lower amounts of resources. She might be in a position to raise taxes if there was a perceived demand by the voter-consumers. Indeed, their relatively limited bundle of services appears acceptable. We have labeled this situation as "Reactive" in Figure 8.4. She could, from a resource perspective, address demands, if requested, without creating a noncompetitive tax rate. Newer towns on the fringes of an urban area may be representative of this situation.

It is the final situation that is the most revealing. Our elected official could be in a community that already has higher rates of taxation than her neighbors. Unfortunately, that high tax effort yields fewer tax resources than for those same neighbors. Our elected official in this case would be in a community that is minimally meeting consumer demands but maximally taxing voters. She and her fellow officials are suffering the worst of both worlds. They would be unable to justify the higher rates of taxation to the voter with the delivery of adequate services to the consumer. The "voter" would be upset with the high rates of taxation while the "consumer" would be dissatisfied with the quality of service. Indeed, one could argue that such a jurisdiction is not competitive and, in market terms, a business failure. We have categorized this situation as "Undesirable" in Figure 8.4. Indeed, no elected official would seek out this condition. These municipalities would be in a condition that would not be one logically chosen by the elected officials. Lacking resources, they would be forced into an unacceptable tax package and a resulting inadequate bundle of services, a plan they would have no reason to design. Few, if any, voter-consumers would seek out such a community. In the absence of legal authority to go out of business, such communities would be noncompetitive. Scale economies aside, individuals deciding to locate in these communities would have to contribute more in taxes than they would get back in services in order for the community to improve its fiscal position.

There are 128 municipalities in the Pittsburgh-area study that can be aligned on a scale from 1 (most fiscally stressed) to 128 (most fiscally healthy) using the criteria of tax rate and tax yield. The municipality ranked 1 would have the highest rate of taxation generating the lowest yield, while municipality 128 would have the lowest rate of taxation generating the highest yield. For assessment purposes, municipalities were divided into four groups. The 32 most fiscally healthy were labeled "stately" and the 32 least fiscal healthy were labeled "stressed." The 32 below the stately were labeled "stable" and the 32 immediately above the stressed were labeled "strapped."

Although attaching labels to the four classes of communities carries subjective connotations, those labels have heuristic value in presenting the subsequent analysis. Indeed, validating both the scale and the subjective labels assigned is important and necessary. With 20.3 percent of the non-Pittsburgh population in Allegheny County, communities in the "stressed" category have 52 percent of all families in poverty; 53 percent of all violent crimes; and 43 percent of all vacant housing units (Miller 2002). The median family income in stressed communities is 50 percent of the median family income in the stately communities. Communities in the "stressed" category have 15 percent of the workforce but 24 percent of the unemployed. Further, in 1987, Pennsylvania adopted the Municipal Fiscal Disparities Act, which serves as a Chapter 11 reorganization process for "bankrupt" municipalities. To date, eight communities in the study area have petitioned to be declared a distressed municipality as defined in the act. On the scale, those municipalities all fall in the "stressed" category. Indeed, they rank first, second, third, fourth, fifth, sixth, eleventh, and twelfth.

Overall, the population of Allegheny County dropped by 4.1 percent during the decade of the 1990s. However, not all municipalities lost population. The city of Pittsburgh and those municipalities classified as stressed lost 9.5 and 9.7 percent respectively while those municipalities classified as stately grew by 7.6 percent. This pattern of hollowing corroborates the broader statewide demographic changes documented by the Brookings Institution (2003).

In 1995, the first year of the revenue-sharing program, just under $31 million was allocated to the municipalities in the county. The city of Pittsburgh received the largest share, $18.6 million or 60 percent. The balance was fairly evenly distributed between the other municipal groups. Between 1995 and 2005, the available funds for the revenue-sharing program increased by 21.6 percent to $37.6 million. Most notable in the data is the low rate of growth for the city of Pittsburgh (8.3 percent) compared to the other groups of municipalities (36.9 percent to 46.4 percent). Pittsburgh's share dropped from 60 percent to 53.4 percent in 2005.

The component of the revenue-sharing program that allocates revenues from the pool to the county's 128 municipalities was designed to be redistributive, more heavily benefiting those communities with a diminished capacity to generate tax dollars. The distribution formula has two parts. First, the formula measures the base share a government receives from the revenue-sharing program by identifying that government's total taxes collected as a percentage of all of the taxes collected by all of the governments participating in the program. This can be understood as a municipality's proportion of the total taxes collected countywide. For instance, a particular municipality that collected 2 percent of the total taxes collected by all the municipalities would be theoretically entitled to 2 percent of the available revenue-sharing funds.

The second part of the formula adjusts that percentage by each municipality's relative wealth. Wealth is measured as the ratio of a particular municipality's per capita assessed value to the average assessed value of all of the municipalities. In the case above, if the community had one-half the per capita wealth it would receive twice as much as it would have received if the formula was simply based on relative tax effort. The municipality with 2 percent of taxes collected and one-half the relative wealth would receive 4 percent of the available revenue-sharing funds. Conversely, if the municipality with 2 percent of taxes collected had twice the relative wealth, it would receive 1 percent of the available revenue-sharing funds. On this measure the proceeds for both 1995 and 2005 indicate that the program is achieving its desired outcomes. In 1995, stately municipalities received $9.46 per capita while municipalities in the stressed category received twice as much ($18.86 per capita). In 2005, the range for the same two categories was $12.63 to $29.31 per capita.

The allocation for the city of Pittsburgh grew much more modestly during the period but still represents twice the per capita allocation of even the stressed municipalities group. That is primarily a function of the part of the formula that establishes the base allocation—total taxes. As a major metropolitan city six times the size of the next largest municipality in Allegheny County, its tax effort is significantly larger, dwarfing those other municipalities. When the revenue-sharing program was conceived, it was probably with the understanding that utilizing a factor as tax effort would yield a greater distribution of the revenue-sharing funds to the city than other measures, such as population, that could have been used as the base calculation.

Although tax effort gave Pittsburgh a greater initial allocation because of its tax effort position in 1995, the city of Pittsburgh's tax effort has been significantly reduced over the last 10 years. As the city has addressed its severe financial condition by reducing costs, limiting revenue increase, and entering a state program for fiscally strapped municipalities, its taxes have actually decreased in relation to the taxing levels of all the other jurisdictions. Indeed, all other categories of municipalities saw a relative increase in tax effort as Pittsburgh's effort declined by 8.9 percent. This decline also accounts for the city's relative modest growth in total disbursements from the pool (the total pool increased 21.6 percent while Pittsburgh's increase was 8.3 percent).

The revenue-sharing program, by virtue of its redistributive formula, has a differential impact on communities. In 1995, the revenue-sharing allocation constituted 3 percent of stately municipalities' budgets and 11.1 percent of stressed municipalities' budgets. For the city of Pittsburgh, although large on a per capita basis, the percentage allocation (5.5 percent) falls between the other categories of municipalities.

Between 1995 and 2005, the overall change in the impact of the revenue-sharing program was surprisingly modest. For stately municipalities, the revenue-sharing program dropped from 3 percent to 2.4 percent of budget, stable municipalities from 4.9 percent to 4.4 percent, strapped municipalities from 7.8 percent to 7.2 percent. Stressed municipalities and the city of Pittsburgh increased from 11.1 percent and 5.5 percent to 11.8 percent and 6.2 percent respectively. Modest does not mean insignificant. It is clear that the city of Pittsburgh and the county's stressed municipalities are becoming more dependent on the program.

A more thorough analysis of how the allocation formula has operated over time reveals that its two principle components work in opposite directions that serve to keep the overall distributions relatively the same (Miller and Easton 2008). Whether a municipality sees a growing or shrinking proportion of the program depends on the interaction between its relative tax effort and its relative fiscal position. The annual formula recalculation will result in a maximum increased allocation share for a municipality when a municipality increases its share of the total taxes (+) collected countywide and experiences relative economic decline (–). If both factors, (+,+) or (–,–), are heading in

Table 8.1

Percent Change (2005/1995) in the Two Key Components Determining Allocation from the Allegheny County Revenue-Sharing Program

Change	Municipalities Grouped by Financial Condition				City of Pittsburgh
	Stately	Stable	Strapped	Stressed	
In Relative Fiscal Stress	−4.6%	−1.1%	4.5%	24.5%	2.2%
In Relative Tax Revenues	29.2%	11.9%	9.7%	1.2%	−8.9%

the same direction, the change in allocation will depend on the intensity of the change of each factor. Finally, that municipality experiencing a relative decline in tax effort (−) and an increase in relative wealth (+) should see a significant reduction in its revenue-sharing allocation.

Analysis of the change in those factors is presented in Table 8.1 and indicates that stately municipalities are the ones most likely to be increasing tax efforts and stressed municipalities are continuing to lose ground in relative wealth. Municipalities in the stately category saw their relative share of total tax effort increase by 29.2 percent between 1995 and 2005. As a practical response to growing populations (they were the only group with population growth) and increasing service demands, these communities were much more apt to see their total collected taxes grow at a faster rate than nongrowth municipalities. At the same time, the stressed municipalities saw little relative tax effort growth but received more from the revenue-sharing program because economic conditions deteriorated. Overall, stressed municipalities saw a 24.5 percent increase in the gap between their relative wealth and that of the average of all the communities. This suggests that economic growth is occurring within Allegheny County in such a way that the economic gap between its richest and poorest communities is growing at a significant rate.

If revenue distributions to Allegheny County municipalities through the Act 77 formula are studied as a snapshot from any given year along the policy's history, the breakdown appears to approximate what its creators envisioned; that is, communities with a diminished capacity to generate tax dollars benefit more heavily. Indeed, municipalities that fall into lower categories of fiscal health by any measure consistently receive the most Act 77 dollars per capita. The more subtle interactions between formula variables over time have created a scenario that is far less straightforward. Over time, a municipality's expanding or shrinking share of the tax dollars dispersed countywide depends on the interaction between two factors: relative tax effort, which determines its base share of the program, and relative fiscal position, which determines how the base share will be adjusted to reflect need. Therefore, the biggest gainers are not only poor communities that experience economic decline, but also rich and growing communities that expand tax collections. In the end, the formula tends to reflect the well-documented underlying phenomenon of an ever-widening gap in financial condition between those two classes.

It is safe to assume that reinforcing this polarization was not among Act 77's original policy aims. Likewise, it is fair to assume that the formula could be made more redistributive by adjustments that would make it less likely to reward tax growth in well-to-do municipalities and more likely to direct funds to the stressed communities where they are needed most. If Act 77 continues to distribute revenue using the current formula, its ability to expand assistance to the trailing communities, including Pittsburgh, will continue to diminish as the deteriorating tax base in those jurisdictions means they are entitled to an ever-shrinking base share of the allocation.

Concluding Thoughts and Things to Ponder

Fiscal regionalism is more a promise than an integral part of today's metropolitan regions. As our assessment of the plans has demonstrated, there are unanticipated consequences associated with their implementation. But the knowledge of such nuances simply paves the way for the next generation of fiscal regionalism strategies to be improved and better able to serve the needs of the region. That said, the bottom line is that they work. Indeed, for regions that have employed them, they generally have served the purpose their designers envisioned.

The biggest limitation on the growth of fiscal regionalism is today's antitax political climate. Generally, the fuel of fiscal regionalism is a new tax or the expansion of an existing tax and, as such, it is extremely difficult to convince elected officials to advance the proposition.

Things to Ponder

1. Why does it make sense for regions to share in the economic benefit of the urban city?
2. In the text we assert that local politics places a high value on having lower tax rates than surrounding communities. Why is this?
3. Do you think that the fiscal regionalism strategy in Minnesota is fair to both affluent and struggling municipalities?
4. What cultural assets in your region could be fiscally combined to benefit from revenue sharing?
5. How do you think the threat of annexation affects the possible fiscal regionalism propositions in American cities?

9

Reshaping Counties and Integrating Regional Special Districts

High Risk but Great Potential

Seemingly the levels above municipal governments are county governments and special districts. While these two types of governments are quite different we have chosen to address their roles in metropolitan governance together because both play relatively limited roles in the broad sweep of public policy making. We describe counties as "dark continents." While they play critical public service delivery roles in much of the United States, they are often forgotten in discussions of effective public service. In much of the United States, county government is relegated to responsibility for the "leftover" activities: providing services for scattered parcels of unincorporated lands, or necessary, but not very visible, public functions such as recordkeeping (birth records to land deeds), or quite literally, back roads. Some parts of the country have always minimized the importance of county government, but even the parts of the country that historically valued the county seem to be diminishing its role.

On the surface, special districts are quite different. They are created to offer specific, often technical, services in a defined geographic region. Special districts provide critical public services across the country, from water and sewer services to K–12 public school education.

What connects these two types of local government? Put simply, it is land. There are special districts that are contiguous with a single municipality (public school districts), but most special districts are larger than a single municipality and many serve multiple counties. They are *regional* governments even though the distinct and/or limited public services they provide mean that they do not offer the array of services of a city or town. This chapter explores whether the geographic basis of these governments makes them regionally relevant even though they are limited as service providers.

County Government

Geographically, the largest units of local government are counties. The term "county" includes those entities called "boroughs" in Alaska and "parishes" in Louisiana. County governments exist in all states but Connecticut and Rhode Island.

Two distinct images of counties have emerged as part of the U.S. political system. Historically, in New England and to a lesser degree the mid-Atlantic states, towns and villages, even in rural settings, were the primary organizing units. County government was seen as a subdivision of the state or colony (see Chapter 2). Shortly after independence, the newly formed states divided themselves into administrative units (counties) for purposes of delivering state-level services. The most extreme version of this is Massachusetts, where the boundaries of the counties are fixed in statute by listing the municipalities that fall within that geography. As a result, counties were not self-constituted governments and became, in the minds of local inhabitants, more remote and less interesting forms of local government. Similarly the governing responsibilities of these counties are limited. Counties rarely provide direct citizen services. For example, county governments in Massachusetts have two functions; running a jail and record keeping (everything from birth certificates to deeds). When Connecticut abolished its county governments in the 1960s they were replaced by regional planning agencies.

In the South, where larger-scale agricultural development was more prevalent, the county was more apt to be the primary unit of local government in all but the more highly developed urban centers (Adrian and Fine 1991). Although not formed from the bottom up, designation as a county seat represented a significant economic opportunity for a number of communities.

Communities lucky enough to be designated as the "county seat" became the trade center; the central point where the local political elites congregated; the site of the year's biggest event, the county fair; and the place of institutional memory for the local inhabitants through its record-keeping function (Adrian and Fine 1991). Particularly in rural areas, county government served as the access point for most citizens to governmental services and opportunities.

This stark contrast in the fundamental building blocks of local civil society in the United States can best be dramatized by comparing practices in Georgia and Massachusetts. Georgia is representative of a number of southern states that employed the "county unit system" (Marando and Thomas 1977). In this system, each county was entitled to at least one representative in the state legislature. This organizing principle elevated the importance of county government in the state political process and afforded rural constituencies a far greater role in state policy than they would have had otherwise. In Massachusetts, towns constituted the Colonial Congress. Zuckerman (1970) asserts that such a constitution had the effect of reducing the [State] House of

Representatives to a virtual congress of communities and establishing a town's "inalienable right to representation." Such a relationship in Massachusetts led Tocqueville (1953, 57) to comment, "It is important to remember that they [the townships of New England] have not been vested with privileges, but that they have, on the contrary, forfeited a portion of their independence to the state." Indeed, early deputies to the state legislature were actually town employees (Zuckerman 1970).

The Dark Continent

County governments have a checkered past. They have been referred to as the "dark continent of American politics" (Gilbertson 1917) and the "forgotten government" (Marando and Thomas 1977). James Bryce (1922, 605) captured the predominant academic notion of the role of county government when he said, "the system which prevails in the southern states need not long detain us, for it is less instructive and has proved less successful. Here the unit is the county." Marando and Thomas (1977) note that power concentration in the North is usually referred to as a more value-neutral "city hall," while similar concentration of power in the South is referred to as a heavily value-laden "courthouse gang."

Bryce's impact, among others, has led to a lack of respect for county government as a fundamental institution within the U.S. governmental system among academics. There are three reasons for this image. Initially, this relegation to footnote status may have more to do with the way in which county governments are managed and the functions they undertake as opposed to their relevance as units of local government. When urban problems attract the attention of the nation, it is city government and city mayors who are called upon to address them. While city governments are dealing with important problems like poverty, county governments have been left to address other less interesting and less important issues like the tarring of county roads. Further, county governments often reflect the rural/suburban constituency of a territory and stand in contrast to the willingness of the city governments to deal with those urban problems. As a result, the image of county government as a sleepy, patronage-riddled organization resistant to change is frequently reinforced in the eyes of the public.

Second, one of the theoretical bases for the organizing of metropolitan areas focuses on drawing boundaries around the smallest relevant service area for the delivery of a particular public good. This theory, sometimes referred to as public choice, relegates county governments to "not critical" status in the governance of metropolitan America. Indeed, they are merely "another potential supplier of urban services, along with special districts, municipalities, and private firms" (Schneider and Park 1989, 345). Although Schneider and Park go on to demonstrate that urban counties are playing an increasingly important role in the delivery of public goods in urban areas, the image within the theoretical framework of public choice serves to minimize the significance of that role.

Third, and perhaps the most significant reason for the lack of a positive image of county government, rests in its existing structure and its general unwillingness to change that structure. The primary structure of county government is the commission. Tracing its origins to Pennsylvania in the early 1700s, this structure is little changed and still the predominant form for more than 2,000 of the nation's 3,100-plus counties (Blair 1986). Under the commission form of government, the legislative and executive functions are concentrated in a small, elected board, usually referred to as the board of county commissioners. It is not uncommon for the commission to have only three members. In Ohio, the commissioners are both legislators and executives, with commissioners being assigned as the heads of various (and potentially multiple) agencies. In some states, this board even has some judicial powers.

In addition to the board, many of the administrative functions of the county are handled through a separate set of elected officials, commonly referred to as row officers. For instance, in Pennsylvania and Ohio, most counties elect most or all of the following: a district attorney, who serves as the chief criminal prosecutor; a clerk of courts, who serves as the chief record-keeper of the criminal courts; a controller, who serves as the financial watchdog of the county finances; a coroner, who serves as the chief medical examiner in determining causes of death in suspected criminal cases; several jury commissioners, who serve as coordinators of lists of citizens for jury selection; a prothonotary, who serves as the chief record-keeper of the civil courts; a recorder of deeds, who serves as the administrator of the deeds records system; a clerk of orphan court, who serves as the chief record-keeper of the orphan courts; a register of wills, who maintains jurisdiction over the probating of wills; a sheriff, who serves as the officer of the court; and a treasurer, who collects the revenues (primarily taxes) for the county.

The term "row office" originates from the physical structure of most courthouses. Upon walking into a courthouse, one encounters a neat "row" of offices. Legend has it that President Harry Truman, upon entering the courthouse in either Allegheny or Fayette County, Pennsylvania, looked up at the signs and said what everyone else was thinking, "What the hell is a prothonotary?" Indeed, Truman's frustration captures the public's general confusion over county government. Not only is a prothonotary an obscure administrative position, the public is asked to choose at the polls between two candidates for a position they can hardly understand or even pronounce. Yet row officers in most states are elected officials with considerable patronage power and the ability to thwart the interest of the commissioners who are more broadly elected to represent the interests of the public.

In theory, the structure of most county governments reflects an idealized notion of citizen government. The commissioners serve as both legislators and administrators, making sure the interests of the citizens are protected, while the election of the row officers guarantees closeness of the administration to the public. In practice, particularly in more urbanized areas, this structure has led to the image of inaction, patronage, and irrelevant elected offices.

The Modern County: Emerging from the Dark Continent

Early Origins: Lakewood Plan

In 1951 the city of Long Beach, California, released a report recommending that Lakewood be annexed to Long Beach. This and other efforts by Long Beach to annex Lakewood's property prompted the Lakewood Taxpayers' Association and other groups to lobby to incorporate the community as a city. Lakewood citizens formed the Lakewood Committee for Incorporation, seeking to incorporate about seven square miles of property, including some 70,000 residents, 105 miles of paved and lighted streets, and the Lakewood Center shopping center.

The Lakewood Plan was the "instruction manual" for incorporation. The Plan specified which municipal duties would be handled by the community as well as which would be handled by the county, respectively. This was not merely a "two-tiered government" but a unique experiment in contract government. Accordingly, the Lakewood City Council would pass laws, set policy, make a budget, and do community planning. However, it would also tap into existing county services by contracting for street construction and repair, animal pound regulation, health laws, building inspections, tax collection, library services, schools, and fire and police protection.

On March 9, 1954, Lakewood was incorporated as a new city. From its start it contracted out most of its municipal services. Although Lakewood's largest contracts are with the County of Los Angeles, they also contract with other municipalities, nonprofits, and the private sector. While few communities "contract out" all but elected functions, as is done in Lakewood, the idea of using a regionally provided service, such as one from a county government, as the basis for *local* service delivery, starts with this contract. This is the precedent that makes models such as Broward and Miami-Dade County service-sharing operations possible.

Two-Tiered Government

The idea of a two-tiered government configuration is most closely associated with the United Kingdom. Under this arrangement two tiers or levels (essentially the county and the municipality) undertake distinct tasks. There are relatively few government functions performed simultaneously by both "tiers." There is minimal overlap of responsibility between the two. Even where there is potential overlap as in permitting, building inspection, and law enforcement, the tasks are constrained by political boundaries. Thus, for example, a county permitting program would only be in force in unincorporated areas of the county. In other cases, the "law enforcement" responsibility of the county sheriff would be limited to traffic on county roads, the incarceration of prisoners or the patrol in unincorporated areas. These are the legal and jurisdictional arrangements that are common in the weak county government of the Northeast and Midwest.

As mentioned in Chapter 5, a different model of two-tiered government has emerged in Florida via charter change in Miami-Dade County (at the time of the charter enactment in 1957 it was Dade County) and by political and administrative agreement in neighboring Broward County. These are two-tiered in a very different sense than the jurisdictional division borrowed from the United Kingdom. Under the charter in Miami-Dade and by interlocal agreement in Broward there exist two "full-service" governments. Under the Miami-Dade Charter, the county performs the same functions as any incorporated municipality. To highlight the expanded responsibility of this new governance model, the Dade County Sheriff's Office, formerly headed by an elected sheriff, became the Dade County Police Department with an appointed chief. Furthermore, the chief executive officer for the newly reorganized county was to be a county manager, with roles and responsibilities virtually identical to those of a city manager in a classic council-manager government. The charter was changed in the first decade of this century to create the elected position of county mayor, with the manager dropping to the role of chief *administrative* officer appointed by the mayor instead of the county commission. The important change is in refashioning the county government by borrowing the municipal template. At the time of the charter change, more than 50 percent of the land and more than 50 percent of the population of the county was in unincorporated areas (Sofen 1961). Changes in the last two decades resulted in a large number of new, mostly small municipalities, but the county remains responsible for large tracts of land and a substantial population of more than 1 million people. (Based upon the 2010 U.S. Census Bureau information, approximately 1.3 million people live in the 39 cities, towns, and villages within Miami-Dade County but another 1.1 million still reside in the unincorporated areas of the county.)

The core idea was that through two equal governments all the residents of the county had access to the same public services whether they resided in a municipality or in the county. Services were intended to be indistinguishable. The difference was in who received the property taxes. At least at the start (the 1960s) the expectation was that more new municipalities would slowly take over most, if not all, of the land in the county. The county government would shrink, not in breadth of responsibility, but in the numbers of persons served.

There were, as it turned out, two flaws in this prediction. First, the quality of services offered by Miami-Dade County were equal (and by sheer economies of scale sometimes better) to those offered by the municipalities. There were few incentives to migrate toward the creation of new municipal governments. Second is the fiscal distress that has become part of everyday life for all local governments for nearly two decades, which spurred the development of service sharing programs (see Chapter 5). Oddly, the push for "privatization" and service sharing generated new interest in the creation of new, often small, municipal governments. The quality of county services became the impetus for the carving of new communities out of developments in unincorporated areas. Those new municipal governments could simply contract for services with neighboring communities, or more likely Miami-Dade County government. While no new community adopted the full "Lakewood" plan, big-ticket activities such as water and law enforcement would remain with county, but now under a contract. The calculus for remaining within the county changed, but it was premised upon the continued existence of the county offering *municipal* services. Today some 39 municipalities are found within Miami-Dade County, up from the 22 in 1957.

The experience of Broward was quite different. The change in the delivery of services was largely driven by the municipal governments (generally the city managers). Broward was quite different from Miami-Dade County. While its population is only about two-thirds of Miami-Dade at about 1.75 million (U.S. Census Bureau 2010), it had much stricter laws with regard to encroachment on the Everglades. As a result, the area available for development is barely half that of Miami-Dade. Much of the development of Broward occurred in the 1950s and then a second spurt in the 1970s. All 28 of its municipalities used some variation of the council-manager form of government. By the 1990s barely 10 percent of the "developable" land was still unincorporated. The Broward County government was structurally a typical Florida county government, but because unincorporated lands were scattered across the county (often in small pockets nestled between municipal boundaries) it provided a range of public services, most notably sanitation, law enforcement, a regional library, and fire/EMS services. By the late 1980s through both informal and formal interjurisdictional agreements, municipalities in

Broward already had a vibrant service-sharing exchange. While on occasion the county would be the contract partner, the City of Ft. Lauderdale was the likely partner, particularly for law enforcement services. On the other hand the state legislature authorized the county to create a "port authority" (later renamed Port Everglades) in 1927, which operates both a commercial port and a major intermodal transportation hub (trucking and ships) while also being connected by rail to the airport. The port is one of the largest container ports on the Atlantic seaboard. The investment in infrastructure and then support services (especially law enforcement and fire/EMS) gave the county considerable expertise (and staff) in these areas.

In conversations that began during the monthly meetings of the Broward County City Management Association, the idea of a different model of a two-tier government began to emerge. One of the first ideas was that the scattered parcels of unincorporated land were difficult to serve. A proposal began to coalesce whereby the contiguous municipalities would annex the unincorporated land so that there would be no unincorporated land remaining. In 1999 special legislation was drafted that made completion of annexations by 2010 mandatory. The next task was to address the now "redundant" county employees. Relatively few of those employees were needed by the municipalities that annex lands; on the other hand those employees and most particularly the fire/EMS service was viewed as an asset to be protected. The solution was to be more inclusive in contracting out service-sharing arrangements to make use of the skilled and knowledgeable county employees.

These stories represent two different approaches and understandings of a two-tiered government. In both cases the strict notion of dividing the provision of services is not followed. Central to the provision of public services is the use of shared service and interlocal agreements to extend the expertise and skill of employees at the county level and make them available at the municipal level. In fact this arrangement works only because the expertise existed at the county level. In the parts of the country where county governments have limited breadth in service delivery, this arrangement could not emerge because there would not be a core of experienced employees upon which to build shared service arrangements. Thus, even though a Broward County would seem much like a county in the Northeast (no unincorporated land to serve), it is quite different than a New York or Massachusetts county in the capacity and capability of its employees. Therefore, it is a more viable and valued partner for municipal governments.

The "Urban" County

In much of the country, counties and municipalities are distinct governments. This goes beyond the classic two-tiered government arrangement with relatively sharp demarcation of services. In much of the country the act of incorporation legally removes the municipality from the county. It is geographically within the county, but politically it is separate. In most states the act of incorporation means that a different part of the state's code now controls governmental affairs. But what about counties that are, by geography as well as service demands, more like a municipality than a traditional county? This was the issue facing the Virginia legislature in the 1960s. In northern Virginia forming the western part of metropolitan Washington, DC, there were two small governments, Arlington County and the City of Alexandria. Both were roughly the same size and population but by the requirements of the state code they were quite different. Three elements of the urban government are pertinent, as noted in the Virginia Code.

1. Adoption of Urban County Executive Form

Any county with a population of more than 90,000 may adopt the urban county executive form of government in accordance with the provisions of Chapter 3 (§ 15.2–300 et seq.) of this title. (1997, c. 587)

2. No Unincorporated Area to Be Incorporated After Adoption of Urban County Form of Government

After the date of adoption of the urban county executive form of government, no unincorporated area within the limits of such county shall be incorporated as a separate town or city within the limits of such county, whether by judicial proceedings or otherwise. (Code 1950, § 15–384.72; 1960, c. 382; 1962, c. 623, § 15.1–785; 1968, c. 797; 1997, c. 587)

3. City May Petition to Become Part of County

After the date of adoption of the urban county executive form of government, a city contiguous to or within the limits of such a county may petition, by action of its governing body, to become a part of the county on terms set forth in a resolution adopted by the board. Passage of a referendum within the petitioning city shall constitute approval of the city becoming a district of the county or a part or parts of one or more districts and action of the board shall constitute final approval thereof by the county. (Code 1950, § 15–384.73; 1960, c. 382; 1962, c. 623, § 15.1–786; 1997, c. 587)

To date only Arlington County has adopted this form. Thus Arlington is both entirely urbanized and has no towns within its boundaries. The county is the only general-purpose local government and is thus similar to a unitary authority, or city-county consolidation.

City-County Consolidation

Rated by Walker (1987) to be the most difficult form of intergovernmental cooperation to achieve, the formal city-county consolidation has a long history going back to the very early part of the nineteenth century, marked by a surge in such reforms through the 1960s and 1970s (Hall 2009). Importantly, and possibly prophetically, the successful efforts of the nineteenth century were the product of legislative enactment. However, all but one such effort in the twentieth century came about by referendum.

City-county consolidation is at once both simple and complicated. "When a city government and a county government unify, they eliminate their separate legislative and executive position and instead become one government. Though it varies state by state, often city-county consolidations have simultaneous status as a city and as a county, with the powers to execute the functions of both" (Sellers 2010, 7). The problem of "simultaneous status as a city and a county" is two-fold; first, as with every merger, the organizational cultures require time to establish new work patterns that bridge the differences of organizational culture, and second, the legal ramifications of a city exercising "county" authority and vice versa is a more complicated statutory path than might be apparent. In the former case, organizational cultures are partly driven by the technical competencies needed to effectively carry out organizational functions. Any time new tasks are added or organizations are merged the cultural differences that shape organizational behavior must be reconciled. A number of studies conducted throughout the creation of the U.S. Department of Homeland Security, because of the organizational culture differences among FEMA, Border Patrol, and intelligence agencies, are testimony to this problem (Executive Office of the President 2003). While merging two building departments, or two fire departments, may not be a problem, merging a police department with its law enforcement duties and a sheriff's department with its responsibility for incarceration is quite another matter. Also, in certain functional areas such as economic development, the merged agencies may have been rivals and competitors before the merger. In the latter case, state rules with regard to the legal authority, particularly concerning taxation, varies between municipal and county governments. State formula for funding various local government activities may well be different for municipalities and counties. Deciding whether a consolidated government is a "city" or a "county" may affect shared revenue from the state.

To better understand the process of consolidation we will examine three such efforts. First is the consolidation of Jacksonville, Florida, with Duval County. The second consolidation is that of Indianapolis, which is the only city-county consolidation completed after the end of the nineteenth century that was created through legislative enactment rather than referenda. The third case study examines the multiple *failed* attempts to consolidate Memphis, Tennessee.

Jacksonville, Florida

In 1968 the voters of Duval County adopted a new charter that created a consolidated government of which the City of Jacksonville was the centerpiece. The first proposal to merge or consolidate the municipalities and county government came during the Depression and was first authorized by an amendment to the Constitution of Florida in 1934. No action was taken until a new charter was developed by the legislature in 1967 (subject to voter approval). This change took place at the same time that the Florida Constitution was amended to add a home rule provision. According to the Consolidated Jacksonville Charter:

> The first legal step to consolidated city-county government for Jacksonville occurred in 1934 when the Florida Constitution was amended to permit merger of Duval County and all of its cities. That government matured only after a legislative-directed study commission drafted a Charter with widespread public approval which was adopted as the Charter in 1967. The government was not the metropolitan form of Miami-Dade County, which had retained the county government, nor was it the chartered-county form later permitted by the Florida Constitution when it was revised in 1968. It essentially eliminated two governments (city and county) and replaced it with one.

Initially all five municipalities in the county were redefined as urban service districts. Subsequently the smaller communities in Duval County—the three beach cities and the town of Baldwin—were reconstituted as urban services districts: they were permitted elements of local control, but they henceforth would look to the new City of Jacksonville for the former functions of county government, and could draw on essential urban services such as police and fire from the central government. Through judicial and legislative action, these communities were restored to their municipal status. Today the City of Jacksonville acts in the manner of a county government and they continue to function as municipal governments.

The legal status of Jacksonville as the successor government to Duval County is reflected in the retention of several elected and appointed offices mandated by the Florida Constitution as constituent parts of county government. Thus, Jacksonville retained the offices of sheriff, property appraiser, tax collector, supervisor of elections, and clerk of the circuit court. In this sense Jacksonville is both a city and a county government.

Indianapolis–Marion County

Indianapolis is notable for the fact that the consolidated government was created as the result of a legislative enactment rather than a vote of the public. The Indianapolis approach (Unigov) also served as the basis for the consolidation in Louisville more than three decades later. According to Gamrat and Haulk (2005, 5):

> Indianapolis merged with Marion County in 1970. The new government was called the UniGov. . . . the merger of Indianapolis and Marion County was accomplished through the state legislature. The Indiana law creating the merger allowed for the consolidation of powers of the mayor and county executive as well as between City and County councils. It did not mandate the merging of departments, agencies, or other taxing districts.

The consolidation of Indianapolis and Marion counties is incomplete at best. The only functions that were specifically assigned to the county by the law were economic development, public works, parks, transportation, and some areas of public safety. At the time of the merger there were four cities (of 22) that opted not to join the consolidation (Beech Grove, Lawrence, Southport, and Speedway). These cities all have their own elected officials and provide services to their own residents. In 2005 the City of Indianapolis and Marion County still had several separate departments and separate budgets that had to be approved by the consolidated 29-member council.

The incomplete nature of the consolidation was the result of the original motivation for the merge: improving Indianapolis's image and spurring economic development in the downtown area.

> When the Indianapolis-Marion County governments merged in 1970, the primary goals were to redevelop downtown and make Indianapolis a destination city. To accomplish these goals, the new UniGov crafted a master plan and created an economic development agency that would provide logistical and technical support to prospective businesses looking to relocate to Indianapolis. They then set out to market the new city to sporting ventures, both pro and amateur. . . .
>
> The UniGov merger has had the desired effect of spurring publicly funded projects in Indianapolis in the three plus decades since its commencement, using a lot of tax money in the process. However, all has not

been unambiguously successful . . . the fastest growing areas in Indiana and the Indianapolis region are those beyond the consolidated city. In addition, a large portion of the jobs created in downtown Indianapolis are low paying and in the service sector, and the public sector remains one of the downtown areas largest employers. (Gamrat and Haulk 2005, 7–8)

Even before the Great Recession created financial problems in Indianapolis, the reality was that the consolidation was successful as an image makeover, but less so as a financial transformation. "Reform" meant consolidation of the remaining departments and townships into UniGov. The arguments for merger could be repeated across the country; too many tax-exempt properties and too many people living outside of the city are using its amenities. While the population of the consolidated city of Indianapolis has risen 4 percent over the last 10 years, population has been increasing faster in the areas just outside of the consolidated city. Counties surrounding Marion County experienced population growth of 24 percent over the same period. Garmat and Haulk (2005, 13) conclude that "merging the city and county in 1970 did not make the merged city more attractive than the suburbs as a place to live."

City of Memphis–Shelby County: The Other Side of the Coin

To better understand the dynamic of city-county consolidation it is necessary to look at an effort that was not successful. The City of Memphis has taken city-county consolidation to the voters three times in the last 50 years. The first merger proposal was rejected both in the city and in the county, but twice since then the proposal has been approved by a wide margin in the city and defeated in the county. State law requires that both "jurisdictions" approve the merger for it to be accepted. Analysis of the voting suggested that separate votes have been instrumental in defeating consolidation. Consolidation proponents have tried to bring suburban leaders on board with the effort, but mayors in outlying cities maintain their opposition. That stance, coupled with the separate vote requirement, has stymied consolidation efforts.

There has been an interesting twist in the most recent attempt at consolidation (2010). That effort was initiated in 2009 by the Shelby County mayor (later mayor for the City of Memphis), who conducted a series of "listening tours" in 2009 to learn what the public would want from a consolidated City of Memphis–Shelby County government. Following these meetings, the county commission and the Memphis City Council both approved resolutions to create a charter commission.

The expectation was that the merger would lead to cost savings to offset the fact that the two governments had the highest combined property tax rate in the state. The proposal was not without controversy. Many, but especially those outside Memphis, had several concerns with the future operations of a unified government, which the charter commission attempted to address. Because one of the issues centered on whether the city and county school systems would be consolidated, the charter included a provision preventing this action unless approved through a separate referendum. The charter was completed in August 2010, leaving proponents only a couple of months to educate citizens about the proposed government before the November election. The result was all too familiar: the charter passed in Memphis by 51 percent but was strongly rejected outside the city, with 85 percent voting no.

The latest twist was when the Memphis school board voted to relinquish its charter, forcing consolidation with Shelby County schools. State legislation passed in 2011, creating a new, merged school board and a transition team. The impact of a consolidated school system on a future city-county consolidation attempt is unknown as several issues, including school funding, are still unresolved (Sanford, Hudson, O'Looney, and Gordon 2012).

The "Other" Regional Governments: Special Districts

The expression "herding cats" is often used to describe a situation in which the pieces of the puzzle defy categorization or ability to manage. The variation in role, responsibility, and geographic reach of special districts makes them difficult to categorize. Since special districts have widely divergent, yet narrow and often technical roles, and are constrained by somewhat unique geographic boundaries, managing them is indeed like herding cats. Nonetheless, there are a few general observations that can be made about them. First, they represent the largest group of local governments, with 37,381 such districts in 2007. Second, they have accounted for 90 percent of the growth in total new local governments between 1952 and 2007. Third, they tend to be narrowly focused, serving a single purpose; for example, in 1997, 92 percent of special district governments were undertaking a narrowly defined, specific function or responsibility. Fourth, their formation usually arises from the perceived need of participants to solve a particular problem rather than as the result of a desire to address a set of complex and interrelated problems or issues in a metropolitan area.

As presented in Chapter 5, there are two broad types of special districts. The first is generally designed to have a service territory approximately coterminous with a particular city or town government or a part of that single jurisdiction. Occasionally, that service area takes in parts of several communities. These special districts function as extensions of individual communities acting in a capacity that is isolated from the broader region of which they are a part. The second type of special district reflects a more regionalized perspective. For instance, the county government may establish a special district to serve all of the county territory or a significant percentage of the municipalities within the county. A second example is when a number of municipalities create a special district to serve the needs of the municipalities, collectively.

Bollens (1957) and Blair (1986), among others, have analyzed why the U.S. system accommodates the proliferation of special district governments. First, there is often a mismatch between the area that desires or needs a particular service and the existing political boundaries of the general-purpose governments in the area. The notion that the boundaries of the whole community would be changed to accommodate a need for a particular service is usually an unacceptable option. Second, there is often an inability on the part of the existing general-purpose local government to have either the power or the financial capacity to undertake a desired service. Third is the lack of a willingness or administrative capacity on the part of the existing general-purpose government. For instance, a rural-dominated town government may have no interest in becoming part of a public water system that primarily services an urban area, even though a portion of the citizenry may support such an activity. Indeed, such a situation leads to the fourth explanation: the group of citizens interested in the service being delivered may also desire control over the governance of the delivery system. The creation of the special district serves the purpose and interest of both the existing general-purpose government and the citizens that desire a service. In a situation where the common interests of government and citizen are served, it frequently is the case that the local government itself acts as the advocate for the creation of the special district. Fifth, officials in general-purpose governments, not wanting to appear to be expanding government services, particularly to voters who will not receive the service, can encourage special district formation to satisfy citizens who want a service without alienating those who do not want to bear the cost of the service. A sixth explanation, particularly in rural areas, centers on the desire of citizens to have some public services, but not to the degree that would require a general-purpose local government. A seventh explanation, offered by Bollens (1957, 15), is the "unadorned self-interest or selfishness of some groups and individuals." This notion of self-interest is more fully articulated by Burns (1994), who argues that a number of general-purpose and single-purpose governments are formed as a direct result of business interests. Whether to produce a more favorable tax climate, a more consistent cash flow, or to better define the market, it is the interests of businesses and not necessarily the political interests of the citizens of the territory that are furthered. Burns demonstrates that the business interests, operating behind the scenes, often provide the financial and legal support necessary for citizens to create a new special district government.

Blair (1986) adds several more explanations. He refers to a "psychological attraction" in which the special district matches a tax or fee with a service in a well-defined area in a parsimonious manner that resonates well with the citizens' sense of correct behavior. Special districts are often associated with a desire to professionalize the management of the service and appeal to a citizen's sense that the service should be delivered in an efficient and businesslike manner. Also, special districts can sometimes be used as a tool to avoid annexation to a larger city.

The picture painted in this analysis is one in which the special district operates as an independent unit of government. There is another category of special district that operates as a wholly owned subsidiary of the parent government. There are two circumstances in which a government would want to create another corporation (special district) to finance or operate a service. The first occurs when a government needs a financing mechanism for a service that keeps the capital cost separate from the debt of the general government. Often referred to as a financing authority, the government creates the special district to serve as its financing arm. As an example, the City of Pittsburgh created the Pittsburgh Water and Sewer Authority to issue debt to finance capital improvements to the water storage and distribution system. In municipal finance, two broad types of debt can be issued to fund such infrastructure improvements: (1) so-called full faith and credit debt, in which the bonds are backed by the underlying value of all the real estate in the governmental jurisdiction, and (2) revenue bonds, for which the revenue stream comes from the ratepayers. Revenue bonds are generally more speculative than the full faith and credit type and were selected as the debt instrument for the Pittsburgh improvements. Creating a separate district removes the debt financing from the city's books.

The second circumstance occurs when it is desirable to have the operating expenses removed from the direct operation of the city. In the case of the Pittsburgh Water and Sewer Authority, the need for rate increases to cover the capital and operating costs was, politically, difficult as long as those increases had to be approved by city council. The financing authority was subsequently converted into an operating authority. This meant that a separate board, insulating both the city council and the mayor from direct political fallout, now would make decisions about rate increases. The authority, at an operational level, continued to be treated as a department of city government. Indeed, departmental meetings of the city include department heads and executive directors of several authorities.

Such a relationship is possible through the selection process of the authority. In the case of the Pittsburgh Water and Sewer Authority, the board was appointed by the mayor and included several department heads of city government. Although board members have a fiduciary responsibility to the authority, significant leeway exists, such that the interests of the city are protected along with the interests of the authority.

As a general rule, the more a single government unilaterally controls selection of the board, the more likely that authority will act as a wholly owned subsidiary of the parent government. Conversely, decreased involvement of a single government in the selection process leads to an authority that acts as a separate and independent government. At the other end of the continuum, where governments have the least control, is when the governing board is directly elected by the voting public.

There are two other methods of board selection that should be noted. These methods generally are used when the district involves a number of municipalities directly or its coverage area encompasses a number of municipalities. Ex officio members, who are on the board by virtue of their current positions, may constitute board membership. For instance, public works directors of participating municipalities may serve as the board for a special district that serves those municipalities. A second method is for each participating municipality to elect a member to the board. For instance, each participating municipality may elect one of its council members to serve as a board member on the special district.

A cautionary note on the wholly owned subsidiary should be mentioned. Special districts are corporations vested with powers derived from that incorporation, which obligates a board member to protect the interests of that corporation. As a result, the wholly owned subsidiary may, over time, drift away from the parent government.

Any overall assessment of special districts in the United States should include the issue of whether such institutions create a "democracy gap." Clearly, in the case of the wholly owned subsidiary, the expectation is that the special district would continue to operate as though it were simply a department of the city. Democratic principles of citizen involvement in government are not the major objective of such a formation. Instances in which special districts are constituted by ex-officio members or members elected from the existing local governments are only marginally better. The special districts may be responsive to other democratically created institutions, but they do not significantly enhance citizen engagement. Accountability of board members is only partially related to service on that particular board.

Many elected boards face the serious problem of finding a sufficient number of candidates to create competition for board membership. Voter turnout tends to be significantly low and voter turnout of less than 5 percent is not unusual

(Burns 1994). Given overlapping jurisdictions, multiplicity of districts, and lack of clarity of where boundaries exist, voters are often confused and frustrated. It is often difficult for them to understand the issues and even whether or where they should be voting.

Balanced against the issues surrounding the democracy gap of special districts are the utilitarian values that are served by the creation of special districts. Bollens (1957, 15) suggests they are a "mixed blessing." On one hand, they are a practical response to delivering specialized services to a relevant community. On the other hand, they do not necessarily enhance general accountability to citizens.

School Districts

Interestingly, the highest expense category of local governments is education, yet the discussion of school districts constitutes a relatively small part of most textbooks on the subject of local government. Further, most school districts are independent local governments. Of 15,834 school districts, 14,422, or 91 percent, exist with an elected board and taxing powers. Of the dependent school districts, the majority are departments within a municipal government. These school departments are concentrated in the New England states of Connecticut, Maine, Massachusetts, and Rhode Island.

The reasons for this light treatment are not obvious, but several can be offered. First, the management form and structure of independent school districts is comparatively uniform across the United States. That form consists of a generally small (5 to 11 members) elected board that serves the legislative function and a school superintendent who serves the executive function. While school superintendents are elected in a few parts of the country, in general they are selected on the basis of professional training and background in school management. A loose comparison would be to view the organization of school districts as if all municipal governments had adopted the manager plan as their organizational design.

Second, although education policy and management is a highly complex field, the issues in school policy are not as diverse as with municipal or county governments. They tend to be focused on the internal management of the schools. Avenues for cooperation are limited.

On occasion the needs of municipal governments and school districts overlap. As funding from the states has become less secure and consistent this form of partnership has become more frequent. One such example is the partnership between the City of Akron (Ohio) and the Akron Public Schools (APS). It first should be noted that the school district is a prototypical special district. While its service boundaries are coterminous with that of the city, they are distinct governments, with separate taxing authority. The primary revenue source for the APS is the property tax, with state funding a close second.

In 2001 the state government, in response to the perceived need to upgrade the physical infrastructure of the state's public schools, embarked on an ambitious partnership whereby the state would fund upwards of 65 percent of the cost of new construction of public schools. The program created by the state was an all-or-nothing arrangement whereby every school in a district would either be replaced or remodeled. The urban (and some rural) schools were the most likely to have the oldest infrastructure and, therefore, the most likely candidates for this capital program. Unfortunately, in addition to the all-or-nothing requirements the state also required that the school districts identify and guarantee a revenue stream to support their share of the capital project at the time of the application for funds. The APS was one of several urban districts caught between a rock and a hard place. It could not confirm, from identifiable revenues, that funding would be available for the life of the bonds. The state-mandated property tax laws made this impossible for cash strapped urban and rural district. The APS essentially had three options:

- Forego participation
- Find a funding partner
- Join another entity with the resources (i.e., become a city department)

When school districts coincide with city boundaries the temptation is for the city to take control. That is what happened in Cleveland. Rather than follow the Cleveland model the City of Akron and Summit County chose a quite different direction. The Summit county executive and the mayor of Akron announced that the city would back an unprecedented ballot initiative to increase the county sales tax to fund construction and remodeling in all 18 school districts in the county. Despite wide support in the business community and among elected officials across the county the ballot initiative passed only in the City of Akron, failing in every other community (*Akron Beacon Journal* 2003b). The proposal was dead, but the need for funding remained. The mayor of the City of Akron shifted gears and now sought an Akron-only solution (*Akron Beacon Journal* 2003b). This time the proposal was to increase the city income tax with the additional funds being transferred to the school district for the construction of new schools that would simultaneously serve as community centers. In May 2003 this proposal passed, permitting the school district to undertake the largest school construction and remodeling effort in its history (*Akron Beacon Journal* 2003a). At the time of its enactment this was a new idea, but a decade later the idea of using school facilities for other public uses is more common. Certainly the scale of the project, including every public school building in the city, was unprecedented. This model, which used city revenue to fund a school building program while the school district remained independent, is still unique.

Special Districts as Technical Silos

As noted, most special districts operate at the subregional level and provide limited services. Following upon the distinctions drawn earlier, it can be argued that there are four forms of special districts/technical silos. The first distinction is between subregional and regional districts. An example of a subregional district would be a water and sewer district that may include only the unincorporated parts of a county, or maybe only a single municipality. A regional district would be a large, likely multicounty district such as the Metropolitan District Commission (MDC) in Massachusetts, which was created nearly a century ago to address the water needs of greater Boston and stretches across an area almost equal to one-third of the state.

The second distinction is between the governance models used. At one end of the spectrum are districts that are essentially a subunit of the government that authorized it. For example, the above-referenced MDC is technically a state agency and was formed by a special state law. The jurisdiction and responsibilities of the MDC are established by that law. As such the MDC is geographically within eastern Massachusetts but is overlaid on top of the various local governments with which it shares "space." Their respective authorities are distinct from each other.

At the other end of the spectrum are districts that are creatures of the local governments within which those districts operate. Although technically an RGO (see Chapter 10), rather than strictly a special district, the Southwest Pennsylvania Commission is a good example because it existence is the result of an agreement among the constituent local governments. The commission is a partner with the governments that created it.

There are common relationships that shape the operations of special districts. Three dimensions dictate the operations:

1. Size
   - Small geographically
   - Large geographically

2. Basis of Authority
   - Distinct authority and constituency (overlay)
   - Partnership with shared constituency

3. Internal Control
   - Staff dominated
   - Board dominated

While there are many examples of all these forms, certain types of special districts are more likely to fall into certain cells. For example, special districts limited to a small geographic area generally operate apart from other governments, whereas large special districts may be of either model. Depending upon the state laws that created them, regional transportation districts may operate based on either the partnership or the overlay model. But regional planning agencies typically use the partnership model.

The models differ also in the decision-making processes and methods used to implement their respective missions. Simplistically, the staff-dominated models are more likely to have a small board, but the locus of technical expertise is within the staff. The model mimics to some extent the council-manager model. In the board-dominated model policies related to the nature of the partnership are more important. The board is likely to be large and have persons who represent constituencies (elected officials representing their respective governments are one version). This model has many of the characteristics of a state legislature with the staff subordinate to the direction of the delegates.

Implications of Special District Models for Governance

The most common special district model is the small, geographically distinct overlay model. The overlay model generally is controlled by a commission type of decision-making arrangement; a small board or commission with legislative responsibility. This governing board may be either elected or appointed. While any generalization is perilous, it is likely that large model special districts will have an appointed board and small districts will have elected boards, but in both cases the board is small in number of members. Just as with the broader commission model of government, the board may define policy, but policy choices and operational practices are likely in the hands of the staff, who are hired based upon their technical competence.

In board-dominated arrangements, the interactions among the district constituencies are of critical importance. The assumption is that the local governments are the stakeholders. Classic models of legislative decision making prevail; the board may have to rely on staff input, but that staff input comes from a wide range of sources. The "staff" is likely to come from the same governments that the board members represent. Analysis is conducted to support the policy preferences of the board representative.

There is a broader issue of governance in the use of special districts. With the possible exception of school board elections, the election of the governing board is at the periphery of the election cycle. These are inevitably nonpartisan elections and, therefore, not linked to the internal contest of primaries, nor do they seem to capture the imagination that local government elections occasionally engender. Political scientists often note the phenomena of the decline in turnout for "down ballot" offices. Special district board elections are exactly the type of elections that these analysts have in mind when they describe the lower number of votes cast at the end of ballot than for the more contentious and well-reported races for national and state offices. Sadly, special districts are likely to be skipped because the public has no idea who the nominees are and may have, at best, a vague idea what the board does.

Having missed the election, the public is even less likely to attend the public meetings of these special district boards. Only local insiders have any sense of the potential importance of the decisions of these boards. Those decisions are not so much done in the dark as they are in silence. While the parties that benefit from the technical capability of the district may attend the meetings, giving them an opportunity to provide "public" comment prior to decisions, the broader public does not attend, leaving them without a voice in decisions. The excuse for this lack of participation is often the technical nature of many of these decisions. After all, what do most of us know about the efficacy of one type of pump versus another to move water through irrigation ditches, the appropriate diameter of a waste water pipe, or the proper level of bacteria allowable in "treated" sewage before it is reused? On the other hand, these are organizations with the authority to assess, tax, and charge fees to fund those decisions.

Too Many?

One of the dilemmas for special districts is their proliferation. Whether it is in response to local tax limitations, as is the case in Florida, or specific needs for a product or service, as in the irrigation districts throughout the Great Plains and Southwest, the need for the service provided by such entities is not in doubt. The main issue is whether or not it is necessary to create a new special district for each new problem. Even with the school district consolidation efforts of the 1960s and 1970s, essentially all the growth in "governments" for some 40 years has been in the increase in special districts (see Table 4.1 in Chapter 4).

As the name itself implies, special districts are created to serve rather narrow and specialized purposes. With the exception of public school facilities, the infrastructure and support facilities rarely can be made part of another facility, or repurposed. The very uniqueness of each service provided makes the multiplication of such districts more likely. Even where a region might be home to several similar districts (sanitation, water, and sewer districts come to mind), there are geographic and political barriers to consolidation of such districts into single larger districts, but this does not address the more common problem of the proliferation of distinct special districts. Having addressed the problem in a piecemeal fashion to begin with, it is harder to put the genie back in the bottle and create mega regional service departments to replace the special districts. Service sharing across a region is the only likely alternative.

The Management of Technical Services

One of the presumptions of organization theory is that organizational culture and folk wisdom about how an organization *should* work is driven by the background and experiences of those in the organizations (Morgan 2006; Weick 2001). Those who are comfortable with the outlook and behavior expectations that represent the dominant organizational culture will be attracted to this type of organization. Those of a technical and scientific orientation will find that organizations exhibiting the characteristics of support for science (technically driven decision-making and research-based analysis) are attractive places for a career. On the other hand organizations that are more fluid in their rules and apply a variety of methods in decision making will be less attractive places to work.

The problem in government is that while many start their careers in the former organizations, as they progress they find themselves working at the "margin" of the organization in interorganizational and intergovernmental settings (Cox, Buck, and Morgan 2011). In the latter setting political, budgetary, and transorganizational analysis replaces narrow technical analysis. The transition from "staff" to "manager" is never easy, but in this environment knowledge and understanding of politics and the managerial ability to lead and implement programs trump technical knowledge and skills (Cox and Pyakuryal 2013).

Such managers are likely to reject or object to decisions that are no longer based upon technical competence. Their very identity as a professional is based upon a narrow technical expertise that seemingly is rejected in this intergovernmental setting (Cox, Buck, and Morgan 2011). Calls for regional cooperation that may require more than a link to like-minded technical professionals is going to be problematic. In such circumstances managers who are trained to deliver specific services will have trouble seeing value in a work setting in which multiple programs are merged. The idea of regional government potentially is a threat to their understanding of professional competence.

Concluding Thoughts and Things to Ponder

At the outset of this chapter it was noted that the one thing that regional special districts and counties shared was land—often land that transcended municipal boundaries. The logical question is whether or not this is a sufficient basis for making either of these types of local government a key actor in regional and metropolitan governance. Both types of governments have been active participants in shared services efforts; counties primarily at the department level and special districts at the district level. However, the shared service efforts are necessary for quite different reasons.

Zeemering and Delabbio (2013) suggested that budget considerations are critical, but that technical innovation, complementary strengths, transferring knowledge and skills, and service quality may also be important. City-county consolidation and the Virginia experiments with independent cities and urban counties were driven primarily by budgetary and only secondarily by service delivery reasons. On the other hand many county department-to-department and district-to-district shared service efforts have more to do with service delivery and complementarity of strengths.

The interests of those in the technical silos remain narrowly focused on knowledge transfer and service quality. Only where these benefits can be demonstrated will a special district look for partners to share services. These efforts enhance what the special districts already do; that it is a regional approach is relatively unimportant.

Things to Ponder

1. Nearly three decades ago David Walker suggested that city-county consolidation is the most difficult of all the forms of metropolitan collaboration. What are the barriers to consolidation?
2. We have labeled special districts as "technical silos." Special districts typically stretch across multiple jurisdictions, yet the technical nature of the functions of these districts does not make them good partners in metropolitan cooperation. Why?
3. What are the sociocultural and political explanations for opposition to annexation?
4. Why have county governments seemed to lag behind in metropolitan initiatives?
5. Why did the creation of independent cities become so popular in Virginia, but the concept of the urban county languish?
6. Regional cooperation as chronicled by the National Association of Counties has been more frequent in smaller counties. What are some of the sociopolitical factors that might explain this?

10

Representing the New Kid on the Block

Regional Governing Organizations

Virtually all metropolitan regions have one or more formal organizations that have been created to address common problems and issues facing the region. The question is no longer whether such organizations exist, but the degree to which they play a meaningful role in their respective regions. We associate the term "proto" with something that is in its early or first version and the term "quasi" with something that resembles something else. Whether an organization will turn out to be the prototype for a fully functioning regional governing institution or forever be something that resembles such an institution, but without the ability to play a meaningful role in regional affairs remains to be seen. With that caveat, we use the term regional governing organization (RGO) to describe these institutions.

RGOs go by a number of different names. They include, among others, council of governments (COG), regional planning commission (RPC), regional council (RC), and associations of governments (AOG). Another institution often categorized as an RGO is the Metropolitan Planning Organization (MPO). An MPO can be an RGO or it can be a designation given to a COG, RPC, RC, or AOG. The confusion of multiple names and lack of clarity in roles is understandable in that the idea for such an organization is in its infancy. We are in the sorting out phase, trying to attach a conceptual framework to an emerging practice.

Historical Development of the RGO

The genesis of RGOs stems from both the urbanization and suburbanization of the United States and can be traced to the early years of the twentieth century. As more governments came into operation and more citizens moved into those governments, public problems grew beyond the boundaries of any one government. Given the structure of federalism in the United States, no one and everyone was responsible for developing cross-boundary systems and protocols to address issues that were no longer capturable or solvable within a single jurisdiction.

It was difficult for the federal government to take on such a role in that local governments, even in a metropolitan area, are creatures of the states. As such, the federal government was severely limited in its ability and willingness to intervene. States, often dominated by rural and suburban interests, lacked the capacity and willingness to create new ways to work together. Center cities were more than likely to take a go-it-alone approach and isolate themselves from the rest of the region. Suburbs, often created to insulate themselves from the issues of the center city, might talk to their neighboring suburbs but not the city.

In that milieu, two relatively distinct paths to today's RGOs emerged. Both were federally initiated. The first originated out of the need to coordinate transportation both within and between metropolitan areas. The interstate highway system, primarily a post–World War II development, responded to the increasing mobility offered by the automobile and, indeed, connected metropolitan areas together. This federal initiative gave legitimacy to the role of the federal government in the domain of transportation. As the federal government assumed the role of connecting metropolitan areas, it was a logical next step to consider connecting the parts of a metropolitan region. In addition, the federal government had the financial resources to address the significant infrastructure needs and, unlike many of the states, an interest in addressing such needs.

Although a number of entry points to demonstrate this federal involvement could be selected, the Federal-Aid Highway Act of 1962 best serves to demonstrate the emergence of the federal government's role. The act required that transportation projects in urbanized areas with populations of 50,000 or more be based on a continuing, comprehensive, urban transportation planning process undertaken cooperatively by the states and local governments. This requirement institutionalized nascent organizations of governments or forced local governments and their respective states to create such an organization.

The 1964 Urban Mass Transportation Act extended the federal role into mass transit. Two important features of the act include the availability of federal aid to develop mass transit systems and financial incentives for the preparation of metropolitan transportation plans. As a result, by the mid-1960s, an effort was under way within the arena of transportation (highways and mass transit) to develop, fund, and build infrastructure that required cross-boundary discussions that were primarily planning activities and heavily subsidized by the federal government.

In 1973 states were allowed to withdraw portions of the funding designated for the interstate highway system and use the freed-up allocation to fund public transit and highway projects within metropolitan areas. The federal legislation specified that such planning and coordinating would be undertaken by local elected officials. The idea that the federal government could dictate and delegate responsibility to local governments without approval and consent of the states was challenged primarily as a states' rights issue in the courts. The courts upheld the right of the federal government to empower such institutions. In so doing, the courts acknowledged that a wide variety of local institutions, including COGs, RPCs, AOGs, RCs, counties, and cities, could be authorized to receive funds from the federal government. The courts, as did the legislation, gave power to metropolitan regions only when that power was exercised by local elected officials.

A second path was a more general response to the growing complexity of U.S. metropolitan areas. The Housing and Urban Development Act of 1965 amended the urban planning assistance program established under the Housing Act of 1954 (Section 701) by authorizing grants for the purposes of comprehensive planning to be made to "organizations composed of public officials whom he (the Secretary of HUD) finds to be representative of the political jurisdictions within a metropolitan or urban region." The federal government, treading carefully on the issue of states' rights, used the power of funding to encourage joint planning activities. The federal interest was to plan for the broad set of public needs of urban areas, not just transportation. Issues of housing, social equity, and quality of life were equally important. The 1966 Demonstration Cities and Metropolitan Development Act, as amended in 1968, created what was known at the time as the A-95 review process. This process required that all applicants for federal funding for a wide variety of economic development and infrastructure projects submit their plans for review by "an area-wide planning agency." As a result, the emerging regional institutions were given voice, albeit advisory, in the growth of their respective regions.

Both paths shared the belief that the appropriate local institution was one made up of the local governments in the region and those governments' elected officials. That said, these two paths to today's RGOs has created two very different visions of what constitutes the purpose of the RGO (see Figure 10.1). The first is transportation centric; that is, a metropolitan region is tied together by its transportation network. In this regard, it is important to coordinate other aspects such as housing, economic development, and water and sewer infrastructure to maximize the effectiveness and efficiency of the transportation system. The second path is governance centric. In this regard, a region is a complex geopolitical entity that needs governmental coordination of a number of key components including transportation, housing, economic development, regional assets, and water and sewer infrastructure.

During the 1970s and 1980s, the distinction was not all that material. RGOs

Figure 10.1 **Two Approaches to the Organizing of Regional Governance Organizations**

Transportation Centric RGO

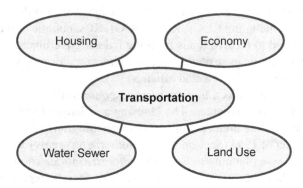

Governance Centric RGO

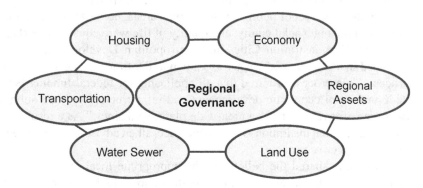

tended to develop a transportation focus as clear responsibilities, authority to plan, and relatively reliable funding steered many in that direction. Development of a governance focus was slower as funding opportunities were limited in part because a clear consensus on how and where to act did not exist. Regardless of focus, RGOs were generally limited to an advisory role. Federal and state transportation departments often tolerated the presence of a regional entity. Local and state governments saw a wall 10 feet thick and 100 feet high that divided the worlds of the city and the suburb. The idea that an RGO could effectively integrate those two worlds had yet to catch on in all but a handful of regions.

ISTEA: Creator of the Modern RGO

The distinction between transportation centric and governance centric became material with the passage of Intermodal Surface Transportation Efficiency Act of 1991 (ISTEA). This legislation consolidated previously disparate federal transportation policy (highways, airports, waterways, mass transit, railroads, and bridges) into a relationship between the federal government and a single organization within each of the metropolitan regions in the United States. Such a local organization receives the federal designation of being the Metropolitan Planning Organization for that region. Each metropolitan region is responsible for identifying the local organization that will serve as their MPO. The game changer with ISTEA rests in how federal funds are to be allocated within that metropolitan region. The MPO was vested with the power to actually decide, not just recommend, which projects were undertaken and when. The effect of such a decision is to invest in an MPO with new and very real powers, albeit transportation focused. These powers strengthened the role of the MPO within the region and between the region and the state and, in particular, its Department of Transportation (DOT). In many regions, it was the states' DOT that had often exercised unilateral, some would say dictatorial, decision making over transportation funding. In many states, tension still exists between the state and MPOs.

To be an MPO has several meanings. Most important, it is a designation as the institution of elected local officials under federal transportation policy with important rights, responsibilities, and duties to act for and on behalf of the region. Secondarily, it could also be the name of the organization. For instance, Iowa has the Des Moines Metropolitan Planning Council. MPOs are not necessarily synonymous with RGOs and not all RGOs are MPOs. Only 18 percent of MPOs are freestanding organizations (Government Accountability Office [GAO] 2009). Indeed, the same GAO study reported that at least 71 percent of all MPOs are housed within an existing agency such as an RGO or a local government (city or county).

One way to work through this confusion of titles and designations is to think of the responsibilities of the RGO in terms of a transportation component and a component of many other activities regional in scope. Different mixes of these two components by particular organizations create three general types of RGOs. The first are regional organizations that are predominantly focused on transportation. As such, they would be designated as MPOs. A second type would be regional organizations that are exclusively governance in that they have not been designated as the MPO but engage in a number of issues affecting the region. They would meet the requirement of being run by local elected officials. The third type would be regional organizations that undertake both transportation (the MPO function) and governance responsibilities.

This distinction between transportation and governance is dramatized by virtue of the existence of two separate RGO groups. More than 450 regional organizations belong to the National Association of Regional Councils (NARC), whose members include "multi-purpose, multi-jurisdictional, public organizations *created by local governments* to bring together participants at multiple levels of government to foster regional cooperation, planning, and service delivery" (emphasis added). Its mission statement is:

> The National Association of Regional Councils (NARC) serves as the national voice for regionalism by advocating for regional cooperation as the most effective way to address a variety of community planning and development opportunities and issues.

NARC's roots in local government are significant. It was created in 1965 by the National League of Cities and the National Association of Counties as a service to those local governments. In 1967 it became a separate organization of the newly forming RGOs.

The importance of transportation planning, particularly post-ISTEA, led to the formation in 1994 of the Association of Metropolitan Planning Organizations (AMPO). Unlike NARC's agenda, AMPO's mission is quote narrow:

> AMPO is the transportation advocate for metropolitan regions and is committed to enhancing MPOs' abilities to improve metropolitan transportation systems.

AMPO's roots are in transportation and the technocratic and procedural rules necessary to comply with federal and state requirements to engage in transportation planning.

General Profile and a Few Examples of RGOs

Generally, RGOs are not very large organizations, nor do they serve particularly large populations. In a GAO survey of MPOs, 52 percent served regions of less than 200,000 population; 36 percent served populations between 200,000 and 1 million; and only 11 percent served populations of over 1 million (GAO 2009). That said, those 11 percent of RGOs serve 49 percent of the total U.S. population. Perhaps more telling is the employment size of RGOs. The same GAO report indicated that MPOs in regions under 200,000 population employed, on average about 3 individuals while MPOs in regions over 1,000,000 population averaged about 50 employees.

These organizations are primarily overseen by local government officials. Again, using data on MPOs as a surrogate for RGOs, 94 percent had seats for elected municipal officials and 81 percent had seats for county commissioners (Bond and Kramer 2009). The same analysis showed that a typical governing board of 17 representatives consisted of 7 municipal officials, 3 county commissioners, 1 countywide elected official, 1 State Department of Transportation representative, 2 open seats, 1 public transit representative, and 2 seats dedicated to a host of other governmental institutions.

Bryan and Wolf (2010) summarized the primary functions of most RGOs as providing services in two broad categories. The first category of activities can be found virtually in every RGO to one degree or another. These activities reflect the traditional "meet and discuss" role and include endeavors such as:

- manage federal and state planning and review requirements,
- facilitate identification of regional issues,
- operate as technical data source and center,
- provide technical and planning consulting services, and
- provide legislative monitoring and lobbying.

The second category is not nearly as common but is growing in popularity. A number of RGOs are taking on operational responsibilities for delivering a broad array of public goods. Transit systems, water and sewer infrastructure, and parks are a few of the responsibilities in this category.

What follows is a more detailed look at four of the larger RGOs. Most observers point to the Metropolitan Council in Minneapolis and Metro in Portland, Oregon, as exemplars of the modern RGO and its potential to serve in a regional governance capacity. Both these RGOs have an active but indirect relationship with the local governments in the region. In contrast the Mid-America Regional Council (MARC) in Kansas City and the Southwestern Pennsylvania Commission (SPC) in Pittsburgh are RGOs composed of the region's local governments and, as such, have an active and direct relationship.[1]

The Metropolitan Council: Minneapolis and St. Paul, Minnesota

The Metropolitan Council in the Twin Cities is the largest and most active RGO in the United States. Its 2012 budget was $780.3 million and it has a staff of 3,700. It is the regional provider of number of public goods, most significantly public transit and waste water operation and management.

As a region with not one, but two, center cities, cross-boundary cooperation was clearly more self-evident and necessary. Historically, by the mid-1960s, the two cities—Minneapolis and St. Paul—had worked together to secure major league baseball, football, and hockey teams. Their cooperation became more significant upon the completion of the interstate freeway between them. Slowly, the two cities saw regionwide opportunities and challenges that required greater regional cooperation between them and a growing number of local governments within the region. In 1967, the Minnesota legislature voted to create a regional planning and coordinating body, the metropolitan council, for the two-city seven-county area. Since then, the metropolitan council has grown to become the institution that develops, advances, and finances regional goals and infrastructure investments.

From a governance perspective, the region is divided into 16 geographic districts and each district is represented by a council member appointed by the governor of Minnesota. A seventeenth member is also appointed by the governor to serve as chair. The governor's appointments are subject to confirmation by the state senate. The role of the state in selection of the council creates a distance between the local governments and the council that makes local governments indirect participants in the activities of the council. That said, most of the council members have local government experience. It is important to note that having local government experience is not the same as representing the interests of local government in the process of regional decision making.

Metro: Portland, Oregon

Metro in Portland, Oregon, is the second largest RGO in the country and the only RGO in which voters directly elect representatives. Metro's 2012–2013 budget was $520 million. It has a workforce of more than 1,600 employees, including specialists such as park rangers, economists, teachers, scientists, zookeepers, designers, planners, and cartographers. Fifteen major offices/centers serve the Metro.

The history of Metro goes back to 1957 when Portland and the three urbanized counties around Portland organized the old Metropolitan Planning Commission from which some of Metro's responsibilities have been passed down. The modern Metro is an expanded version of the original Metropolitan Service District that area voters approved in 1970. In 1969 and 1970, an essential set of new government institutions were formed to meet regional needs. They include County Metropolitan Transportation District (1969), Portland Metropolitan Area Local Government Boundary Commission (1969), and the Metropolitan Service District (1970).

Voters approved the present-day Metro in 1978, and the agency went into operation in 1979. A major responsibility is regional land-use planning. Metro's initiatives include the 2040 Growth Concept (1994), The Future Vision Plan (1995), the Regional Framework Plan (1997), and the Regional Transportation Plan (2000). Metro also plays a significant role in operating waste management and regional facilities, managing parks and open spaces, and planning and coordinating for natural disasters.

The Metro council consists of a president who is elected by voters throughout the region and six district councilors who are elected every four years in nonpartisan elections. Elections are held concurrently with the Oregon statewide primary in May of even-numbered years. Metro councilors may not be elected to more than three consecutive full terms and no more than two consecutive full terms for the Metro Council president. Since Metro councilors are elected directly, they tend to represent a broader range of community interests than just those of local governments. As such, the connection between local governments and Metro, like the Met Council in the Twin Cities, is, at best, indirect.

MARC: Kansas City

Kansas City's MARC is large by RGO standards with a 2012 budget of $65 million and a staff of 157. It was formed by combining the Metropolitan Planning Commission and the Mid-America Council of Governments in 1972. Since its establishment, MARC has adopted the first long-range transportation plan for the region (1975), which became known as the Transportation 2020 Plan in 1995 and formed various committees: the City/County Administrators Committee (1979), Solid Water Committee (1983), Stormwater Management Committee (1984), Metropolitan Council on Child Care (1989), Kansas and Missouri Metropolitan Culture District Commission (1997), and Kansas City Regional Purchasing Cooperative (2002).

MARC's main functions are coordinating policies that lead to progress in the region, developing regional plans for transportation, environment, and emergency responses, allocating resources for regional systems, providing cooperative services between local governments, as well as advocating for regional issues at the state and federal levels. It also promotes consensus and commitment to regional solutions by engaging the public in decision making, conducting research, and providing technical support to local leaders.

MARC currently serves nine counties and 119 cities. The MARC board of directors consists of 33 locally elected leaders from the nine member counties and the six largest cities in the region.

The Southwestern Pennsylvania Commission

The Southwestern Pennsylvania Commission (SPC) serves as the RGO for the Pittsburgh metropolitan region and its 2.3 million inhabitants. It represents a more typical RGO in a larger metro area with a budget of slightly less than $10 million and a staff of around 60. Its mission statement acknowledges that it is "a forum for collaboration and planning" (traditional planning roles); it also states that the SPC is a place "of public decision-making" (new governance role). Later the statement reads, "The Commission has the authority and responsibility to make decisions affecting the 10-county region" (Southwestern Pennsylvania Commission 2013).

SPC was formed in 1962 as the Southwestern Pennsylvania Regional Planning Commission (SPRPC), an organization serving as a regional advisory committee for six counties: Allegheny, Armstrong, Beaver, Butler, Washington, and Westmoreland. In 1992, the Southwestern Pennsylvania Regional Development Council (SPRDC) was formed as a nine-county local development district to provide services such as financial, technical, and information assistance to smaller organizations and municipalities. It was administratively housed in and operated by SPRPC. In 1998, a merger of the SPRPC and SPRDC was approved by the member counties. The merger of the two organizations was completed in 1999, and the new organization became SPC.

SPC has expanded beyond its original borders and added new members. In 1999, Indiana and Greene counties officially joined the transportation planning area by becoming full members of SPC. Fayette County followed in 2002. There are currently 11 members in the organization: 10 county governments and the City of Pittsburgh. Each member appoints five commissioners, creating a board of 55 commissioners that is supplemented by a number of state and federal officials.

What is particularly interesting is the connection between the commission and the constituent governments. Pennsylvania is typical of states that have the county commissioner form of government. In that form, (usually) three elected commissioners serve as the legislative and executive branches of government. All counties except Allegheny have that form of government. Of the 27 county commissioners in nine counties, 26 are SPC commissioners who represent nearly 50 percent of the voting representation on the commission. For Allegheny County, which operates with a mayor (county executive)-council form of government, the county executive leads the delegation that usually includes at least one county council member. The delegation from the City of Pittsburgh is led by the city's mayor and includes a representative from the city council.

Two important changes are under way. Over the years, the dialogue among these elected officials has shifted from the purely parochial protection of individual governments' self-interests to a more enlightened discussion about the needs of the region. Such enhanced regional dialogue has not yet resulted in a transformation of the commission into an RGO that can impose its will on constituent governments, but the potential exists.

A 2010 development dramatizes this transformation. Historically, the Pennsylvania Department of Transportation (PENNDOT) had the power to make sure the Transportation Improvement Plan (TIP) reflected its priorities; indeed, it has never been clear whether the final TIP was a state or a regional document. That said, it is the document that identifies the short- and long-term transportation projects of the region, and SPC has the responsibility to produce it. After the long and often arduous public engagement process to arrive at a TIP, PENNDOT has been able to make last-minute changes to the document that have been docilely accepted by the SPC. But during the most recent approval process, PENNDOT's last-minute changes were met with stiff opposition from the SPC as a whole. At the core of the resistance to these changes was a maturing belief that it was the SPC, acting as a regional institution that was responsible for reflecting the needs and priorities of its citizens. The message was very clear to the state: PENNDOT is an important institution in helping to shape the TIP, but one that should be participating like any other institution.

A second factor is SPC's growth in stature within the civic and private sectors. It is now viewed as the institution that is representative of the major local government in the region. As the City of Pittsburgh has gone from containing 25 percent of the region's population to 12 percent, its influence within the region has declined. The City of Pittsburgh is now the third largest local government in the region, behind Allegheny County and Westmoreland County. The largest local government, Allegheny County, exercises its cross-boundary relations through SPC because that institution is governed primarily by the region's county governments. The result has been for the region's other sectors to see SPC as a way to access the local governmental arena.

Issues Confronting RGOs

Issue 1: Representativeness

RGOs have grown out of informal and voluntary institutions with few formal voting protocols. As they were constituted by local governments operating in a "meet and discuss" environment, unanimity of action was more likely to be obtained through informal consensus rather than formal voting. Governments participated voluntarily and could withdraw support for action they deemed undesirable. As such, they generally adopted a one-government, one-vote model, much like the U.S. Senate, wherein each state has the same number of votes. As a result, most RGOs were skewed toward rural, suburban interests over the interests of the urban cores. For instance, the voting distribution for the SPC in 1995 gave the core county 24 percent of the vote, even though it contained 58 percent of the population and 64 percent of the market valuation of the region. Conversely, the smallest county had 3 percent of the population and 12 percent of the voting power on the commission.

When the stakes were relatively low, such a distribution was probably tolerable. However, when an organization skewed heavily to its rural hinterlands becomes invested with allocating billions of dollars of development funds, its decisions can reflect its rural bias and an unwillingness of the organization, on a voluntary basis, to redistribute power.

The result has been significant challenges to RGOs, particularly related to developing democratic decision-making rules (Benjamin, Kincaid, and McDowell 1994; Miller and DeLoughry 1996; Orfield 1997; Lewis 1998). Sanchez (2006) demonstrated that urban areas are severely underserved in favor of suburban jurisdictions. Nelson and colleagues (2004) found that the overall commitment to regional transit declined by 1 to 7 percent for each suburban vote added to the board. Orfield and Luce (2009) called for eight major reforms to MPOs with the first and most important recommendation to make "recertification of MPOs conditional on proportional representation (based on population) of central cities, fully developed suburbs, and developing suburbs on MPO boards." Fulton and colleagues (2001) demonstrate how RGOs that are weighted to overrepresent rural/suburban interests lead to greater degrees of sprawl within those regions.

Although slowly and haltingly, the democracy gap resulting from the lack of equal representation is being addressed in some metropolitan regions. The most frequently used innovation in decision-making rules is the development of weighted voting structures that reflect the distribution of population and market value within a metropolitan area. Typically, MPOs use weighted voting when requested by some percentage of the jurisdictions. In a survey of 17 of the largest MPOs, more than half had developed voting structures that reflected the population distribution of the region (Miller and DeLoughry 1996). The mere existence of provisions allowing for weighted voting appears to encourage compromise without actually having to employ the voting technique.

The Southeastern Michigan Council of Governments (SMCoG) can vote twice on the same measure, once on the basis of jurisdiction and then again on a population-weighted vote. Another technique is proportional representation where the number of representatives from each jurisdiction is based on the population of that jurisdiction. The Mid-America Regional Council in Kansas City, Missouri, and the Northeastern Illinois Planning Commission in Chicago are representative of this technique. A third technique is representation on the basis of equally sized population districts that are drawn irrespective of political jurisdictions. Such an approach exists in very few locations, most notably in Portland Metro.

Issue 2: An Assembly of Local Governments or Representatives of the Parts of the Region

Related to the first issue is a more fundamental question of how best to represent the interests of the citizens in a regional forum. One approach is to have those interests represented through the constituent local governments of the region. This is the predominant method employed by RGOs and is supported by federal transportation policy. A second approach operates on the assumption that the interests of the constituent local governments are not necessarily the interests of the citizens as a whole. As such, representatives to the RGO should be directly elected by the citizens, as is the case with Portland Metro.

Frustrated metropolitan reformers often see RGOs built on elected officials of local governments representing the interests of local government as "letting the fox loose in the chicken coop," as the old adage goes. Perhaps reform comes more slowly but RGOs are connected to the building blocks of the region (i.e., local governments) in this fashion. A directly elected regional government, disconnected from the local governments, creates two new problems. The first is a chasm between the RGO and local governments that will still need to be addressed and minimized. Local governments will not necessarily stop doing what they have been doing for the last couple of centuries. As a result, the second problem is the potential to simply create another layer of government that finds an ecological niche in an already highly fragmented system. The more fragmented the system, the easier it is for that system to fragment further in an effort to solve the problem of fragmentation.

Issue 3: The Battle Between Local and Regional Land-Use Authority

One of the defining responsibilities of local governments (cities and towns primarily) is the ability to determine land uses within their respective jurisdictions. This responsibility includes the legal authority to develop and implement community comprehensive plans and to legally enforce those plans through its police powers to protect the health and safety of its citizens. Such a responsibility is a double-edged sword. On one hand it enables local governments to translate community wants and expectations into action. It empowers local governments to have a significant role in the lives of its inhabitants and to allow its inhabitants to shape the purpose and nature of the community in which they reside. To that end, it is a right deeply ingrained in history and culture. It is also legislatively and judicially considered to be settled law.

The other edge of the sword, however, has created metropolitan regions wherein land-use decisions are made and executed at the local government level with no real history, tradition, or legal authority for the region to have a say in those local decisions. A plan for the metropolitan region cannot simply be the sum of the independent land-use decisions made by local governments. Such a system, where everyone is in charge, often means no one is in charge.

The emergence of the RGO can be seen as a slow, often halting, seldom comprehensive effort to develop a new relationship between local and regional land-use authority. The weight of history, law, and tradition is on the side of the local while the reality of modern America and need for coordination is on the side of the regional. If the balance was 95 percent local and 5 percent regional in 1960, it is probably 85/15 today. Getting closer to 50/50 will require a significantly expanded role of RGOs and the development of more effective means to create consistency between local and regional planning such that the desirability of locally engaged communities coexists with the advantages of coordinated regional authority.

There have been several efforts to assess the degree to which cooperation is occurring at the metropolitan regional level. Hitchings (1998) uses three criteria to classify metropolitan regions into four broad categories. The first criterion is whether an official regional plan exists. If the region has a plan, the second criterion is whether a regional organization has been given responsibility to oversee local government compliance with that plan. If the organization has oversight responsibility, the third criterion is whether that regional organization can require changes in local plans to be consistent with the overall regional plan.

When those three criteria are used to assess the current state of land-use responsibility of RGOs in America, RGOs fall into one of four categories that Hitchings labels as ad hoc, advisory, supervisory, and authoritative. Ad hoc regions are numerous and, in those regions, local governments work together on specific land use issues but do not have a written plan that coordinates physical development at the regional level. Advisory RGOs look much like ad hoc regions except that they *do* have a regional plan. However, there is generally inadequate means to implement that plan except the willingness of local governments to adhere to the plan on a voluntary basis.

All but a handful of RGOs fall into one of the two categories noted: supervisory and authoritative. Supervisory RGOs are delegated the responsibility of administering the regional plan. The actual implementation of the plan is still done at the local level, but the regional body oversees compliance and reports progress. Authoritative RGOs, of which Met Council in Minneapolis and Metro in Portland are the only members, have the statutory authority to develop the regional plan and then to require changes or force compliance with that plan on the part of local governments. Indeed, these two RGOs have been called "unique" (Stephens and Wikstrom 1999, p. 101). Part of this uniqueness lies in the distance between the regional organization and the constituent local governments. Rather than organizations of local governments, the Minnesota and Portland organizations are created externally and separate from their local governments.

A few states have been taking more aggressive actions to encourage planning and coordination among governments in metropolitan regions. Until recently, Pennsylvania municipalities could plan together, but in the end, each separate municipality had to "accommodate" all uses within their territorial boundaries. This meant that for the 130 municipalities in Allegheny County, each had to provide industrial, commercial, and housing areas within their individual communities. Recent state legislation allows municipalities to jointly plan, but utilize the entire area of the participating municipalities for the accommodation of all land uses. As a result, a number of communities can treat themselves as a planning district such that some communities may not have any industrial uses at all, while others take on that role for the broader territory.

Concluding Thoughts and Things to Ponder

Perhaps the title of this section should be "What do I want to be when I grow up?" Indeed, RGOs have been born and exist in virtually every metropolitan region in the United States. Their champions are necessity and the federal government, particularly in the guise of transportation policy. They generally are constituted by local governments in the regions and, in that capacity, exist as the one authoritative place where local governments can be convened to address issues and concerns facing the region as a whole. That said, it's not clear whether RGOs will become the platform for regional decision making in the public interest or, as many are now, the place where local governments protect their private interests in a regional setting. It is unsettling that the two most sophisticated RGOs are not constituted by local governments but by gubernatorial appointment in Minneapolis-St. Paul and direct election in Portland, Oregon. Neither of those forms is likely to be rapidly emulated or easily adopted in other regions. Perhaps the slow, deliberate approaches in Kansas City and Pittsburgh are more reflective of the likely trajectory of RGOs as they careen into their "teens."

As we have noted, many RGOs, particularly at the staff level, see themselves as the region's transportation planner. That perspective is certainly reinforced through federal policy, which defines MPOs as transportation centric. MPOs are rewarded by the federal government based on their efficiency and effectiveness in conducting transportation planning. To that degree, RGO bureaucracies respond by elevating transportation to the center of their priorities. The rules for being an MPO are very clear across all metropolitan regions. However, the rules for being an RGO are not very clear at all. The end result is an organization whose "comfort zone" is to stay within the orthodoxy of transportation centricity.

State governments have been slow to empower RGOs or to clarify their status within a regional decision-making framework. That is not an observation unique to RGOs, but applies to most regional instruments, such as tax sharing or land-use authority. States don't want the federal government to dictate relationships between local governments even though the federal government is in a position to do so.

Nothing described in this chapter suggests the need to "throw the baby away with the bathwater" quite yet. The RGOs are, at best, proto- or quasi-governance institutions. But given time, they can mature into institutions that coordinate the new metropolitan region.

Things to Ponder

1. How did ISTEA change the role of MPOs in regionalism?
2. Why was transportation centric the first naturally evolved form of RGO?
3. To what extent has the transportation-centric nature of MPOs inhibited them from playing a broader metropolitan governance role?
4. What are the strengths and weaknesses of RGOs versus individual local representation?
5. The two versions of representation have considerable consequences for effective metropolitan governance. What do you think is the most equitable way to define representativeness on the governing board of an RGO?

Note

1. We have included MARC as it appears to be more advanced in assuming operational responsibilities and SPC as more representative of the majority of RGOs in larger metropolitan areas. One of the author's role as commissioner in SPC provides a unique insider perspective to our understanding of the changing nature of RGOs.

11

State Government Versus Local Governments

Creative Tension or Inherent Conflict?

In Chapter 5 we examined the role of the states vis-à-vis local governments in a regional and intergovernmental context. Yet we also noted that Dillon's dicta had a long-ignored and misunderstood codicil. While he affirmed the capacity of the states and their legislatures to direct and control both the scope and substance of local government practices, he also suggested that he was not sure why legislatures would seek to intervene in this manner (see Chapter 2, p. 16 for the quote). Historically and legally the formulation made sense, as did the cautionary note that followed it.

It is more the dismissal of this cautionary note, rather than the fact of Dillon's Rule, that has shaped state-local interactions in the more than 140 years since that judgment. All too often the suggestion that the legislature *should* give local governments a primary role in their own governance has been ignored. Even when states have acted in response to local needs (especially fiscal needs) by creating broad grants of authority that required no further legislative enactment, the acts themselves have been somewhat ephemeral, being modified or even abolished when it suited the legislature. For most of our history, rural political interests that were antithetical to those of urban areas dominated legislatures. In this chapter, we discuss how *Reynolds v. Sims* changed that by introducing the one-person, one-vote concept to legislative districting. However, the positive impact on urban areas was short-lived as the suburbs began to outstrip the center city in population, shifting legislative control to the suburbs.

This chapter examines the intergovernmental dynamics of regional and metropolitan governance as seen through the dark lens of continued assertions of state control over local governments. To accomplish this task we will examine some of the same topics addressed in earlier chapters (especially 4, 5, and 10), including fiscal relations, interorganizational service agreements, legal frameworks for intergovernmental partnerships, annexation, city-county partnerships, and formal multijurisdictional purposive and governing structures. The frame for this new analysis is more analytic and less descriptive than the earlier chapters and, as suggested above, the emphasis will be on the negative aspects of the relationships.

Through the Glass Darkly: State-Local Fiscal Relationships

As was implied by the historical examination of intergovernmental fiscal relations in Chapter 3, the relationship between state and local governments was relatively stable for decades after what is thought of as the key change—Dillon's Rule. Certainly, until World War II it could be argued that there were essentially only two fiscally important levels of government: first local governments and then, after World War I, the federal government. Dillon's Rule may have affirmed the constitutional importance of the states in governance and intergovernmental relations, but few states had an impact on the policy agenda of the nation. The "laboratories of democracy" claim aside, even the innovations in governmental, economic, and social regulation and practice that earned a few states high marks was a markedly brief interlude between the laissez-faire approaches of the nineteenth century and the growing assertion of federal authority from the Depression to the present. In both fiscal affairs and in terms of public policy, the time from the end of the civil war until the late 1950s can be summed up by the simple assertion that the states were an afterthought at best and often irrelevant in the promotion of positive change. Three changes at the local level illustrate this. First is the development of a charter city/home rule movement in response to Dillon's Rule. Second are the mid-to-late nineteenth-century actions that significantly expanded the boundaries of large cities. Third is the city management movement. While Dillon's Rule requirements may have mandated some level of state legislative concurrence in these endeavors, they are noteworthy for being local movements with little regard for the states. While students of the Progressive Era are often taught about state and national initiatives, it is the bureau movement in the urban areas, civil service, the planned city, and the profession of city management that are the era's indelible results.

Despite the changes in labor laws and the regulatory environment that are the product of state efforts at the beginning of the twentieth century, the economic and social dislocation of the Depression resulted in the creation of federal-local partnerships to address unemployment, housing, and other problems. As noted in Chapter 5, the states were viewed as a hindrance, not a help.

Bolstered by districting systems that favored rural community interests, state governments would remain a "sideshow" until almost the last quarter of the twentieth century. The period spanning the 1960s and 1970s was one of the only times in our political history when a large number of state legislators and governments came together to affirm a central role in policy making for the states. These initiatives came on the heels of political changes that reflected the growing urbanization of most states, not merely the corridor states of the Northeast, Midwest, and Pacific Coast. The landmark *Reynolds v. Sims* (377 U.S. 533 1964) mandated that state legislative districts contain populations that are as near equal as practicable. Gone were legislatures with slanted districts that favored rural counties and communities. By the 1970s, legislatures began to reflect the predominantly urban character of the states. This confluence of court-mandated redistricting and an urban and progressive political agenda brought the states into the discussion about policy and governance. Educational reform, new and innovative programs for housing, and efforts to limit the negative impact of regressive taxes, such as the property tax, were aggressively pursued.

The 1960s and 1970s were a period noted for many cooperative endeavors between increasingly urban-oriented legislatures and the metropolitan areas of the states. There was a burst of activity in addressing educational, organizational, and social issues linked to cities and urban areas. States became much more heavily engaged in the funding of public education; again in an effort to control property taxes. Importantly, these efforts often generated funding formulae that were biased toward poor and/or urban communities. The concept of the "homestead exemption," whereby the assessment on housing was lowered or limits were placed on property tax payments, was introduced. While such exemptions were available across any state, the assumption was that housing values were higher in urban areas and, therefore, urban homeowners (especially the elderly and those with moderate incomes) would derive the greatest benefit from such programs.

There also was an effort to revive regional public mass transit. While the bulk of the funds to modernize and expand public transportation came from the federal government, state-authorized transit districts were created. Major expansions and renovation of systems in Chicago, New York, and Boston as well as new integrated subway/rail and bus systems for Miami, San Francisco, and Washington, DC, were opened in the 1970s. This period was also the first, albeit short-lived, "golden era" for regional and metropolitan government. According to information generated by Hall (2009), of the 24 successful city-county consolidation efforts between 1947 and 2000, half were approved in the decade from 1967 to 1977.

In 1965, Florida created the most broad-ranging local government tax reform effort of any state. The state mandated a homestead exemption of $25,000 per home. Given that the average price of a home in Florida at that time was $25,000, this law effectively exempted the majority of Florida homeowners from paying property taxes. The impact of this change has been lost in the nearly five decades since that legislation was enacted. No legislature then, nor at any time since, has provided funds from state sources to replace the lost revenues from the exemption. Local governments were forced to raise tax rates, which led to a new set of rules from the legislature limiting the mill rate, which spawned a new round of special districts that had authority to tax up to the same mill limit. Property tax bills are notorious for having four, five, and even six local government entities all collecting funds from the property tax. The idea that a sanitation district or a water district would ever need the same dollar amounts in tax revenue as a municipality or county seems strange to contemplate, but the statute makes this assumption.

In part because of the policy debate over lowering property taxes, the public concluded that state and local taxes were in general too high. The public's focus was not on services, but on tax rates. By the late 1970s, the debate in the states shifted from offsetting the burden of regressive taxes to simply cutting taxes. Beginning with Proposition 13 in California and Proposition 2.5 in Massachusetts, the capacity of states and local governments to increase taxes was limited by statute and/or constitutional amendment. In both campaigns to approve these referenda, the target was the perceived extravagance of the respective state governments. Yet the effect of these laws was to limit *local* sources of revenue. Both Proposition 13 and Proposition 2.5 limited the ability of local governments to generate new revenues. Similar tax limitation proposals in Ohio made virtually all local taxation (except city income taxes) subject to sunset provisions and limits on revenue rather than rates. These restrictions have created a cycle of tax referenda even when the expenditures are under control. This affects school districts and special districts, as well as smaller communities. Briefly the effects of such limitations were minimized. For example, increases in state transfers to local governments masked the massive change in taxing capacity of Proposition 13. In a pattern repeated across the country (Cox 2009), by the middle of the 1980s the state has become less generous with local aid, opting to address its own budget issues, slowly constricting local governments' capacity to fund local services.

The funding for a wide variety of programs (especially the programs that were the crowning achievements of the 1970s: social services expansion, public education funding reform, and local government revenue sharing) were cut or at least limited in growth. "Reform" became synonymous with program and tax cuts. Politicians know that even to suggest a tax increase was likely to incur the wrath of the general public and a sure way to lose the next election. For most of the first decade of this century, public opinion has been decidedly against any government action. The response to the recession of 2001 was not to increase spending, but rather to make more cuts. Even as the nation entered the second recession of the decade in 2008, public sentiment and legislative actions continued to favor even further cuts. A good example is the reaction of the Ohio legislature to an Ohio Supreme Court decision in 1999 that concluded that the state was in violation of the constitution because it was not funding public primary education at the required levels. Since then, the original complainants have been back to the state supreme court four times because the legislature simply refused to change the funding formula. The legislature ignored all five court rulings. Clearly, there was little sentiment to adjust state expenditures upward, even though it should have been apparent to everyone that local property taxes were increasing in order to make up for the state dollars that had not been appropriated. Tellingly, the proponents of the funding change have given up the fight.

By the middle of the first decade of this century the intergovernmental fiscal house of cards had collapsed. Yet the demand for further cuts at the federal and state levels, even though it potentially meant higher local property taxes, continued. The public simply did not believe that taxes would or should go up, and, given the reluctance of all politicians even to discuss tax increases, this belief was affirmed in the mind of the general public. Cries for new funding, especially for school districts, fell on deaf ears. In an era when the expenditures of both state and local governments could not be balanced against revenues without significant funding from the federal government or the states, every cut to balance the budget at one level created an imbalance at another. This was not a system in equilibrium, but one in which spending outstripped revenues at all levels.

Over time, the assumptions and expectations that framed the informal tax system adjusted to reflect the realities of practice. By 2001 the assumption was that taxes collected by higher levels of government were not to be distributed through the intergovernmental system but rather distributed based on expectations that reflected the policy goals of the agency that wrote the check. The sense was that this was their money being collected by them and given to local government to serve their purposes. As such, funding provided by higher levels of government was targeted to narrow program goals that were in jeopardy if recipients attempted to tailor the funding to their needs. There was a growing reliance upon competitive grants rather than simple transfers and formula allocations to fund projects (Cox 2009).

The system had become highly regulated and rigid, but it worked from the standpoint that no state or municipality could provide the breadth of services and programs these entities were able to offer without these intergovernmental transfers and grants. However, as long as the funding priorities of recipient governments aligned with the conditions of the awards, even the slow erosion of the share of funding from one of the participants could be tolerated.

This arrangement was fragile; it depended on the funding sources (the federal government and states) to continue, jointly or independently, to maintain the funding stream. The last two decades of the twentieth century were an economic and financial disaster for all levels of government, especially municipalities. Each level of government operated on the assumption that their fiscal policy decisions had no consequences for others. The federal government cut taxes even though the lost revenues created still larger deficits. Intergovernmental transfers became luxuries that could not be afforded because of deficits, created in part by tax cuts. Although they are rarely allowed to operate with a deficit, states nonetheless followed the same practices as the federal government. Multiyear tax cuts were enacted, which created deficits that had to be corrected by deeper and deeper program cuts. Funding for local governments and public education became luxuries that had to be sacrificed in order to meet the mandate of balanced budgets. The downward spiral of budget cuts went beyond the expectations of doing more with less and seemingly had a momentum of its own. Most devastating for recipient governments was that these cuts occurred in programs that were most visibly their responsibility—schools, roads, and public safety. The displeasure of members of the public was felt by those closest to them—local governments.

We entered the twenty-first century ill-prepared economically and politically to address the problem. The present situation began against a backdrop that Osborne and Hutchinson (2004) described as one of ever-increasing costs associated with health care and public safety needs, an aging population, and pension plans juxtaposed against continued resistance to tax increases, increased demand, and need for public assistance programs, which have placed new stresses on state and local governments. They noted that state governments were passing their problems down to cities and counties, with deep cuts in local aid, while the federal government dug a fiscal hole so rapidly that future cuts and unfunded mandates for states and localities are inevitable (Osborne and Hutchinson 2004).

It would seem that from a fiscal standpoint we have a pattern of one step forward and two steps back. Beginning in the 1960s the states begin to recognize the importance of local governments per se and the political dilemmas associated with urban life in particular. Even at the best of times, when the state became a fiscal conduit for local funding, the issues were addressed at the municipal or even neighborhood levels with little regard for metropolitan areas as anything but a geographic place. When issues were addressed at a metropolitan level it was likely to be driven by functional concerns such as primary and secondary education, mass transit, and environmental degradation, rather than as a matter of governance. Support for local governments grew from the 1950s into the start of the new century, but the funding often was program or project specific and offered little with regard to the governments that received the funds. A simple example demonstrates this point: the wave of school district consolidations that swept the country in the 1960s and 1970s was focused on the economy of scale problems of *rural* schools, not education quality or even education funding (funding formulae did not alter because of the consolidation efforts).

Interorganizational Service Agreements

Local governments have sought for several decades to find more fiscally prudent and cost-effective means of delivering services. Frederickson and colleagues (2004) identified interorganizational (or interlocal) service agreements as a key initiative for reducing the cost of service delivery. Much of the work has been done at the functional level resulting from the networks of city managers and department heads in a region. Less complex than formal processes (Walker 1987), these efforts often linked similar communities (i.e., communities that shared geography and often economic and sociological characteristics). Thus, these networks often emerged first as suburb-to-suburb connections, not across the broad reach of a region. The statutory authority for such activity often precludes a broader reach. Thus a broader effort would have to go through the same approval process (potentially including a vote by the citizens of each individual community) that a bilateral or trilateral arrangement would require. Requirements that joint operations be conducted in contiguous communities effectively can be thwarted by a negative response from one geographically sensitive municipality (see Chapter 2).

Ohio added a requirement to its distribution of local government funds that municipalities must actively pursue interlocal service agreements, with the further mandate that costs be reduced upon implementing the agreement. Those who do not combine services would sustain a deeper cut in local government funds. The pressure to "cooperate" now tilts the process toward small, narrow functional partnerships, which have the benefit of being easy to create but may have little fiscal or governmental impact. Broad-ranging and complex partnerships may produce more effective service delivery, but are all but impossible to create and implement before local government fund cuts take effect. The catch-22 in this process is that the state demands interlocal agreements be undertaken first. But budget cuts in anticipation of savings from implementation of interlocal agreements are already occurring. This leaves little room for anything but minor tinkering and/or noncontroversial, quick turnaround agreements that produce relatively small budget advantage. In other words, interlocal agreements that might well have occurred are "incentivized." But more complex and innovative agreements that will take longer to develop and implement, but also may yield significant savings, will be ignored. Quick fixes are rewarded while more useful approaches are set aside because they are too time-consuming and/or too risky. The state interest is less in effective government services through interlocal agreements than the *appearance* of change. Though the state has encouraged more interlocal agreements, the incentives potentially discourage broader arrangements.

Intergovernmental Partnerships

One of the preferred mechanisms for interorganizational service agreements is through intergovernmental partnerships. While today most states offer general statutory authority to undertake such partnerships, often these partnerships are initiated by local governments. The states play catch-up by first enacting special laws to approve such a partnership and then later creating a general statutory framework. In Chapter 5, the development of joint economic development districts in Ohio was presented. As the city of Akron moved forward with this innovative program, opposition emerged in the state legislature. The legislative perspective dwindled only when the district was presented as an alternative to annexation. Thus, with some reluctance the legislature approved special legislation that authorized the program. Within a few years a general enabling legislation that was little more than a slightly modified version of the original special legislation was approved. Three of the four Akron joint economic development districts were created under general statutory authority.

Other cities have also created such districts. The general statute gained legislative approval because it was viewed by many as the lesser of two evils. The legislature accepted the argument that creating these regional revenue-sharing economic development entities would reduce the likelihood that core cities would attempt to annex more territory. As far as the legislature was concerned, the primary beneficiaries of such development districts were small communities and townships, not cities. In reality, had the legislature perceived that the benefits flowed to the city (as they perceive is the case with annexation), the general statute may well have failed.

Annexation

Walker (1987) classifies annexation as "middling" in difficulty, but depending upon the perspective and goal this may belie the political hazards implicit in efforts of core cities to annex. As outlined in Chapter 5, the annexation process is fairly straightforward. As long as both sides agree, the process can be completed in a relatively expeditious manner. However, there are significant sociological and political barriers to annexation, especially when the annexation involves a center city or an inner core city and a suburban or exurban community. Many of these barriers could be addressed by changes in state law. What is missing is any political interest in promoting the expansion of the center city or inner core city. Norris, Phares, and Zimmerman (2009) offer *sixteen* political considerations for the failure of efforts for metropolitan government. They go on to offer three more economic and financial considerations and offer this pessimistic conclusion:

> as demonstrated by the sixteen (and there may be more!) principal factors affecting metropolitan governance, the very structure of the American political system and many of the values underlying it strongly bias that system against either metropolitan government or governance. Certainly, the political system is biased against metropolitan government. There are no such governments in the United States today, despite more than fifty years of calls to establish them. There is a bias against metropolitan governance, if by that one means coordinated actions among all or nearly all of the local governments in a region to address the tough issues facing the region or substantial parts of it. (34–35)

Lorch (2001) recounts some of the political and fiscal concerns with annexation in a list that is reminiscent of the Norris et al. list. At the core are objections from the suburban ring communities about the loss of "community" upon being incorporated into a large, supposedly less responsive government and the expectation that they will become burdened with higher costs of government.

State legislatures controlled by suburban constituencies base policy decisions on the negative stereotypes of the inner city—crime, drugs, poverty, education, housing and fiscal disparities (Norris et al. 2009). Furthermore, they reflect the bias for single-family dwellings that populate the suburbs—they, no less than their constituents, reside in the suburbs because of a preference for a lifestyle that they see as threatened by becoming part of a larger government unit. The limits of outward expansion are the limits of the private commute. As Norris et al. suggest, it is the "pro-sprawl," not the pro-regional, forces that have the political clout. Annexation serves the purposes of the suburb by bringing into their governance orbit like-minded residence at the fringe of the metropolitan area.

Under such circumstances annexation rules become a buffer *from* the city, not a means to join the inner city. The rules in most states are designed to facilitate the incorporation of relatively small parcels of property in unincorporated areas into small, incorporated, governments. Such annexation practices effectively fence in the urban core cities, which are no longer adjacent to unincorporated lands. As has been discussed previously (see Chapter 7) both the center city and the older, inner suburbs (the urban core), are surrounded by incorporated municipalities. As long as the rules of the game in annexation are written to facilitate the transfer of unincorporated properties into incorporated municipalities, those "surrounded" communities have no ability to use annexation.

Can the rules be altered? The simple answer is yes, but just as Norris et al. (2009), Lorch (2001), and Hall (2009) attest, the rules favor groups that are the political majority, who rarely support these approaches.

Urban Counties and Independent Cities

Virginia, while far from the most urban state in the country, nevertheless took aggressive action to address issues related to metropolitan governance in the 1950s and 1960s (see Chapter 5). The good news is that these models exist, but the bad news is that other legislatures have not used the two models of urban counties or independent cities as the basis for metropolitan reform in their own states. Even within the Commonwealth of Virginia it is the independent city form that has had the most use. Effectively, the development of independent cities has come at the expense of county governments. In a few instances (Virginia Beach and Norfolk, for example) the independent city form was used to prevent broader metropolitan initiatives (Virginia Beach merged with the county, which gave it the resources as an independent city to hold off merging with Norfolk).

The more interesting experiment was the creation of an urban county. Because no other governments could operate within the urban county, this represented a true regional government. On the other hand, the one example of this form is Arlington, Virginia, which is barely larger than a typical midsized city in both population and geography. The prototypes for the two models are the neighboring governments of Alexandria and Arlington. They are very similar in size and in form of government, yet one is an urban county and the other is an independent city. Arlington essentially is too small to be a good model for the urban county form. Other counties in Virginia are more easily swallowed by an independent city rather than becoming urban counties. There are great benefits to the city-county merger, regardless of whether it is the county or the city that becomes the governmental seat of authority. Nevertheless, from a national and metropolitan perspective basing metropolitan governance on the county rather than the city seems to make more sense. There is little interest in promoting this version of the models. Despite the long-standing use of the county as the basis for public services (see Chapter 2), the independent city arrangement, which often leads to the abolition (technically a merger) of a county, seems preferable to the state. While not a totally accurate characterization of the situation, the end result of these companion models is that the independent city model is seen as "reforming" a weak government type (county government), not as a metropolitan governance initiative.

Formal Multijurisdictional Purposive and Governing Structures

Much of state policy with regard to local governments has been to encourage the growth of special districts. Whether it is the wording of tax limitation laws, referenda that restricted the local capacity to generate revenue, or the all too frequent serial approach to public problem solving, if there is a growth industry in the public sector, it is in the development of special districts. The emergence of the special district is hardly new. Regional transit districts and multigovernment water districts first emerged in the late nineteenth century. School districts have an even longer history. Then, as now, the attractiveness of such districts is in the ability to concentrate technical expertise on the solution to a perceived problem. The issue often is less in problem definition than in the geographic scope of the problem. There is a tendency to define the district through preexisting geopolitical boundaries, rather than an examination of the geographic "scope" of the problem. Many special districts have a core urban center as their base, but the extent of the district will be defined by existing political entities (defined as designated municipalities or designated counties). This makes political sense for the state (and unfortunately for government statisticians), but may not make sense in terms of addressing a problem. A simple test to judge the economic reach of a core city is to look at the geographic boundaries of subscriptions to the major center city daily newspaper. People want news about their local community, but they also want news about the community where they work (and thus affects "lifestyle" and other choices). This simple rule of thumb is a more accurate indicator of the economic region for which a core city is the economic center, than boundaries defined by the U.S. Census Bureau (which simply combines counties to define an SMSA), or the boundaries of Regional Planning Districts (also clusters of counties), or school districts, which in urban areas never reach across county boundaries and may be divided at the municipal level. Political geography dictates special districts even when the districts logically reflect different boundaries.

Why is geography such a barrier? History and common usage are certainly factors in the affinity that people seem to feel for local governments, communities, and neighborhoods. Whether the district is already large, such as county-based school districts in the South and Southwest and regionally identifiable districts such as park and transportation districts, or they are quite small, as in neighborhoods or political wards in cities and townships. People base their political identity on those boundaries. Anyone who has gone through the political trauma of state legislative district and city ward redistricting can attest to this attachment. While over time these districts can become little more than historic artifacts, people often see them as the lowest common denominator when defining larger districts. Thus, such artificial and historically irrelevant boundaries are the basis for most regional efforts even when the projects themselves bear little resemblance to that geography. Once the pattern is set in the minds of the public, geographically more relevant districts become all but impossible. Claims to historic meaning trump economic and political realities.

Special Districts

The idea of a "special district" is complicated both in a legal, jurisdictional sense and in a functional sense. As noted in Chapter 9, special districts are not easily classified beyond the simple notion that they provide a narrow function, or provide a specific service. Thus, we labeled them "technical silos." These organizations also differ in the extent to which they possess the legal authority to generate revenues from taxing authority and/or user fee charges. Thus, certain special districts (including school districts in most of the country except New England) have full taxing authority (generally to tax property and levy fees), while the vast majority of special districts receive funds through transfers from other governments and/or get a share of a tax levied by another government (income taxes or sales taxes). Even though special districts may serve a narrow function (a park district or an irrigation district, for example), the revenues that support the district are more broad-based. The true cost of service may not always be apparent. For example, in South Florida, where schools are county-based and special districts have proliferated, property owners get a single property tax bill. Upon closer examination the bill includes levies by 3, 4, 5, or even more governments and districts. We noted in Chapter 3 the paradox that public school districts are still thought of as under local control, but if one were to trace the revenues that support those schools, it is quite likely that state revenues provide the bulk of the funding and in a few cases local funding trails even federal support. Similarly, special planning districts, which were often created in response to federal or state mandates, are supported by funds that are predominantly federal and state with little or no funding (only participation in decisions) by local public agencies.

Both the state and local governments in the region in which the special districts operate display some ambiguity about the role of special districts as distinct units of government. The functions performed are not necessarily in question, but the sources of revenue to support the district functions make the form and structure of regional entities a more complex political choice for both the local governments and the states. The general legal authority to create small, functionally specific districts exists, and to some extent there continues to be support at both the local and the state levels to create these districts as responses to immediate and *localized* need. However, there seems to be much less interest at the state level in the kind of large regional efforts typified by the Southwest Pennsylvania Commission or the RGOs.

City-County Partnerships

While it would seem that the states would have little stake in city-county partnerships, even city-county consolidation, the reality is that legislatures are reluctant to sanction such efforts. While most states have sanctioned a general grant of authority, the general rules seemingly favor the opposition to such efforts. Thus, for example, the standard format for city-county consolidation requires an affirmative vote in all political jurisdictions for the consolidation to be approved. Thus, as the National Association of Counties (NACo) found in a study of such efforts for its annual report in 2012 (Sanford et al. 2012), most such efforts in all but small, semirural counties fail because of opposition from the suburbs. Depending on the population and voter interest in the core city, a majority of the county voters may approve consolidation, but it is not approved because of the suburban vote. Much as the rules of procedure of the U.S. Senate require 60 of the 100 senators to permit legislation to be released from a committee for a floor vote, a minority controls the decision process. If one municipality, no matter its population, votes "no," the consolidation fails.

The legislative authority for such consolidation rarely permits a "partial" approval, whereby if contiguous communities vote to consolidate while others reject it, the municipalities where the consolidation was approved could proceed. At this point an all or nothing arrangement means that in large geographically, economically, and politically complex environments there is little chance for such efforts. When Jacksonville, Florida, merged with Duval County, three other municipalities within the county were included in the new government. The original referendum merged the four municipalities, but the vote involved only two governments—the city of Jacksonville and Duval County. Duval County became part of the "new" city of Jacksonville government. The four municipalities, of which the "old" city of Jacksonville was one, became subunits of the new city government. That choice was quickly reversed and those three units reverted to separate municipalities. Splitting the three beach communities from the city of Jacksonville required that charter language reaffirm that state law regarding municipal-county relations had to be reintroduced. State-mandated municipal-county fiscal and administrative relations would be handled by the "new" city of Jacksonville, because, for these purposes, it was simultaneously Duval County. Given the small populations of the three small municipalities involved, this changed little from an administrative standpoint. Yet for all that, the separate identity of these communities trumped a constitutionally permitted merger.

When the 28 municipalities in Broward County, Florida, decided in the late 1990s to create a semiformal two-tiered government model, the municipalities requested that the proposal be presented to the state legislature for review. Opposition to the proposal emerged, but the bipartisan support within the Broward County delegation meant that the opposition gained little traction in Tallahassee. More interesting is that it was not clear whether the legislature could stop the arrangement, or even if it needed to be presented to that body, but no one wanted to risk not getting approval in advance of the effort.

Concluding Thoughts and Things to Ponder

The urban agendas of the states and metropolitan areas infrequently intersect. While some of the blame/explanation can be laid at the doorstep of Dillon's Rule and the historic reluctance of the U.S. Supreme Court to intervene in state legislative affairs, and particularly on redistricting, the reality is that the states have rarely been active partners in a regional or metropolitan agenda. For example, even when Hall (2009) suggests a "third wave" cycle of interest in metropolitan governance, he discusses the new leadership of the large cities and the possibility of a more aggressive and positive *federal* agenda. The states are rarely seen as active or positive contributors to the resolution of metropolitan issues. To be more blunt, it is the interests and concerns of suburban legislators, whom in many states seem as disinterested in urban and metropolitan issues as their rural-dominated counterparts that controlled state politics into the 1950s that dictate the legislative agenda. While it might be tempting to suggest that many states are overtly hostile to urban interests, there is insufficient evidence to make such a claim. Certainly, the time when an "urban" agenda was a major part of the legislative agenda is in the past, but some of the changes made during the 1960s and 1970s are still relevant. Efforts to promote public mass transit, to tilt K–12 education funding toward urban districts, and to help both the poor and those of moderate means find adequate housing are quite literally the agenda of a prior century. While the financial straits of many states have been exacerbated by the Great Recession, by escalating health care costs, and by cuts in support for both state and local governments by the federal government are well documented, the reality is that general (as opposed to project- or program-specific) funding for a wide range of local government programs has been on the decline for several years.

Things to Ponder

1. How did Dillon's Rule affect the relationship of cities with their surrounding regions?
2. Why do you think programs such as social services and public education are the first to see cuts in an economic recession like that of 2008?
3. How do tax cuts at the federal and state levels affect local municipalities? What challenges do they face because of this?
4. Why are states reluctant to sanction city-county partnership efforts and how do these partnerships fare in the face of this adversity?

12

The Conflicted Role of Professional Municipal Managers

Help Build or Insulate from the Metropolitan Region?

Local government managers know they should be engaging and often do engage with surrounding communities. At the 2008 International City and County Management Association (ICMA) annual conference held in Pittsburgh, a panel discussed the role and nature of cross-jurisdictional collaborations in the future of local government. A group of experts presented a balanced but tepid response to how the profession of city management should approach regional problems. Their message was clear—"the first priority of a city manager is internal and a manager should look outside only when no internal option exists." The practitioners in attendance were out in front of the experts as they spoke most passionately of the need to risk personal consequences to accomplish multijurisdictional goals.

The managers attending the session were certainly not typical of managers in general as they tended to represent center cities, but there was a consensus among the panel and the practitioners that professional local government managers *should* play a role in addressing regional problems. This proposition is bolstered by an emerging body of work that suggests managers and mayors are beginning to consider the impact their decisions have on residents of other jurisdictions (Matkin and Fredrickson 2009). That said, many noted the difficulty in communicating the benefits of multijurisdictional cooperation to officials, especially elected officials in *other* municipalities. Furthermore, none of the managers present were able to clearly articulate the skills or policy tools necessary to build consensus around or achieve multijurisdictional or regional goals. They understood the importance of a healthy region but could not articulate how to balance the good of the region with the good of their respective communities. It is unclear what incentives, training, and education are necessary so that managers are equipped with the necessary tools to make outcomes as positive as possible for their communities and the broader regions of which they are a part.

Why is this so? Imagine for a moment a simple, two-dimensional matrix

Figure 12.1 **Likely Outcomes from the Interplay of Regional Interests and Local Interests**

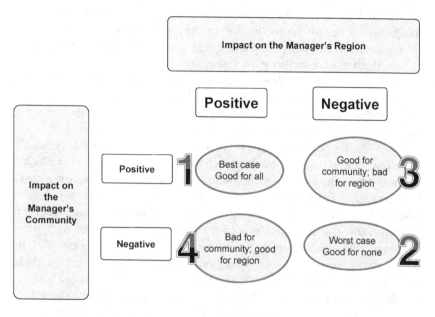

involving the interests of a local government that employs the manager and the region of which that local government is a part (see Figure 12.1). Local government actions or agreements could have one of four possible impacts on that local government and its region. In the first (Scenario 1), the outcome is positive for the local government and positive for the region—the ideal situation and asserted goal of any transaction. Coming to such an agreement should be relatively easy assuming all parties have full information about the expected outcomes. In the second (Scenario 2), the results are negative for the local government and negative for the region creating a lose-lose situation—an unlikely event unless imposed by some outside party. Indeed, we have presumed that such a scenario would knowingly never be adopted and, as such, we will dispense with further discussion of it.

It is the third and fourth possible outcomes that are the most intriguing. In the third (Scenario 3), the impact on the local government is positive, but the impact on the region is negative. This is a form of regional consumership in that the local government is taking advantage of the region only when it is in its interest. Examples of this might include aggressive fiscal mercantilism (attracting economic development through predatory tax policies) or campaigning against policies that overcome local resource disparities like regional tax-base sharing. In many regions this is "business as usual," but it raises important questions for managers. Is the manager professionally free to advance such an outcome? Are there perverse incentives in the system that reward such behavior? What options exist for the manager to work toward mitigating the negative consequences on the region? How are the interests of the region and community weighed? These questions and the tools needed to engage them require further exploration.

In the fourth outcome (Scenario 4), the impact on the region is positive, but the impact on the community is negative. This is a form of regional citizenship wherein the interests of the whole require citizens to put their interests aside. An example is tax-base sharing. As we noted in Chapter 8, tax- and revenue-sharing programs have been shown to be universally beneficial to those few regions that have adopted such methods. Many regions have looked at, for instance, the Twin Cities tax-base sharing program, but have rejected it for their region. In most cases, regional opposition came from municipalities who saw themselves as contributing more in assets than they would receive in benefits. These municipalities' objections were often voiced by the manager as the community's spokesperson. Should a manager be rewarded or punished for supporting or failing to block such regional action? What strategies might be applied to minimize the local negative effects? Furthermore, one must consider whether they are preparing their elected and appointed officials to be able to engage in a healthy discussion (citizenship) regarding such outcomes.

Unfortunately, we have yet to build the institutional or conceptual framework to make Scenario 4 work. Neither of the two current prevailing themes on crossjurisdictional relationships provides insight or assistance in identifying actions and behaviors that address this fourth scenario. Neither of the institutional structures that prepare and serve city managers incorporates Scenario 4 other than at the margins. Both themes implicitly assume that the only operationally important outcomes are those in which both the region and local government benefit or in which the local government benefits even if there is a negative cost to the region. They are Scenarios 1 and 3 specific.

Both those institutions are rooted in the prevailing themes. The practice of management is driven by theory and training. To that end, there are two pillars upon which a manager is acculturated into the profession: training and practitioner norms. Academic training is primarily delivered through graduate schools loosely connected by the Network of Schools of Public Policy, Affairs, and Administration (NASPAA). Practitioner norms and values are primarily articulated by the ICMA. A review of the academics and practices of these two organizations reveals an almost exclusive focus on Scenarios 1 and 2. Dealing with Scenario 4 is, at best, seen as a nice idea with limited practical value.

But the future of successful regions that balance local and regional interests requires Scenario 4 solutions. Like a family, all cannot agree on the best course all the time. There are times when some have to compromise for the good of all.

Weakness of Prevailing Cross-Jurisdictional Themes

The first theme is the idea of networks wherein participants engage in cross-jurisdictional activities with each other on a voluntary basis. The second theme is derived from economic reasoning or collective action. As individuals transact with each other to derive desired goods and services, institutions such as local governments transact in exactly the same manner and behavior. Bundled under the banner of institutional collective action (ICA), local governments seek to maximize the greatest net benefit in their relations with other institutions.

Networks have particular salience to the world of local government. Boundaries are often difficult to change for political and cultural reasons but few real world problems conform to those inviolate borders. Agranoff (2006) notes that there are multiple types of networks with differing expected outcomes and advantages. The four most prominent forms of networks are (1) informational—sharing information and technologies to make voluntary changes among partners possible; (2) developmental—exchanges coupled with "education and member services" to foster individual agency implementation; (3) outreach—developmental efforts supplemented by "blueprinted strategies for program and policy change that [lead] to an exchange or coordination of resources"; and (4) action networks—formally adopted interagency agreements on service delivery adjustments (Agranoff 2006, 57). Bilateral and multilateral mutual aid agreements and the assumption of services by other agencies are collaborative, but do not fall within Agranoff's definition of networks.

One common thesis in the network literature is that the skills associated with collaborative approaches are unique and therefore different from those of traditional management, which inform managers on how to operate within a single organization (Kikert and Koppenjan 1997; Kettl 2002, 2006; Agranoff and McGuire 2003; Goldsmith and Eggers 2004; Koppenjan and Klijn 2004; McGuire 2006). The researchers argue that networks are more deliberative; focus on reaching consensus (versus authoritative decisions); are less hierarchically authoritative, with the presence of partners (versus superior-subordinate); and have less clear legal authority with fewer direct consequences for those who "defect" (Agranoff 2006). Furthermore, Agranoff indicates that the vast majority of managers' time is still focused on concerns within their own organizations. Discussing barriers to collaborative efforts, Kettl (2006, 16) notes, "there is manifest evidence that government at all levels has not ensured that its managers develop skill sets to keep up with the rapidly evolving tools they are responsible for using."

The second theme explaining current practice in interjurisdictional relations is represented in the political economy literature on the organization of metropolitan regions, or ICA. ICA conceptualizes local government (or homeowners associations, special districts, and other forms of public service-delivery institutions) as a form of public household that represents a group of citizens who share a common sense of purpose or want (Oakerson 1999; Feiock 2009). Each public household is a local public economy and these local public economies engage in collective action and behave in a way that mirrors how individuals act as they seek self-interests. Managers, as representatives of their constituencies, are expected to engage in intergovernmental transactions as a utility-maximizing exercise. Like all utility-maximizing exercises, regional solutions suffer from the problems of multiple transaction costs, defections, and free-riding strategies (Olson 1965; Axelrod and Axelrod 1984; Ostrom, Gardner, and Walker 1994).

Cross-jurisdictional options for service delivery will be chosen only if transaction costs are decreased and the expected utility is greater than for internal alternatives. Basolo (2003) uses this perspective to note that regional solutions have largely been limited to areas with high fixed costs or apparent economies of scale, such as waste management, water and sewer, and public transportation. Attempts at cross-jurisdictional solutions to regional problems are also hampered by Jeffersonian desires for local autonomy and local economic interests that spur intraregional economic competition and limit cooperation (Basolo 2003).

The key, then, to most collective action problems is mitigating the transaction costs involved so that regions can realize the potential benefits of shared services and coordinated policies. Feiock (2008) identifies four types of transaction costs as barriers to multijurisdictional agreements. Information costs, which concern the clarity of partners' preferences, increase as the number of players increase, yet decrease when potential partners are homogeneous. Agency costs are tied to internal principal-agent problems and can be reduced by long tenure of officials and evidence of stable local institutions. Negotiation/division of benefits costs deals with the ability to negotiate mutually beneficial deals and how the spoils of multijurisdiction agreements are divided. These costs are also reduced by homogeneity and symmetry in political strength (Heckathorn and Maser 1987). Finally, enforcement costs are reduced by repeated interactions and close proximity—these reduce the chances of partners reneging once a deal is struck. Interestingly, ICA turns to network theory to reduce many of these costs because bilateral and multilateral relations across many areas create social networks that clarify potential partners' preferences (information costs) and allow agencies to build reputations as good partners, thus reducing agency, negotiation/division, and enforcement costs (Thurmaier and Wood 2002).

ICA theory also highlights concerns for professional managers, especially in their relations to elected officials. Managers may attempt to negotiate agreements only to have elected officials veto their efforts by not passing legislation necessary for implementation (Tsebelis 2005; Feiock 2008). Elected officials may be more myopic than managers due to the former's higher rates of turnover and short election cycles and the desire to keep voting blocs stable (Clingermayer and Feiock 2001; Feiock 2008).

> The underlying political dilemma associated with regional governance is that local officials need to give up some authority to achieve regional coordination, but they may then be held accountable for regional policies that are contrary to the preferences of their local constituents. (Gerber and Gibson 2005, 12)

However, the literature also notes that managers may enhance their careers if they can claim and capitalize on the benefits of collaborative efforts (Stein 1990; Feiock 2004; Carr and LeRoux 2005; McCabe et al. 2008).

Both these theoretical approaches are more descriptive of how the systems work, as opposed to prescriptive; that is, how the systems might work, particularly as to how those approaches might improve the ability of managers to advance Scenario 4 outcomes. Unfortunately, theories often merely explain current practice and are slow to catch up to a significant restructuring in intergovernmental relations that is occurring. This point perhaps explains why some of the managers at the ICMA conference were well ahead of the theorists. These managers understood that the present norms of acceptable cross-jurisdictional behavior was neither responsive not appropriate for today's interdependent region.

The Inwardness of the Model City Charter

Local government theory and practice has long been focused inward. Nowhere is the internal focus on the management of a particular local government more dramatic than in the Model City Charter. A charter is a local constitution that governs the organization of the branches of its government, its finances and tax structure, and the relationship among its citizens, elected officials, and administration. The Model City Charter, sponsored and developed through the National League of Cities (NLC), represents the current thinking of practitioners, experts, and academics on what a good local government should look like. It is often used by localities as a framework for designing government as it aids in deciding questions such as whether to have a city manager and, if so, what his or her powers should be; how many elected officials should the government have and which ones; and whether elections should be by district or at large.

The charter's roots date back to the late nineteenth century, when reformers desiring to develop the "best" form of government first laid out their vision. The initial version called for a mayor-council form of government with the mayor directly elected, at-large elections for council, an independent civil service commission, and nonpartisan elections. Since the 1915 version, the council-manager form has been the recommended form of government.

There is no set period in which the charter is automatically updated. However, it is a living document and the realities of "doing government" eventually lead to a sense that the document should be reviewed and updated. Such an event has occurred seven times with updates occurring in 1915, 1927, 1933, 1941, 1964, 1989, and 2002.

Prior to the eighth edition (2003), there was virtually no reference to the metropolitan region as part of the Model City Charter, which simply acknowledged that when it is prudent for a government to advance its citizens' desire and interest through intergovernmental involvement, it should do so. The eighth edition made the first modest acknowledgment of the region but subordinated the interests of region to the interests of the municipality. Specifically, the commentary to section 1.03, Intergovernmental Relations, states,

> The nature of intergovernmental relations is rapidly changing. Most cities are integral parts of the region. In that regard, engaging in cooperative intergovernmental relations is fundamental to the effective functioning of the city and the region of which it is a part. Although the purpose of engaging in intergovernmental relations is primarily to further the ends of the city, the health of the region should also be of concern to the city. (NLC 2004, 4)

Later, in section 4.04, Land Use, Development, and Environmental Planning, it is recommended the city council be charged with determining "to what extent the comprehensive plan and zoning and other land-use ordinances are consistent with regional plan(s)" (NLC 2003, 29). The commentary that supports the charter clause simply states,

> Most cities are integral parts of metropolitan and other regions. The planning and development policies of a city have implications beyond its boundaries.

The overall health of a Metropolitan region is dependent on some integration of local and regional planning. In addition to establishing appropriate processes and relevant agencies, the city should seek consistency with regional plans in its planning endeavors. (NLC 2003, 30)

Aside from these two modest references to the city's relationship to the region of which it is a part, the balance of the 79-page Model City Charter is internally focused. This observation is not meant to say the issues covered in the charter are unimportant. To the contrary, they are extremely important as concepts and ideas that have been nurtured for more than 100 years within eight editions of the charter. However, these issues instruct a city on how to operate internally, not on how to operate externally. As a result, both the profession and culture of local government has been directed inward.

Additionally, cross-jurisdictional relations are but an extension of inward directedness of local government interests. When those local interests are served by regional engagement, even to the extent they may not be "healthy" for the region, action is both acceptable and desirable (Scenario 2).

The Inwardness of ICMA

ICMA is clearly the leading organization of local government professional managers in the United States and is recognized globally for representing the best and the brightest of local government managers. Much of the overall strength of local government in the United States is derived from the ability of local governments to be effective business and political enterprises. Taking that into consideration, perhaps the "I" in ICMA should be changed to "Internal." That is not meant to be overly critical, but to identify the origins and roots of city management. The profession of local government management grew out of internal concerns with inefficiency, corruption, and incompetence in urban areas (Fredrickson, Wood, and Logan 2001). Beginning with the first professional manager—hired in Staunton, Virginia, in 1908—municipal governments called on city managers to administer their internal affairs. Because local government administration focuses on running individual governments, the knowledge base has mostly developed in a number of identifiable areas—such as finance, management, and personnel, with subfields in police, fire, public works, and parks management. In those early days, local governments were like islands, and it was presumed that if each local government operated efficiently, the system of islands, as a whole, would be fine.

ICMA was organized in 1914. Its major activities include publishing reference material; training, connecting, and credentialing managers; and completing consulting work, often to develop professional local governance in emerging democracies. ICMA publishes *Public Management (PM)* magazine, which delivers practitioner-focused articles on local government operations. IMCA also runs ICMA Press, which publishes books, reports, research results, and training material for managers, students, and government associations. Additionally, ICMA holds an annual conference that draws a worldwide audience of professionals for networking, workshops, educational sessions, field demonstrations, and speakers designed to equip managers with the tools necessary for addressing contemporary issues of local government.

The connection between ICMA's mission and professional development in local government is strong and clear. Their rich and important substantive contributions include democratic, institutional development in manager-council governments and a strong concentration on the ethical dimensions of municipal management. To that end, ICMA's training materials provide a comprehensive reflection of professional norms, standards, and priorities among those who study and practice local government management.

A qualitative review of recent ICMA Press and ICMA Annual Conference offerings indicates that managers receive training on issues that are almost exclusively *internal*. Topics in both the published offerings and conference training sessions are divided by practice area, including (among others) finance and budgeting, policy facilitation, personnel, strategic planning, public safety, service delivery, and technology. The overarching theme is one of individual government performance and how managers can apply professional tools to maximize the efficiency and effectiveness of operations in their particular jurisdictions.

In its 2007 Resource Catalog, ICMA Press advertised 58 titles—4 subscriptions, 27 books, and 27 reports. Only four involved issues beyond internal management. ICMA's monthly magazine provides local government managers a wealth of information and guidance on a wide variety of timely and ongoing concerns, including regionalism. Using their online index, we searched for any local government articles or statements ICMA classified as dealing with "regionalism" from January 1990 through October 2009. The results indicate 69 articles or announcements dealing with multimunicipal efforts. Fourteen of those instances concerned awards or nominations for awards through ICMA's Program Excellence Award in Community Partnerships, itself a sign that ICMA is cognizant of regional and multisector collaboration. Another 33 articles provided sample plans for local governments to follow, with public safety (7), code enforcement (6), general administration (5), economic development (5), and innovations (5) being the primary subjects. In addition to the publication of two case studies, 15 articles were presented spanning regional topics such as city-county relations, city-city collaboration, and coordination of public safety services.

It is important to put this emphasis in context. By contrast, there were 665 articles on public safety, 373 concerning finance and budget, and 337 that focused on public works issues during the same period. Surprisingly, a recent "state of the profession" article coauthored by a number of respected leaders in the field of local government management is virtually silent on the regional milieu in which most municipalities operate (Keene et al. 2007). Instead, the authors focus on the important value professionals add within their jurisdictions in service to elected officials and community members. This is only one article, but it suggests that the "thought leaders" in the field continue to focus primarily on single-jurisdiction issues and skills.

ICMA's convention training sessions share this consistent internal focus. At its annual conferences, the organization provides formal educational workshops and forums under the title ICMA University. A review of 2005, 2006, and 2007 conference programs determined that 63 separate topics were offered over three years, all of which ICMA classified as addressing at least 1 of its 18 "practice groups" or skill areas. None of the practice groups focuses directly on regional issues or multimunicipal coordination.

The descriptions of ICMA university workshops that appear in the conference programs suggest no more than 4 of 63 total topics in recent years appear to address multijurisdictional problem solving. Most, like ICMA Press publications, focus on improving individual government performance by providing practical tools for problem solving. Typical examples include "Improving Service Delivery and Reducing Costs," "High-Performance Organizations: Becoming Stewards of the Whole," and "Leadership: An Art of Possibility."

NASPAA: Serving the Customer What the Customer Wants—Inwardness

The Network of Schools of Public Policy, Affairs, and Administration has been intertwined with ICMA in at least one very important way. To realize the idea of a professional local government manager as represented in the Model City Charter and the development of the council-manager plan, a formal means to professionally train and credential the manager was needed. Doctors have medical schools, dentists have dental schools, and lawyers have law schools. A number of graduate schools started to offer a master's in public administration (MPA) degree that translated the professional expectations of the manager profession into a graduate-level curriculum. These schools focused on improving government's internal management and organized to form NASPAA, which has become the standard-bearer of shaping and improving education in public management. NASPAA maintains accreditation criteria for colleges and universities that offer graduate degrees in professional public service. Its 290+ member institutions offer programs specializing in policy, administration, and nonprofit management. Despite some encroachment from business and law schools in the last few decades, the MPA remains the traditional terminal degree in local government management. Therefore, long-term changes in the educational backgrounds of future local government managers are likely to be affected by the accreditation standards and substantive recommendations of NASPAA.

Curriculum is one component of NASPAA's nine formal accreditation standards. However, because it serves a wide variety of institutions and aims to accredit primarily on a basis of mission, NASPAA does not require that accredited schools offer any specific coursework. Rather, it establishes five "common component areas" to prepare students for professional public service leadership in organizations. None of the common component areas focuses on external skills or responsibilities. Instead, they include the following: policy and program formulation; implementation and evaluation; decision making and problem solving; human resources; budgeting and financial processes; information management, technology applications, and policy; political and legal institutions and processes; economic and social institutions and processes; and organization and management concepts and behavior. All are geared toward developing a strong internal focus. NASPAA does not require that schools spend an equal amount of time and resources on each area, nor does it require that a program supply all of the courses itself. Perhaps due to the latitude NASPAA gives graduate programs in patterning their own paths of study and specialization, NASPAA does not prescribe any topic areas that explicitly involve thinking beyond jurisdictional boundaries.

NASPAA has not completely ignored regional thinking. It also publishes a series of nonbinding guidelines intended to address more specific issues in professional public service education. These include advice on diversity, internships, and developing program specializations, among other topics. One guideline, written in 1992 by the ICMA/NASPAA Task Force on Local Government Management Education, discusses the professional demands placed on local government managers and offers advice for tailoring a graduate program to prepare them accordingly. In addition to specific curriculum suggestions (e.g., courses in policy analysis, political accountability, planning and administrative values), the guidelines suggest cultivating competence in relations extending beyond jurisdictional borders, including interlocal, interregional, local-state, and local-national interaction, as well as involvement with private and nonprofit entities. This appears to be the only mention of regional problem solving in professional public service education. While the task force guideline highlights the importance of regional thinking, it does not speak to which competencies are important or how managers are to balance the needs of their own community with those of the region.

Testing Attitudes

The following analysis reinforces the previous discussion regarding the internal focus of the profession of local government management and its professional and academic institutions, ICMA and NASPAA. A representative sample of appointed and elected local government officials in western Pennsylvania were asked about their (and their governments') willingness to participate in several programs that are controversial, but also retain the existing structure of local governments. The questions were particularly interested in whether respondents who had obtained a graduate degree in public administration and/or were members of ICMA reacted to these programs more sympathetically than those who were not trained or educated within those institutional frameworks.

The two issues were designed to test attitudes toward Scenario 4 outcomes. The first issue dealt with collective decision making undertaken by a group of municipalities. Voluntary organizations of municipalities, often referred to as councils of governments (COGs), have a rich tradition in a highly fragmented state like Pennsylvania. They are voluntary and cannot compel participation in activities by recalcitrant members.

The proposed reform respondents were asked to evaluate the possibility of municipalities to collectively decide a best course of action. Once made, the decision would be binding on all members, even those who voted against the proposal. As an example, if six of the nine municipalities, representing 60 percent of the total population of all nine, voted to have a joint police department, that decision would be binding even if the three municipalities, representing 40 percent of the population, were opposed. Under present rules, the six could form the joint police department, and the other three would not be part of the operation.

This approach is similar to the rules under which the European Union (EU) operates. At the core of the EU is the transfer of partial sovereignty from the constituent governments to a regional authority. Such power sharing is a form of dual sovereignty, a political concept familiar to and embodied in United States political institutions. The regional authority (EU) can impose rules and regulations on constituent governments when a super majority of those constituent governments decides it is in the best interest of the whole. As such, the EU is not simply an aggregation of each government wherein each government has the ability to veto actions unilaterally. Conversely, the associational rights connected with each nation allow each member to manage its own affairs.

Our presumption was that either ICMA- or NASPAA-trained managers would be more likely to understand that such a program retained the existing structure of local government and local government decision making while recognizing the needs of the bigger region of which each municipality was a part. The question was framed as follows:

> How willing would you be to participate in a COG that required full participation in all programs that were approved by the COG?

The second question dealt with an issue frequently discussed in this book: tax-base sharing. As has been previously discussed in Chapter 8, tax-base sharing pools a source of revenue, such as the property tax or sales tax, and distributes the proceeds to constituent local governments on objective criteria that reflect the needs of the region taken as a whole. Its asserted benefit is more effective and equitable impact on economic development and growth. To the degree that the fragmentation of government services and decision making in an urban area prevents any rational approach to the distribution of the gains and benefits from development and growth policies, tax-base sharing helps to mitigate the adverse effects of that fragmentation.

The presumption was that managers trained by either ICMA or NASPAA would be more likely to understand that such a program retained the existing structure of local government by aiding those municipalities not growing as fast as others without unduly burdening the municipalities with higher growth. The question was framed as follows:

> How willing would you be to participate in such a [tax-base sharing] system knowing that from year to year your municipality's contribution to, or benefit from, the program may fluctuate?

While one might hope that managers would be less myopic than elected officials that face reelection on a regular basis, our review of the ICMA and NASPAA literature and training offerings gives no reason to expect this to be the case. A look at the survey data suggests that managers and elected officials view the two Scenario 4 proposals (tax-base sharing and full COG participation) as unacceptable. More than 60 percent of managers and elected officials indicated they would be unwilling to participate in tax-base sharing efforts. In a similar fashion, neither group indicated substantial interest in participating in a council of government that requires full participation in all programs that were approved by the COG.

The majority of ICMA members were unwilling to participate in tax-base sharing systems, just like those who are not members of the organization. In a similar fashion, more than 60 percent of ICMA members were unwilling to participate in COGs that mandated full participation. Those with degrees in the profession (MPA/MPP) are no more willing to participate in tax-base sharing or full council of government programs than those with other degrees. More than 63 percent of both groups indicated an unwillingness to participate in tax-base sharing. At least 70 percent of both groups were unwilling to participate in COGs that require full participation in all approved COG services. In other words, ICMA membership and NASPAA education had no significant impact on moving managers to a better understanding of how to deal with cross-jurisdictional issues that are not perceived to be in the best interests of the community they represent, regardless of the negative impact on the region of which they are a part.

Concluding Thoughts and Things to Ponder

The Model City Charter, ICMA, and NASPAA are representatives of a system that has developed to address the internal affairs of a local government. They deliver what the customer wants, and theory has been developed to support what is wanted in practice. The underlying assumption is that external affairs are useful as a means of advancing the internal affairs of the local government regardless of the impact on that which is external. Conversely, if there are no internal issues that require external engagement, the city should not be engaged in external affairs. The notion that a city has a role to play in regional governance is absent from the current perspective.

The underlying assumption must be altered so that cross-jurisdictional relations are seen as a balancing of local and regional interests (Scenario 4 in our analysis). Behavior that achieves such a goal should be rewarded and education on how to accomplish such an end advanced. As such, new theoretical foundations for cross-jurisdictional relations must be developed. Consistent with Herbert Simon's (a mid-twentieth century organizational theorist and thinker) admonition—we can only design that which we know—regional strategies cannot get on the table if they are not known or understood.

From that perspective, the role of ICMA, NASPAA, and other professional associations involved in local government is critical to structure a manager's understanding and awareness of cross-jurisdictional problems. The field of local government administration is only beginning to recognize the importance of the context of community and region. The context of local government management has changed substantially in the past 30 years due to growing disparities within regions, urban sprawl, threats of terrorism, and global competition (Mitchell-Weaver, Miller, and Deal 2000; Miller 2002; Fraser, Lepofsky, Kick, and Williams 2003; Sparrow 2008). Responses to these changes require multimunicipal and regional solutions to problems, but local government management training has largely remained internally focused.

ICMA, NASPAA, and public administration scholars need to develop, test, and promote intergovernmental regional skills that work. A key research question is: How can the skills managers have developed to deal with elected officials in their own communities be applied when dealing with elected officials in other communities? Research should also focus on whether iterative, small successes in cooperation lead to collaborative experiences between regional communities and subsequent larger endeavors. Finally, a catalog of what forms of collaboration are most common among municipalities and which are most effective would help managers begin to foster an environment of regional cooperation.

Finally, a new edition of the Model City Charter is needed. This time, cross-jurisdictional roles, responsibilities, and obligations should be at the core of the discussions. How the city serves the interests of its citizens *and* the interests of the region of which the city is a part and a building block must be addressed in the new charter. A local government engages in cross-boundary activities as both a means by which city interests are advanced and by which the region is governed. Sometimes the interests of the local government should take a backseat to the interests of the region.

Things to Ponder

1. How are intergovernmental skills different from those directed at inward-focused administrative tasks?
2. What new elements need to be added to a new Model City Charter to accommodate metropolitan governance principles?
3. Figure 12.1 depicts the possible outcomes from regional decisions. How does one avoid outcome number 3 and promote outcome number 4?
4. What are the managerial skills that enhance collaboration and networking?
5. Why do you think politicians are hesitant to give up authority as part of regional solutions?
6. Why do you think administrators are hesitant to give up authority as part of regional solutions?
7. Why is the focus of ICMA education and materials on internal situations and where do we see proof of this?
8. In the survey studying reactions to Scenario 4, why do you think the majority of respondents were unwilling to try such a scenario?

13

Speculation on the Future

From Cooperation to Collaboration?

The terms "cooperation," "coordination," and "collaboration" are similar in that they all mean "working together." However, they are profoundly different concepts. Figure 13.1 indicates the differences between these three methods of working together. At the more basic level, cooperation is highlighted by relatively short time horizons, loose informal relations, complete retention of power and authority by the players, and a shared sense of the transient nature of cross-boundary activity. Coordination is cooperation that has been slightly institutionalized with a longer duration, perhaps some more formal rules and channels of communication, and a sense that the relationship between players is less transient. Like cooperation, coordination still retains all power and authority with the players who can stop working together when doing so appears to be no longer in their interests. Collaboration is coordination on steroids. It occurs when the players virtually create a new structured relationship between themselves that shares power and authority in a way that recognizes the importance and rights of each player as well as the importance and rights of the collaborative taken as a whole. To us, regional governing is not just cooperation or even coordination. Indeed, it is reasonable to argue that regional cooperation and a fair degree of regional coordination presently occurs within our metropolitan areas. Neither of those will suffice to truly govern a metropolitan region. That will require the collaboration of building blocks.

The premise of this book is that local governments are those building blocks. Indeed, it is hard to imagine a metropolitan region where regional decision making occurs without a strong and visible connection to the geopolitical communities (local governments) that all regions in the United States are divided into. As we have noted, the two principles upon which the purpose for and meaning of local government has been built is a double-edged sword. One principle pushes a region together while the other can pull a region apart. The pull of local government as "creature of the citizen," particularly when joined with economic/market models, generates barriers to cross-boundary

Figure 13.1 **The Fundamental Differences Between Cooperation, Coordination, and Collaboration**

Feature	Cooperation	Coordination	Collaboration
Duration	Short	Longer	Long
Relations	Informal	More formal	Very formal
Mission	Not well defined	Loosely understood	Common
Structure	Ad hoc	Program specific	New structure
Planning	Little	Some	Comprehensive
Information	Shared relevant to issue	Open channels	Well defined
Authority	Retained	Retained	Shared
Resources	Separate	Shared	Shared

Source: Adapted from Winer and Ray 1994.

activity that often sounds the death knell for many regional efforts. The push of local government as "creatures of the state" often generates systems that unite local governments.

This push and pull has been treated as a war between competing principles in which champions of each hope to claim victory and eliminate the other. The assumption of each champion is that their cause is just and their opponent's is not. As is the case with most wars, this war is both unwinnable and unnecessary. We advance this idea in the belief that the system of governance in the United States needs local governments to be creatures of both the state and the citizen. Only in this fused state can collaboration replace cooperation and coordination as the means of cross-boundary governing. It is through local government as "creature of the state" that structure, authority, and organization are created in our governance system. It is through local government as "creature of the citizen" that human-scale connection of community to government is made and reinforced.

Americans learn and experience the art of simultaneously ruling and being ruled through their personal ownership of their local government. Indeed, there are more than 500,000 locally elected officials in the United States and 12 million individuals employed by local governments. As an outcome of such a system, to the extent possible, the distance between the rulers and the ruled is minimized. To a citizen, their local government has not been administratively created by the state as a means of organizing a state or metropolitan area. It is not a mere cog in a state or national political party apparatus. Indeed, to think that their local government is but a mere convenience of the state or national party trivializes the very concept of *their* local government. To be just another institution of modern society distant and removed from them is an anathema. Local government is more often "us," and state/federal government is more often "them." Such a strong emotional tie is a function of "creature of the citizen." Judge Dillon was remarkably perceptive in understanding that U.S. local government was not a creature of either state or citizen but of both. As such, they (state and citizen) must be seen not as competitors but as partners in the governing of complex, multijurisdictional urban societies.

Nowhere is the importance of viewing the two foundational principles as partners greater than in the development of the metropolitan region. The messy process of recalibrating decision making up from the individual local government and down from the state suggests that the metropolitan region is the option most likely to emerge as the new focus of decision making. Indeed, the very reason the metropolitan region makes the most practical sense is its ability to capture and employ both foundation principles. We do not use the term "messy" lightly. It effectively captures the uneven process by which a new scale of governance (the metropolitan region) takes on a more defined role in addressing today's urban America. There are some small steps forward, some failed experiments, a few steps back, and no blueprint or game plan to guide the process.

As we careen toward a new way of governance, we have organized our concluding thoughts and observations into three categories. The first broadly covers what we consider to be the encouraging signs in building a framework for regional decision making. The second, and perhaps easier to write, covers the discouraging signs that continue to act as weights on the process. The third summarizes our recommendations for steps that important institutions and actors need to take to develop more effective means of true regional governance.

The Encouraging Signs

The barriers to successful metropolitan governance are many, yet we also believe that the models and prototypes for cross-boundary collaboration do exist. Our discussion of the EU in Chapter 2 demonstrates that shared decision making is possible. Equally important, we believe that the future of the metropolitan region is still in the urban centers. The *necessity* of that collaboration is certainly apparent to many local public officials, even if it is less apparent to those at the state level. It is necessary because both social service and technical service problems are often best handled at a regional or metropolitan level. The perception of the suburbs as an escape from the perceived problems of urbanization represented in the center city is waning. The perception that suburbs are an economic refuge remains, but the unreality of that perception has grown. The increasing use of shared services, the persistence of attempts to create regional governance organizations, and the emergence of center city-alsoUrb coalitions means that a need for such regional enterprises is accepted.

Encouraging Sign 1: Albeit Slowly, the Borders Are Breaking Down

The artificial lines that constitute geopolitical boundaries are of great importance in U.S. politics. We "see" those lines as having political, social, and economic meaning. The battles every ten years over congressional districts, state legislative districts, and city council ward boundaries are legion. Citizens, no less than the public officials directly affected, attach great significance to which side of those boundary lines they are placed. Community and neighborhood identities are shaped by those boundaries. As a city councilman, one of us watched the anguish of identity when persons found themselves on the "wrong" side of the boundary line. It was as though not just their political but their social sense of themselves was altered by this change. Yet the reality is that over time (after two to three redistricting changes) those who fought to stay in district will fight to prevent changes that would correct modifications from another era. Sense of place is in the eye of the beholder.

What this means for proponents of metropolitan governance is that our sense of place can change or expand, especially as social and economic factors make a larger area more "familiar." This is the expectation in the concept of the alsoUrbs. Borders become more porous and thus less relevant to those in the area. Over time the socioeconomic links make the political boundary distinctions less relevant. Cooperative endeavors are now a positive thing rather than a threat to one's identity. Despite the fact that such reforms are still infrequent, few can even remember, much less endorse a return to, a time before coordinated transportation planning through MPOs, before interdepartmental service sharing was a common part of any managers toolkit, or before urban counties or the city-county consolidations of the post–World War II era. They are fully integrated into the political ethos of urban life.

Such incremental changes in political viewpoints are inevitable as the socioeconomic differences among communities disappear. The alsoUrbs represent another change. Rather than a focus on specific services through technical service sharing, the partnership of the communities of interests that are the cities and the alsoUrbs represent the potential for broad, across-the-board collaboration that is a practical and attainable surrogate for consolidation.

Encouraging Sign 2: RGOs Exist in Every Metropolitan Region

The most likely approach for expanding metropolitan governance is through the use of regional governance organizations. Virtually all metropolitan regions have at least one organization that has been created to address common problems and issues facing the region. The question is no longer whether such organization(s) exists, but the degree to which they play a meaningful role in their respective regions.

The champions of RGO development have been and are practical necessity and the federal government. The latter's influence has been primarily in the guise of transportation policy. RGOs are predominantly constituted by the local governments in the regions and, in that capacity, exist as the one authoritative place where local governments can be convened to address issues and concerns facing the region as a whole. However, it is not clear whether RGOs will become the platform for regional decision making in the public interest or, as many are now, the place where local governments protect their private interests in a regional setting. It is unsettling that the two most sophisticated RGOs are not constituted by local governments but by gubernatorial appointment in Minneapolis-St. Paul and direct election in Portland, Oregon. Neither of those forms are likely to be rapidly emulated or easily adopted in other regions. Perhaps the slow and more deliberative approaches in Kansas City and Pittsburgh are more reflective of the likely trajectory of RGOs as they evolve.

State governments have been slow to empower RGOs or to clarify their status within a regional decision-making framework. That is not an observation unique to RGOs but to most regional instruments such as tax sharing or land-use authority. States generally do not want to do much themselves, nor do they want the federal government to dictate relationships between local governments even though the federal government is in a position to so do. Yet as we suggest below, this push from Washington may be what is needed.

The RGOs are still in the early stages of development. They are, at best, proto- or quasigovernance institutions. We believe they can mature into collaborative institutions for the new metropolitan region.

Encouraging Sign 3: Successful Cross-boundary Governance Tools Are Growing

While the numbers seem small, successful intergovernmental collaborations continue to multiply. Even when the impetus and explanation for the change is based on other factors (as with the problem of corruption that drove charter change in Cuyahoga, Ohio), the end result is a streamlined and (hopefully) more efficient government structure. The NACo study (Sanford et al. 2012) of county "reform" reported organizational changes in a number of smaller counties. While these organizational changes were not occurring in large metropolitan areas, the simple fact that small and midsized counties see regional collaboration as a tool for better government is important. The models we have had for decades have been of consolidation and merger in very large urban areas. When those urban areas reach across the metropolitan region they are reaching out to counties and municipalities that have little experience with collaborative endeavors. The search for more avenues to do "more with less" has led smaller governments to consider strategies of collaboration and consolidation. In the long run this means that a greater number of local governments will have had experience in such efforts.

The search for cost-effective service delivery has created considerable impetus. This may explain why efforts for cross-jurisdictional solutions beyond basic interlocal agreements continue to be discussed and debated even though there are few examples of successful change initiatives. Two quite different types of change efforts are worthy of more discussion: tax-sharing and city-county consolidations.

The great experiment with tax sharing is the Twin Cities tax-sharing program. As noted in Chapter 8, the program provides that 40 percent of a municipality's growth in commercial and industrial real estate valuation is diverted from the municipality's direct control to a pool shared by all municipalities in the region. A uniform tax rate is applied to this pooled value, and the proceeds are distributed back to the municipalities on a needs-based formula. The amount a government contributes to the pool has little relation to what it will receive in distributions—a participating government may receive much less than it contributes to the pool, and conversely, it may receive substantially more than it contributes. In this fashion, tax-base sharing serves a redistributive function. Other regions have not followed suit with the comprehensive model of the Minneapolis-St. Paul metropolitan initiative, but others including Dayton, Ohio, Denver, Colorado, and Pittsburgh, Pennsylvania, have tried a version of this effort. These regions chose not to simply mimic the Twin Cities model, but rather fashioned tax-sharing efforts that fit the development needs of the region. Each of these efforts represents successful change in its own right.

Much the same can be said of city-county consolidation. The efforts of the post–World War II period did not yield a single model of how to consolidate. Consolidation has always been a process that could occur at two distinct levels: department-to-department consolidation and government-to-government consolidation. The former efforts are quite common, building as they do upon technical and professional interactions. Merging departments to improve services is something that all but a few rural communities consider. Merging governments is more difficult politically and organizationally (and thus less frequently attempted), but it must also be understood that such efforts are not of one type. UniGov in Indianapolis is quite different from Jacksonville, Florida, and the independent city efforts in Virginia are less fully "metropolitan" in scope, but also more comprehensive at the government level. There remain other governments functioning (providing services and even having their own elected officials) in both greater Indianapolis and greater Jacksonville. The independent cities that have assumed the functions of counties in Virginia are the only governments functioning within those boundaries, but the boundaries themselves may not cover an entire metropolitan region. Again, the important point is not having a single vision of how to consolidate, but that it continues to be explored by governments across the country.

We must judge these efforts as successful. In this we concur (but with some reservations) with Leland and Thurmaier (2010) in their evaluation of city-county consolidation.

Encouraging Sign 4: Regional Special Districts

Special districts are something of a conundrum. As technical silos they do not represent an effective tool for encouraging metropolitan governance. On the other hand they are typically *regional* organizations. Service-sharing initiatives and some department-to-department consolidation have been facilitated by the presence and support of special districts. As we commented in Chapter 9, since special districts have widely divergent, yet narrow, often technical roles and are constrained by somewhat unique geographic boundaries, it is difficult to generalize about them. Nonetheless, there are a few broad observations that can be made. First, they represent the largest single type of local government. Second, they have accounted for 90 percent of the growth in total new local governments between 1952 and 2007. Third, they tend to be narrowly focused, serving a single purpose. Indeed, in 1997, 92 percent of special district governments were undertaking a narrowly defined, specific function or responsibility. Fourth, their formation usually arises from the perceived need of participants to solve a particular problem rather than as the result of a desire to address a set of complex and interrelated problems or issues in a metropolitan area.

As the name itself implies, special districts are created to provide rather narrow and specialized purposes. With the exception of public school facilities, the infrastructure and support facilities rarely can be made part of another facility, or repurposed. The very uniqueness of the service provided makes the multiplication of such districts more likely. Even where a region might be home to several similar districts (sanitation, water, and water and sewer districts come to mind), there are geographic and political barriers to consolidation of such districts into single larger districts, but this does not address the more common problem of the proliferation of distinct special districts. Having addressed the problem in a piecemeal fashion to begin with, it is harder to put that genie back in the bottle and create megaregional public works departments to replace the special districts. At best you will find that service sharing across a region is the only likely alternative.

Why do we count them among the encouraging signs? Because any efforts to consolidate service delivery are positive. Special districts have some geographic limitations that may make some smaller than the size needed to maximize effectiveness, but there is no reason similar special districts could not consolidate to achieve that desired effectiveness. Also, the bar for success for special districts is low. Given the technical nature of the functions of such districts, horizontal links were not likely (no one would suggest merging a school district with a water district, but people do discuss consolidating water districts with other districts and school districts with other districts). As technical silos, they are not the foundation upon which a metropolitan governance framework can be hung. On the other hand, they have the potential to serve as the equivalent of department-to-department merger. If seen more from the latter perspective, the emergence of the RGO as the manager of the technical silos integrates those special districts into a coordinated whole.

Encouraging Sign 5: Regional Governance Innovation and Experimentation Continues

Despite the seemingly dismal track record of the proponents of metropolitan governance, the continuing efforts to accomplish collaborative partnerships are impressive. Spurred by the logic of *necessity*, both elected and appointed local government officials have championed these efforts. As the continuing pursuit of city-county consolidation, the growth of urban counties and independent cities in Virginia, and the plethora of shared service agreements being approved, there are any number of regional entrepreneurs who have successfully taken up the task of metropolitan partnerships, cooperation, and governance. While interest in metropolitan governance arrangements is still stronger among academics than practitioners, there is a growing understanding of the need to explore these arrangements. And, as the NACo study (Sanford et al. 2012) demonstrates, and the stories of the efforts in Indianapolis, Pittsburgh, Louisville (Gamrat and Haulk, 2005) affirm, a common ingredient in these efforts is that there are both political and administrative "leaders" who take the reins of the process. There are innovators in every region. The difference may well be that of timing; the regional agenda is not yet set.

The Discouraging Signs

For every success story there seems to be a counterpoint. Metropolitan governance is not on the political radar of most states. It is not clear whether the states simply don't care, don't want to, or don't know how to create metropolitan decision making. As we noted earlier, they do not have the appetite. Perhaps such regional efforts are simply too far down the priority list to get on the agenda. Even in states that have created general statutory authority for regionalizing activities, it is not always clear whether or not permission to exercise authority will be allowed. The City of Memphis sought three times to create a unified government through consolidation with Shelby County. As the Sanford et al. (2012) assessment noted, the Shelby County case also offers a note of caution: *trying* to meet public expectations and *successfully* meeting them are two very different things. Although the charter commission worked to address the concerns of residents outside the City of Memphis by including several specific provisions, it was not enough to overcome these residents' wariness and outright objection to consolidation.

In every election Shelby County residents voted against the merger. When the "partial" consolidation through the merger of Memphis and Shelby County schools appeared to have a chance for approval (it was approved in 2011), the Tennessee legislature reacted by enacting new mandates to be imposed upon any government merger prior to the implementation of any district-level consolidation. The legislature effectively took control of the merger decision out of the hands of the voters and turned it over to a planning commission created for the sole purpose of developing an implementation plan.

Discouraging Sign 1: The Era of Declining Resources from the State Is Likely to Continue

The changing (and declining) funding by the states for local governments is the backstory of the fiscal havoc caused by the Great Recession. As discussed in Chapter 3, the rules of the game had already changed. Long before that recession, the states were reducing support for local governments, often to support state-level tax cuts. While the recession has been the political excuse/ explanation for the last few years, the pattern of cuts began during much better economic times.

The reality is that state support for general operations of local governments has been declining relative to overall budget changes for two decades. In this the states were simply following the lead of the federal government where revenue sharing remained viable for barely a decade to be replaced by block grant programs. The funding levels for block grant programs have been in decline for more than a decade. The "era of good feeling," during which both the federal and state governments supported urban areas, was but a brief period of time. Unfortunately, it was one thing to be dependent on own-source revenue when government programs were of their own making, but today local governments deliver a wide range of programs developed by the states and the federal government. These new programs mean that local governments are paying an increasing share to support state and federally mandated programs in addition to their own programs. They must pay for those new programs through the same antiquated and regressive tax structures (primarily property taxes) that were not up to the task before the programs were added. This is less a partnership to address important public policy issues than a shell game in which the pea is not under any cup—the local governments lose.

Discouraging Sign 2: The Political Supremacy of Consumership over Citizenship

Market-driven approaches have dominated both academic and political discourse for the better part of three decades. It is not for us at this point to recount that debate, but rather to examine the effect of that approach on problem solving in metropolitan areas. In our view the dominant perspective supported by market-driven approaches is distinctly antimetropolitan. To the extent that local governments continue to depend on tax sources that relate directly or indirectly to consumption (property taxes and fees), the capacity to generate local own-source revenue will be based on the wealth of those in the community. The disadvantages go to lower- and even middle-class communities, which are taxed at proportionately higher rates to generate the same dollars. From a market perspective this simply validates the choice of wealthy consumers to congregate together. Furthermore, this perspective suggests that sharing services, much less more sophisticated forms of metropolitan collaboration, is an inefficient use of resources.

The flaw in this perspective is, of course, that it treats each individual local government as a fully independent and self-supporting island without need of an urban core. At this point those in the suburbs do not see their economic success as the product of the urban core, but rather as self-sufficiency. Even the Great Recession, which hit many suburbs as hard as it did cities, did not dissuade those who sought refuge in those suburbs from the illusion of social and economic independence. Until the interdependence of communities is accepted, the relative ease of tax generation (and the myth of communities as places of the like-minded), will hold sway.

Discouraging Sign 3: Prevailing Notions of How Local Government Works Are Deeply Embedded

The simple reality is that few outside the cities and some alsoUrbs are interested in metropolitan solutions. Even the most optimistic among students of metropolitan governance recognize that except in very few cities, where the city is the center economically and in population, public opinion is against broad activities such as mergers and consolidations. Also, it must be noted that even service sharing is problematic. When done in the administrative shadows as an extension of technical expertise, the public is supportive, especially if the linking of services can produce cost savings. The informal network of mostly appointed officials is active and often successful. However, when service sharing extends to domains in which the public has a strong viewpoint, even service sharing is difficult. The conversion of schools in Akron, Ohio, into "community learning centers" garnered much praise, but the question before the public was support of the Akron Public Schools, not a service-sharing plan. As they had done on other matters, the voters of Akron affirmed their support of the public schools, even though what they were doing was increasing the city income tax. The focus stayed on the schoolchildren and succeeded, unlike the earlier county effort where the suburban residents voted "no" out of distaste for the Akron city government.

There is a well-known saying in public administration, called Miles' law.

Rufus Miles commented on the tendency of persons in an organization to view events through the lens of their profession and/or their organizational position when he said, "Where you stand depends on where you sit." The dynamic of intergovernmental relations within metropolitan regions is very much at play here. Public officials, both elected and appointed, in central cities see the necessity of developing metropolitan solutions to a range of regional issues. Fewer, but still many in the alsoUrbs, see the same necessity. Once you get outside that narrow orbit, the world looks quite different. The relative success and wealth of these suburbs creates an air of invincibility (a trait once shared, but no longer, among the alsoUrbs) in which the political climate is one in which the suburbs believe they can survive without a center city (Savitch and Vogel 2004). From where they "sit" the only threat to a comfortable way of life is to be pulled into the fiscal quagmire of the city. The logic often extends to other suburbs. At the core is a value that is akin to hyper-individualism. The expectation is that others should respect your individualism and that discourse challenging your beliefs are to be avoided. Public discourse is simply an opportunity to announce a position, not to deliberate. In this we come full circle to the classic ideas of representation first presented in Chapter 2.

Discouraging Sign 4: Conceptual Tools to Build Metropolitan Governance Are Still Nascent

While it is not easy to explain how we got into this mess, the emphasis on protection of individual identity and perspective is rooted in how we educate and train public administration professionals. The emphasis on managers as the ultimate decision makers, the ideal of the city manager as the professional analyst who applies the precepts of the economics to reach rational decisions void of political overtones, and a bias toward "business" models of the market (the three legs of the New Public Management) create an organizational culture that emphasizes "them versus us" calculations and a narrow vision of the unit of analysis (never broader than the municipality). Cooperative ventures are accepted only if there is "advantage" to do so. Narrow technical solutions are best because they keep the problem "simple." Crossing the politics-administration barrier (the always rejected but still practiced dichotomy) is viewed as a sign of failure. Finally, most managers are recognized for what they do for "their" local government, not what they do for the greater good of the metropolitan region.

The management theories of Public Choice and the New Public Management place great emphasis on giving managers the authority to act, but this authority is constrained by the form of organization. Managers are bounded in their capacity to act within organizational and governmental barriers. They are kings of their domain within the boundaries and are guided in decision making by the vision (and constraints) of market theory. The market is typically a two-person relationship. In the case of public managers, bilateral relationship can be defined as both "things I control" and "things I don't control." Metropolitan cooperation is by definition something that falls into the category of things I *don't* control. As such, these are efforts to either be dominated or ignored. In either case "cooperation" is not a tool of relationship. City managers often find themselves at odds with metropolitan governance frameworks because it requires giving up a measure of control.

Discouraging Sign 5: The Growth of Special Districts as the Solution to Every Regional Problem

We included special districts among the "encouraging" aspects for the metropolitan regions, yet counties and special districts are not without problems as a basis for metropolitan governance. The special district as a technical silo represents a significant conundrum. On the one hand they are by their very nature a *regional* solution to local problems. On the other hand, as narrow technical matters, the regional is simply a geographic statement, "regional" solutions are a by-product of the work, not an end unto themselves. The technical nature of the work does not lend itself to horizontal linkages. Ten regional special districts do not represent an opportunity to create one consolidated endeavor. These special districts can only expand in one direction (linking more similar units). Thus, special districts do not advance governance per se. They contribute to the more effective delivery of services, but are also invisible governments. How many of us think of the regional water or sewer district as government? As we suggested in Chapter 9, even few who work for special districts think of themselves as part of the public service. In such an environment it is difficult to link these service and product providers into the broader fabric of governance. At best they will be reluctant participants in metropolitan endeavors.

Actions

Strategy 1: Federal and State Support for Urban Coalition Building Between City and AlsoUrbs

The concepts of the SMSA and MSA were useful as reference points for the collection of demographic data from census reports. It was an entry point the federal government could take advantage of and not appear as if they were meddling in state affairs. That said, they are but a broad framework for the realistic reflections of metropolitan regions. We need to develop additional rubrics that define a region in a way that public officials and the broader public can agree. Metropolitan solutions could then emerge from meetings of true regional representatives rather than a congress of persons from clusters of counties that a statistician has defined. We made a start on this redefinition by talking about the urban core as the city and the alsoUrbs. Although descriptively accurate we recognize that this terminology may have relatively little public relations value. The point is that we need to redefine the city in much the same way we think about the place we call home (much as someone from the greater Boston area will say "Boston," not Natick or Gloucester or Ashland or any of the more than 75 cities and towns surrounding the actual city).

Connecting the central city to the region and building the region out from that center is where the fusion of the statistical area and the political area can occur. Such a fusion needs the active endorsement, support, and encouragement of both the federal and state governments. Both levels of government must develop policies and practices that create incentives for true region building. The Department of Housing and Urban Development (HUD) still focuses on and rewards individual center city building, not region building. The result is that center cities live in one world created by HUD policies and practices while the rest of the region lives in another world virtually unrecognized by HUD. Encouraging projects and activities that capture the shared reality of the physical border that separates city and alsoUrb is but a modest example of how HUD policy could change urban perceptions.

No real dialogue presently exists between the federal government, state governments, and local governments on how to build metropolitan regions. However, dialogue does exist among them on how to build metropolitan transportation systems, a process that has arguably created a myopic and potentially stifling sense of regional governing. What is needed is a national dialogue on regional governance, not as a means of building better transportation systems, but as means of governing. The states have the legal authority, the federal government has the financial clout, and the local governments have a growing sense of interconnectedness to make such a dialogue productive. Are the cities and the urban areas that share a common border ready to be the catalyst and framework for that dialogue?

Strategy 2: Promote Fiscal Regionalism

Fiscal Regionalism is more a promise than an integral part of today's metropolitan regions. As our assessment of the plans has demonstrated, there are unanticipated consequences associated with their implementation. But the knowledge of such nuances simply paves the way for the next generation of fiscal regionalism strategies to be improved and better able to serve the needs of the region. But the bottom line is that they work. Indeed, they generally have served the purpose their designers envisioned for regions that have employed them.

The major inhibitor of the growth of fiscal regionalism is today's antitax political climate. Generally, the fuel of fiscal regionalism is a new tax or the expansion of an existing tax and, as such, it is extremely difficult to convince elected officials to advance the proposition. More fundamentally, as long as those in the suburbs believe that they can succeed without an urban core, fiscal regionalism is problematic. Seemingly only when the fiscal distress that afflicts many cities spreads beyond the city and the alsoUrbs into the suburbs will such behaviors change. We can take this a step further by noting that to the extent metropolitan collaboration is seen as relieving fiscal stress, even the wealthiest communities at the fringe of the metropolitan area will want to buy into the process. In the short term programs such as the Twin Cities tax-sharing model are politically unrealistic, but with some modifications (such as redistributions modified by hold-harmless requirements so no one "loses") such programs continue.

The public is suspicious and even cynical about such efforts, but at this point the arguments for improving services rests with the advocates of more metropolitan cooperation, not the antitax ideologues. The key is to frame the metropolitan agenda as an improvement on the effectiveness and reach of public services. Programmatic efforts that affirm the synergistic relationships first between the alsoUrbs and the city and then the alsoUrbs to the suburbs will reshape and redefine fiscal regionalism.

Strategy 3: Strengthen Regional Governing Organizations as More Than Transportation Planners

Earlier in this chapter we emphasized the importance of RGOs because of their potential as protoregional governments. There is a considerable gap both politically and conceptually between an RGO and a metropolitan government. The reality is that we do not need to fill this gap. Expanding the use of RGOs in and of itself is a first step because it addresses the sociopolitical and cultural conflicts within metropolitan regions without forcing an all or nothing choice. Furthermore, the simple experience of collective decision making in an RGO is invaluable in correcting some of the myths and misgivings of suburban opponents of metropolitan solutions. With a narrower agenda, the RGO introduces elements of metropolitan government that are more palatable for opponents of metropolitan government. Specifically, activities that would serve to strengthen RGOs could include the following:

- serving as the coordinator and manager of regional special districts within the metropolitan area,
- serving as the operator for the region's cultural and recreational assets,
- administering tax- and revenue-sharing programs,
- creating consistency between local and regional land-use plans.

Strategy 4: Establish an Intergovernmental Focus for Cities (Model City Charter)

The Model City Charter has stood for more than 100 years as the best and recommended form of local government in the United States. It embodies the collective academic and practical knowledge about what a local government should be. Democracy, representativeness, transparency, engagement, social and economic justice, professionalism, and accountability are but a few of the values that are advanced, reinforced, and carried from one generation to the next. It is not a document to be taken lightly. Only eight times has the charter been amended to capture the changing nature of the world we live in. With all due respect to the charter and the deliberative process that has given rise to it, in one regard, it is woefully out of date. It is virtually silent on how a local government, albeit city, town, or county, works with other local governments to pursue the collective interests of the region as a whole. Under the current model charter, a local government can use the region as a resource to advance its private interests. The eighth edition took the first feeble steps toward addressing a more nuanced relationship of local government to region. Simply put, there needs to be a ninth edition that more definitively establishes a relationship among local governments in pursuit of regional interests. If local governments are to be the building blocks of the metropolitan region, they need to know how to fit together.

Strategy 5: Framing Regional Governing—Not a War Between Foundation Principles, but Effective Governance Through Complementary Foundational Principles

As developed in Chapter 2, there are two distinct and diametrically opposed visions of local government. One holds local governments to be creatures of their citizens. The other that they are creatures of the state. Currently, a battle is playing out in a winner-take-all war wherein one vision will beat out the other. That's a senseless war in which to engage. Local governments are neither always creatures of the state or of their citizens. Rather, they move back and forth between those two visions. Indeed, we want them to be both. This flexibility is both necessary and essential to the success of local governing. The key to regional governance in the United States is the successful management of the competing visions they create separately and the tension they create collectively.

That tension does not require a resolution in which one of the two visions is transcendent. Rather we must understand the value of both visions and apply them as necessary and define those times when a synthesis is needed. It is likely that this type of synthesis represents the pathway toward metropolitan governance (see Figure 1.4).

Three classic political theory questions are:

- Who should rule?
- Where does the locus of authority lie?
- Is that authority sufficient to the task of governance?

In the context of local governments in the United States there are no easy answers to any of these questions. Dillon's Rule, at the very least, implies that the locus of authority is with the states. However, in the development of home rule statements in state constitutions and/or broad statutory grants of authority, local governments on some service delivery and policy matters have considerable leeway within which to operate. On the other two questions, the answers are more ambiguous. The question of who should rule is influenced by political ideological perspectives on the nature of government itself. As the discussion in Chapter 2 points out, local governments in the United States are organized and operate upon two conflicting founding principles (Figure 2.1). The halting pattern of political and institutional reform at the local level is a result of the tension between these two traditions. With few exceptions, the political-cultural tradition has proven to be both powerful and resilient. Partly because of the twin financial crises of the first decade of the twenty-first century, we seem to be at the cusp of another rethinking of intergovernmental relations. The extent to which such changes will succeed and their general direction will be a product of how the two foundational principles are captured in any new policies that emerge. All we can be certain of is that to organize metropolitan areas around either the organic or economic model does not work. The economic metropolis has been the primary driver of regional service delivery. These efforts are at best a starting point, but are not sufficient. On the other hand the organic model of the metropolitan region is one in which the integration of local governments is maximized. This can be accomplished either through reducing the actual numbers of governments or by increasing the mandated collaboration of those governments by some higher level of government. Such a perspective demands a strong interest from state government in reorganizing these creatures of the state, to better serve the interests of the state. There is no evidence that the states wish to become catalysts for such wholesale reorganization of local government.

Strategy 6: The Necessity of an Active Role for the Federal Government

It was a revolution of sorts when the federal government began to directly engage local governments on a range of public policy issues. Great strides were made in transportation, housing, and some social services. Revenue sharing and block grants made directly to local governments make a difference. The requirement to plan through regional organizations has fostered a regional perspective and encouraged regional collaboration. We are suggesting it is time for the federal government to again leapfrog the states and work with local governments, but this time to foster actual metropolitan governance, not merely regional planning and urban services. Oddly, the general grants of authority by state legislatures to encourage "home rule" may be the basis for marginalizing the states. The point is that the major barrier to metropolitan governance is suburban-dominated state legislatures (though we must also acknowledge that the U.S. House of Representatives is as tilted toward suburbs as any state legislature). Only with a push from the federal government (much like those from the Depression and then the 1960s and 1970s) would metropolitan governance have a consistent place on the policy agenda of the states.

Metropolitan Governance as a Bundle of Strategies

We have argued that there is danger in seeing metropolitan governance as consolidated, regionalized government. This nation is too diverse to cling to one-size-fits-all solutions. There is no magic formula for resolving metropolitan issues, nor should there be. We are somewhat more pessimistic about the politics of metropolitan governance, but at the same time we believe that these efforts must continue. Importantly, they may serve as the basis for building a broader acceptance of government-focused strategies for improving the public service. We should add that we are encouraged because the range of tools for regional collaboration continues to multiply. There need not be one way of achieving metropolitan governance. Successful patterns of relationships and collaboration are more varied.

We see the future of metropolitan governance in the broad range of efforts.

None of these efforts in and of themselves are fully and broadly metropolitan, yet each effort represents a piece of the puzzle. Given the political climate, there are states in which even interlocal agreements are problematic. States such as Florida and Virginia, which in earlier decades took the lead in experimenting with metropolitan endeavors, seem unwilling to stretch these processes from governance processes to full governments. While for some this is a less than satisfactory outcome, we see the variety of programs and models as a strength. All metropolitan areas may not require metropolitan governments. Thus, we see metropolitan governance as a bundle of strategies for matching geography and services to improve the effectiveness of local governments. The bundle of strategies are a good start, and the reality is they will be the pinnacle of governance in some metropolitan areas. In others we can foresee more consolidation and more cooperation, which ultimately moves an area toward becoming truly metropolitan. We should expect no more and accept no less.

Bibliography

Adams, C. F., H. B. Fleeter, Y. Kim, M. Freeman, and I. Cho. 1996. "Flight from Blight and Metropolitan Suburbanization Revisited." *Urban Affairs Review* 31, no. 4: 529–543.

Adams, John. 1856. *The Works of John Adams, Second President of the United States.* Boston: Little, Brown.

Adrian, C., and M. Fine. 1991. *State and Local Politics.* Chicago: Nelson-Hall.

Agranoff, R. 2006. "Inside Collaborative Networks: Ten Lessons for Public Managers." *Public Administration Review* 66, no. s1: 56–65.

———. 2001. "Managing within the Matrix: Do Collaborative Intergovernmental Relations Exist?" *Publius: The Journal of Federalism* 31, no. 2: 31–56.

———. 1990. "Managing Federalism through Metropolitan Human Services Intergovernmental Bodies." *Publius: The Journal of Federalism* 20, no. 1: 1–22.

Agranoff, R., and M. McGuire. 2003. *Collaborative Public Management: New Strategies for Local Governments.* Washington, DC: Georgetown University Press.

Akron Beacon Journal. 2003a. "Akron Gears Up for School Projects, Meetings to Help Map Out Construction Plans After Passage of Income Tax Hike." May 8, A1.

———. 2003b. "Mayor: Akron on Own, in Address, He Says Schools Can't Count on County Tax." January 10, B1.

Ammons, D. N., and C. Newell. 1988. "'City Managers Don't Make Policy': a Lie; Let's Face It." *National Civic Review* 77, no. 2: 124–132.

Arizona Revised Statutes. 2005. http://www.azleg.state.az.us/ars/9/00471.htm.

Aurand, A. 2007."The Impact of Regional Government Structure on the Concentration and Supply of Affordable Housing." *Housing Policy Debate* 18, no. 2: 393–430.

Axelrod, R. K., and R. M. Axelrod. 1984. *The Evolution of Cooperation.* New York: Basic Books.

Baker, K., and S. Hinze. 1987. *Minnesota's Fiscal Disparities Program: Tax Base Sharing in the Twin Cities Metropolitan Area: A Research Report.* Minneapolis: University of Minnesota.

Barber, Benjamin. 1995. *Jihad v. McWorld.* New York: Times Books.

Barnes, William R., and Kathryn A. Foster. 2012. "Toward a More Useful Way of Understanding Regional Governance."Conference of the European Urban Research Association, Vienna, Austria, September. http://brr.berkeley.edu/wp-content/uploads/2012/10/Barnes-Foster-Toward-a-more-useful-way-of-understanding-regional-governance.pdf.

Basolo, V. 2003. "US Regionalism and Rationality." *Urban Studies* 40, no. 3: 447–462.

Beach, W. 2000. "Forum: Tax Revenue Sharing Agreements in Michigan." *Government Finance Review* 16, no. 6: 34–36.

Beckman, N. 1964. "Alternative Approaches for Metropolitan Reorganization." *Public Management*: 47.

Benjamin, G., and R. P. Nathan. 2001. *Regionalism and Realism: A Study of Governments in the New York Metropolitan Area.* Washington, DC: Brookings Institution.

Benjamin, R. 1980. *The Limits of Politics: Collective Goods and Political Change in Post-Industrial Societies.* Chicago: University of Chicago Press.

Benjamin, S. B., J. Kincaid, and B. D. McDowell. 1994. "MPOs and Weighted Voting." *Intergovernmental Perspective* 20, no. 2: 31–35.

Berman, D. R., and L. L. Martin. 1988. "State-Local Relations: An Examination of Local Discretion." *Public Administration Review* 48, no. 2: 637–642.

Berube, A., W. H. Frey, A. Singer, and J. H. Wilson et al. 2010. *The State of Metropolitan America: On the Front Lines of Demographic Transformation.* Washington, DC: Brookings Institution.

Bickers, K. N., S. Post, and R. M. Stein. 2006. "The Political Market for Intergovernmental Cooperation." In *Self-Organizing Federalism: Collaborative Mechanisms to Mitigate Institutional Collective Action Dilemmas*, edited by R. C. Feiock and J. T. Scholz, 161–178. New York: Cambridge University Press.

Blair, G. S. 1986. *Government at the Grassroots.* Pacific Palisades, CA: Palisades.

Blakely, E. J., and M. G. Snyder. 1997. *Fortress America: Gated Communities in the United States.* Washington, DC: Brookings Institution.

Bollens, J. C. 1957. *Special District Government in the United States.* Berkeley: University of California Press.

Bollens, S. A. 2008. "Fragments of Regionalism: The Limits of Southern California Governance." *Journal of Urban Affairs* 19, no. 1: 105–122.

———. 1986. "A Political-Ecological Analysis of Income Inequality in the Metropolitan Area." *Urban Affairs Quarterly* 22, no. 2: 221–241.

Bond, A., and J. Kramer. 2009. "E-Government Service Offerings and Website Content of Florida's Metropolitan Planning Organizations." *Transportation Research Record: Journal of the Transportation Research Board* 2119, no. 1: 54–57.

Bowman, A. O., and R. C. Kearney. 2012. "Are US Cities Losing Power and Authority? Perceptions of Local Government Actors." *Urban Affairs Review* 48, no. 4: 528–546.

Brenner, N. 2001. "The Limits to Scale? Methodological Reflections on Scalar Structuration." *Progress in Human Geography* 25, no. 4: 591–614.

Brookings Institution. 2003. *Back to Prosperity: A Competitive Agenda for Renewing Pennsylvania.* Washington, DC: Brookings Institution.

Bryan, T. K., and J. F. Wolf. 2010. "Soft Regionalism in Action: Examining Voluntary Regional Councils' Structures, Processes and Programs." *Public Organization Review* 10, no. 2: 99–115.

Bryce, J. 1922. *The American Commonwealth.* New York: Macmillan.

Bryson, J. M., B. C. Crosby, and M. M. Stone. 2006. "The Design and Implementation of Cross-Sector Collaborations: Propositions from the Literature." *Public Administration Review* 66, no. s1: 44–55.

Buchanan, J. M. 1975. *The Limits of Liberty.* Chicago: University of Chicago Press.

———. 1987. *Public Finance in Democratic Process: Fiscal Institutions and Individual Choice.* Chapel Hill: University of North Carolina Press.

Burke, E. 1949. *Burke's Politics: Selected Writings and Speeches of Edmund Burke on Reform, Revolution, and War*, ed. R. J. S. Hoffman and P. Levack. New York: Knopf.

Burns, N. 1994. *The Formation of American Local Governments: Private Values in Public Institutions.* New York: Oxford University Press.

Carr, J. B., and K. LeRoux. 2005. "Which Local Governments Cooperate on Public Safety? Lessons from Michigan." Working Group on Interlocal Services Cooperation. Paper 4. http://digitalcommons.wayne.edu/interlocal_coop/4/.

Carroll, D., and S. Chapman. 2013. "Government Spending and Employment in Recoveries." Federal Reserve Bank of Cleveland, Economic Trends, April 9. www. clevelandfed.org/research/trends/2013/0413/01gropro.cfm.

Clingermayer, J. C., and R. C. Feiock. 2001. *Institutional Constraints and Policy Choice: An Exploration of Local Governance.* Albany: SUNY Press.

Consoliated Jacksonville Charter. 1992. http://www.fl-counties.com/docs/legal-documents-links/duval.pdf?sfvrsn=0.

Cox III, R. W. 2009. "Seeding the Clouds for the Perfect Storm: A Commentary on the Current Fiscal Crisis." *State & Local Government Review* 41, no. 3: 216–222.

———. 2004. "On Being an Effective Local Government Manager." In *The Effective Local Government Manager*, 3d ed., edited by Charldean Newell, 1–19. Washington, DC: ICMA.

Cox III, R. W., S. Buck, and B. Morgan. 2011. *Public Administration in Theory and Practice.* 2d ed. New York: Longman.

Cox III, R. W., and S. Pyakuryal. 2013. "Tacit Knowledge: The Foundation of Information Management." In *Ethics and Public Management*, 2d ed., edited by H.G. Frederickson and R. Ghere, 216–239. Armonk, NY: M. E. Sharpe.

Dillon, John F. 1868. "The Dillon Rule." *City of Clinton v. The City of Cedar Rapids and the Missouri River Railroad Company,* (24 Iowa 455).

Dolan, D. A. 1990. "Local Government Fragmentation: Does It Drive up the Cost of Government?" *Urban Affairs Quarterly* 26, no. 1: 28–45.

Downs, A. 1994. *New Visions for Metropolitan America.* Washington, DC: Brookings Institution.

Edwards, M. M. 2008. "Understanding the Complexities of Annexation." *Journal of Planning Literature* 23, no. 2, November.

Elazar, D. J. 1984. *Cities of the Prairie: The Metropolitan Frontier and American Politics.* Lanham, MD: University Press of America.

———. 1975. "Suburbanization: Reviving the Town on the Metropolitan Frontier." *Publius: The Journal of Federalism* 5, no. 1: 53–80.

———. 1971. "Community Self-Government and the Crisis of American Politics." *Ethics* 81, no. 2: 91–106.

———. 1966. *American Federalism: A View from the States.* New York: Thomas Crowell.

Ensch, J. L. 2008. "Electoral Systems and Interregional Cooperation: Politics and Economics in Transportation and Metropolitan Planning Organizations." Symposium: Democracy and Its Development 2005–2011, Center for the Study of Democracy, University of California–Irvine.

Executive Office of the President. 2003. Department of Homeland Security. In *Budget of the United States Government, Fiscal Year 2004,* 141–161. Washington, DC: U.S. Government Printing Office. http://www.whitehouse.gov/sites/default/files/omb/budget/fy2004/pdf/budget/homeland.pdf.

Feiock, R. C. 2009. "Metropolitan Governance and Institutional Collective Action." *Urban Affairs Review* 44, no. 3: 356–377.

————. 2008. "Institutional Collective Action and Local Government Collaboration." In *Big Ideas in Collaborative Public Management*, edited by L. B. Bingham and R. O'Leary, 195–210. Armonk, NY: M. E. Sharpe.

————. 2007. "Rational Choice and Regional Governance." *Journal of Urban Affairs* 29, no. 1: 47–63.

————, ed. 2004. *Metropolitan Governance: Conflict, Competition, and Cooperation.* Washington, DC: Georgetown University Press.

Feiock, R. C., and J. B. Carr. 2001. "Incentives, Entrepreneurs, and Boundary Change: a Collective Action Framework." *Urban Affairs Review* 36, no. 3: 382–405.

Florida, R. 2007. *The Flight of the Creative Class: The New Global Competition for Talent.* New York: HarperBusiness.

————. 2004. *Cities and the Creative Class.* New York: Routledge.

————. 2002. "The Rise of the Creative Class." *Washington Monthly* (May).

Foster, K. A. 1997. "Regional Impulses." *Journal of Urban Affairs* 19, no. 4: 375–403.

Foster, K. A., and W. R. Barnes. 2012. "Reframing Regional Governance for Research and Practice." *Urban Affairs Review* 48, no. 2: 272–283.

Fraser, J. C., J. Lepofsky, E. L. Kick, and J. P. Williams. 2003. "The Construction of the Local and the Limits of Contemporary Community Building in the United States." *Urban Affairs Review* 38, no. 3: 417–445.

Frederickson, H. G. 1999. "The Repositioning of American Public Administration." *PS: Political Science and Politics* 32, no. 4: 701–11.

Frederickson, H. G., and G. A. Johnson. 2001. "The Adapted American City: A Study of Institutional Dynamics." *Urban Affairs Review* 36, no. 6: 872–884.

Frederickson, H. G., G. A. Johnson, and C. Wood. 2004. "The Changing Structure of American Cities: A Study of the Diffusion of Innovation." *Public Administration Review* 64, no. 3: 320–330.

Fredrickson, H. G., C. Wood, and B. Logan. 2001. "How American Governments Have Changed: The Evolution of the Modern City Charter." *National Civic Review* 90, no. 1: 3–18.

Frey, B. 1978. *Modern Political Economy.* New York: Wiley.

Friedman, J., and J. Miller. 1965. "The Urban Field." *Journal of the American Institute of Planners* 31, no. 4: 312–20.

Friesma, H. P. 1971. *Metropolitan Political Structure; Intergovernmental Relations and Political Integration in the Quad-Cities.* Iowa City: University of Iowa Press.

Frug, G. 1999. *City Making: Building Communities without Building Walls.* Princeton, NJ: Princeton University Press.

————. 1980. "The City as a Legal Concept." *Harvard Law Review* 93: 1059–1154.

Frug, G. E., and D. J. Barron. 2008. *City Bound: How States Stifle Urban Innovation.* Ithaca, NY: Cornell University Press.

Fukuyama, F. 2011. *The Origins of Political Order: From Prehuman Times to the French Revolution.* New York: Farrar, Straus and Giroux.

Fulton, W. B., R. Pendall, M. Nguyen, and A. Harrison. 2001. *Who Sprawls Most? How Growth Patterns Differ across the U.S.* Report, July. Washington, DC: Brookings Institution.

Gamrat, F., and J. Haulk. 2005. *Merging Governments: Lessons from Louisville, Indianapolis and Philadelphia.* Allegheny Institute Report No. 05–04, June. Pittsburgh: Allegheny Institute for Public Policy.

Gauto, V. 2012."Urban Competitiveness and the Twin Cities Metropolitan Area." *CURA Reporter* 42, no. 2: 3–8.

Gerber, E. R., and C. C. Gibson. 2009. "Balancing Regionalism and Localism: How Institutions and Incentives Shape American Transportation Policy." *American Journal of Political Science* 53, no. 3: 633–648.

———. 2005. "Balancing Competing Interests in American Regional Governance." Unpublished paper, January.http://localgov.fsu.edu/readings_papers/Growth%20 Manag/Gerber_Gibson_Regional_Governancer.pdf.

Gere, E. A. 1982. "Dillon's Rule and the Cooley Doctrine: Reflections on the Political Culture." *Journal of Urban History* 8, no. 3: 271–298.

Gilbertson, H. S. 1917. *The County: The "Dark Continent" of American Politics.* New York: The National Short Ballot Organization.

Giuliano, G. 2007. "The Changing Landscape of Transportation Decision Making." *Transportation Research Record: Journal of the Transportation Research Board* 2036: 5–12.

Goldsmith, S., and W. D. Eggers. 2004. *Governing by Network: The New Shape of the Public Sector.* Washington, DC: Brookings Institution.

Goodman, J. S. 1980. *The Dynamics of Urban Growth and Politics.* New York: Macmillan.

Gorte, R. W., C. H. Vincent, L. A. Hanson, and M. R. Rosenblum. 2012. *Federal Land Ownership: Overview and Data.* CRS Report for Congress R42346. Washington, DC: Congressional Research Service.

Government Accountability Office. 2009. www.gao.gov/new.items/d09868.pdf.

Grassmueck, G., S. Goetz, and M. Shields. 2008. "Youth Out-Migration from Pennsylvania: The Roles of Government Fragmentation vs. The Beaten Path Effect." *The Journal of Regional Analysis and Policy* 38, no. 1: 77–88.

Grassmueck, G., and M. Shields. 2010. "Does Government Fragmentation Enhance or Hinder Metropolitan Economic Growth?" *Papers in Regional Science* 89, no. 3: 641–657.

Hall, J. S. 2009. "Who Will Govern American Metropolitan Regions, and How?" In *Governing Metropolitan Regions in the 21st Century*, edited by D. Phares, 54–78. Armonk, NY: M. E. Sharpe.

Halloway, W. V. 1951. *State and Local Government in the United States.* New York: McGraw-Hill.

Hamilton, D., D. Miller, and J. Paytas. 2004. "Exploring the Horizontal and Vertical Dimensions of the Governing of Metropolitan Regions." *Urban Affairs Review* 40, no. 2: 147–182.

Hamilton, D. K., and P. S. Atkins. 2008. *Urban and Regional Policies for Metropolitan Livability.* Armonk, NY: M. E. Sharpe.

Hamilton County, Ohio. 2004. *Community Revitalization Initiative Strategic Plan.* Community COMPASS Report No. 19–1, March. Cincinnati: Hamilton County Regional Planning Commission.

Hanlon, B. 2009. "A Typology of InnerRing Suburbs: Class, Race, and Ethnicity in U.S. Suburbia." *City & Community* 8, no. 3: 221–246.

Hansberry, J. 2000. "Denver's Scientific and Cultural Facilities District: A Case Study in Regionalism." *Government Finance Review* 16, no. 6: 13–16.

Hansell, W. 2000. "Evolution and Change Characterize Council-Manager Government." *Public Management* 82, no. 8: 17–21.

Harkness, P. 2009. "When the Well Runs Dry."*Governing*, May 1. www.governing. com/columns/potomac-chronicle/When-the-Well-Runs.html.

Harrison, R. J., and D. M. Weinberg. 1992. *Racial and Ethnic Segregation in 1990.* April. Washington, DC: U.S. Census Bureau.

Harrison, S. M. 1926. Round Table on Regional Planning. *American Political Science Review* (February): 156–163.

Hawkins, B. W. 1971. *Politics and Urban Policies.* Indianapolis: Bobbs-Merrill Co.

Heckathorn, D. D., and S. M. Maser. 1987. "Bargaining and Constitutional Contracts." *American Journal of Political Science* 31, no. 1: 142–168.

Hendrick, R. M., B. S. Jimenez, and K. Lal. 2011. "Does Local Government Fragmentation Reduce Local Spending?" *Urban Affairs Review* 47, no. 4: 467–510.

Henton, D., J. Melville, and K. Walesh. 1997. *Grassroots Leaders for a New Economy: How Civic Entrepreneurs Are Building Prosperous Communities.* San Francisco: Jossey-Bass.

Hill, R. C. 1974. "Separate and Unequal: Governmental Inequality." *American Political Science Review* 68, no. 4: 1557–1568.

Hitchings, B. G. 1998. "A Typology of Regional Growth Management Systems." *The Regionalist* 3, nos. 1 & 2: 1–14.

Hobbes, T. 1964. *Leviathan.* Abridged ed. New York: Washington Square Press.

Hoene, C. W., and M. A. Pagano. 2009. "City Fiscal Conditions in 2009." *Research Brief on America's Cities,* September, 2009. Washington, DC: National League of Cities.

Hollis, L. E. 1998. *"Regionalism Today: Background, Timeliness, and Current Practice.* Washington, DC: Urban Land Institute.

Hooker, G. E. 1917. "City Planning and Political Areas." *National Municipal Review* 6, no. 3: 337–345.

Howell-Moroney, M. 2008. "The Tiebout Hypothesis 50 Years Later: Lessons and Lingering Challenges for Metropolitan Governance in the 21st Century." *Public Administration Review* 68, no. 1: 97–109.

International City/County Management Association (ICMA). 1996. *The Municipal Year Book 1996.* Washington, DC: ICMA.

———. 1984. *The Municipal Year Book 1984.* Washington, DC: ICMA.

Jacobs, P. E., and J. V. Toscano. 1964. *The Integration of Political Communities.* Philadelphia: J. B. Lippincott.

Jensen, B., and J. Turner. 2000. "Act 77: Revenue Sharing in Allegheny County." *Government Finance Review* 16, no. 6: 17–21.

Jillson, C. C. 1988. "Political Culture and the Patterns of Congressional Politics under the Articles of Confederation." *Publius: The Journal of Federalism* 18, no. 1: 1–26.

Judt, T. 2010. *Postwar: A History of Europe since 1945.* New York: Penguin Press.

Katz, B. 1998. *Reviving Cities: Think Metropolitan.* Policy Brief No. 33. Washington, DC: Brookings Institution.

Keating, M. 1995. "Size, Efficiency, and Democracy: Consolidation, Fragmentation, and Public Choice." In *Theories of Urban Politics,* edited by D. Judge, G. Stoker, and H. Wolman, 117–134. Thousand Oaks, CA: Sage.

Keene, J., J. Nalbandian, R. O'Neill, S. Portillo, and J. Svara. 2007. "How Professionals Can Add Value to Their Communities and Organizations." *Public Management* (March): 32–39.

Kettl, D. F. 2006. "Managing Boundaries in American Administration: The Collaboration Imperative." *Public Administration Review* 66, no. s1: 10–19.

————. 2002. *The Transformation of Governance: Public Administration for Twenty-First Century America.* Baltimore: Johns Hopkins University Press.

Kikert, W. J. M., and J. Koppenjan. 1997. "Public Management and Network Management: An Overview." In *Managing Complex Networks: Strategies for the Public Sector,* edited by W. J. M. Kickert, E. -H. Klijn, and J. F. M. Koppenjan. London: Sage.

Kincaid, J. 1980. "Political Culture of the American Compound Republic." *Publius: The Journal of Federalism* 10, no. 2: 1–15.

Koppenjan, J. F. M., and E. Klijn. 2004. *Managing Uncertainties in Networks: A Network Approach to Problem Solving and Decision Making.* New York: Routledge.

Ledebur, L., and W. Barnes. 1993. *All in It Together: Cities, Suburbs and Local Economic Regions.* Washington, DC: National League of Cities.

————. 1992. *Metropolitan Disparities and Economic Growth: City Distress and the Need for a Federal Local Growth Package.* Washington, DC: National League of Cities.

Leland, S. M., and K. M. Thurmaier, eds. 2010. *City-County Consolidation: Promises Made, Promises Kept?* Washington, DC: Georgetown University Press.

LeRoux, K., P. W. Brandenburger, and S. K. Pandey. 2010. "Interlocal Service Cooperation in US Cities: A Social Network Explanation." *Public Administration Review* 70, no. 2: 268–278.

Lewis, J. H., and D. K. Hamilton. 2011. "Race and Regionalism: The Structure of Local Government and Racial Disparity." *Urban Affairs Review* 47, no. 3: 349–384.

Lewis, P. G. 1998. "Regionalism and Representation Measuring and Assessing Representation in Metropolitan Planning Organizations." *Urban Affairs Review* 33, no. 6: 839–853.

————. 1996. *Shaping Suburbia: How Political Institutions Organize Development.* Pittsburgh: University of Pittsburgh Press.

Lineberry, R. L., and E. P. Fowler. 1967. "Reformism and Public Policy in American Cities."*American Political Science Review* 61: 701–716.

Locke, J. 1955. *Of Civil Liberty, Second Essay.* Chicago: Gateway Editions.

Lorch, R. S. 2001. *State and Local Politics: The Great Entanglement.* 6th ed. Upper Saddle River, NJ: Prentice-Hall.

Lubell, M., and J. T. Scholz. 2001. "Cooperation, Reciprocity, and the Collective-Action Heuristic." *American Journal of Political Science* 45 no. 1: 160–178.

Luce, T. F. Jr. 1998a. "Applying the Twin Cities Model of Tax-base Sharing in other Metropolitan Areas: Simulations for Chicago, Philadelphia, Portland, and Seattle." In *National Tax Association 1997 Annual Conference Proceedings,* National Tax Association.

————.1998b. "Regional Tax Base Sharing: The Twin Cities Experience." In *Local Government Tax and Land Use Policies in the United States,* edited by H. F. Ladd. Northhampton, MA: Edward Elgar.

Luria, D. D., and J. Rogers, eds. 1999. *Metro Futures: Economic Solutions for Cities and Their Suburbs.* Boston: Beacon Press.

Lyons, W. 1978. "Reform and Response in American Cities: Structure and Policy Reconsidered." *Social Science Quarterly* 59: 118–132.

Mackenzie, W. J. 1961. *Theories of Local Government.* London: London School of Economics and Political Science.

Mansbridge, J. J. 1980. *Beyond Adversarial Democracy*. New York: Basic Books.

Marando, V. L., and R. D. Thomas. 1977. *The Forgotten Governments: County Commissioners as Policy Makers*. Gainesville: University Presses of Florida.

Matkin, D. S., and H. G. Frederickson. 2009. "Metropolitan Governance: Institutional Roles and Interjurisdictional Cooperation." *Journal of Urban Affairs* 31, no. 1: 45–66.

McCabe, B. C., R. C. Feiock, J. C. Clingermayer, and C. Stream. 2008. "Turnover among City Managers: The Role of Political and Economic Change." *Public Administration Review* 68, no. 2: 380–386.

McGinnis, M. D., ed. 1999. *Polycentricity and Local Public Economies: Readings from the Workshop in Political Theory and Policy Analysis*. Ann Arbor: University of Michigan Press.

McGuire, M. 2006. "Collaborative Public Management: Assessing What We Know and How We Know It." *Public Administration Review* 66, no. s1: 33–43.

McLaughlin, J. P. 2010. *The Temple Municipal Governance Survey: How Pennsylvanians View Their Local Governments*. A Preliminary Report, December. Philadelphia: Temple University, Institute for Public Affairs.

McQuaid, K., M. Bok, D. Y. Miller, and J. James. 1992. *Tax Base Sharing as an Alternative Fiscal Policy in Pennsylvania*. Harrisburg: Center for Rural Pennsylvania.

Miller, D. Y. 2002. *The Regional Governing of Metropolitan America*. Boulder, CO: Westview Press.

———. 1999. "Transforming the Governance of Western Pennsylvania from Town to Region." In *The State of the Region Report: Economic, Demographic, and Social Conditions and Trends in Southwestern Pennsylvania*, edited by R. Bangs. Pittsburgh: University Center for Social and Urban Research, University of Pittsburgh.

———. 1991. "The Impact of Political Culture on Patterns of State and Local Government Expenditures." *Publius: The Journal of Federalism* 21, no. 2: 83–100.

Miller, D. Y., and C. M. DeLoughry. 1996. *1995 Organizational Assessment: A Report to the Southwestern Pennsylvania Regional Planning Commission*. Pittsburgh: The Pennsylvania Economy League.

Miller, D. Y., and J. Easton. 2008. *Assessing Allegheny County's Revenue Sharing Program after 10 Years*. Pittsburgh: University of Pittsburgh Graduate School of Public and International Affairs, Center for Metropolitan Studies.

Miller, D. Y., and J. H. Lee. 2011. "Making Sense of Metropolitan Regions: A Dimensional Approach to Regional Governance." *Publius: The Journal of Federalism* 41, no. 1: 126–145.

Miller, D. Y., R. Miranda, R. Roque, and C. Wilf. 1995. "The Fiscal Organization of Metropolitan Areas: The Allegheny County Case Reconsidered." *Publius: The Journal of Federalism* 25, no. 4: 19–36.

Miller, J. 2013. Bill Pushing Uniform Muny Tax Could Return. *Crain's Cleveland Business,* January 7. http://www.crainscleveland.com/article/20130107/SUB1/301079975/0/SEARCH?template=printart.

Miller-Adams, M. 2009. *The Power of a Promise: Education and Economic Renewal in Kalamazoo*. Kalamazoo, MI: W.E. Upjohn Institute for Employment Research.

———. 2006. "A Simple Gift? The Impact of the Kalamazoo Promise on Economic Revitalization." *Employment Research* 13, no. 3: [1]–2; 5–6.

Minnesota House of Representative's Research Department. 1987. *Minnesota's Fis-*

cal Disparities Program: Tax Base Sharing in the Twin Cities Metropolitan Area, A Research Report.

Mitchell-Weaver, C., D. Y. Miller, and R. Deal. 2000. "Multilevel Governance and Metropolitan Regionalism in the USA." *Urban Studies* 37, nos. 5–6: 851–876.

Model City Charter. A Publication of the National Civic League. 2013. http://www.cgr. org/onebataviacharter/docs/National_Civic_League_Model_City_Charter.pdf.

Moore, M. H. 1995. *Creating Public Value: Strategic Management in Government.* Cambridge: Harvard University Press.

Morgan, G. 2006. *Images of Organization.* Updated ed. Thousand Oaks, CA: Sage.

Mosher, F. 1982. *Democracy and the Public Service.* 2d ed. New York: Oxford University Press.

Mueller, D. C. 1979. *Public Choice.* Cambridge: Cambridge University Press.

Mumford, L. 1961. *The City in History.* New York: Free Press.

Muro, M. and B. Katz. 2010. *The New "Cluster Moment": How Regional Innovation Clusters Can Foster the Next Economy.* Paper, September. Washington, DC: Brookings Institution.

Nalbandian, J. 2002. The Future of City Management Education." In *The Future of Local Government Administration: The Hansell Symposium,* edited by H.G. Frederickson and J. Nalbandian. Washington, DC: International City/County Management Association.

———. 1991. *Professionalism in Local Government: Transformations in the Roles, Responsibilities, and Values of City Managers.* San Francisco: Jossey-Bass.

National Association of Regional Councils. 2013. http://www.narc.org/.

National League of Cities (NLC). 2003/2004. www.nlc.org/onebataviacharter/docs/ National_Civic_League_Model_City_Charter.pdf.

National Municipal League, Committee on Metropolitan Government. 1974. *The Government of Metropolitan Areas in the United States.* New York: Arno Press.

National Research Council. 1999. *Governance and Opportunity in Metropolitan America.* Washington, DC: National Academy Press.

Nelson, A. C., T. W. Sanchez, J. F. Wolf, and M. B. Farquhar. 2004. "Metropolitan Planning Organization Voting Structure and Transit Investment Bias: Preliminary Analysis with Social Equity Implications." *Transportation Research Record: Journal of the Transportation Research Board* 1895: 1–7.

New Jersey Meadowlands Commission. 2013. Tax Sharing. www.njmeadowlands. gov/municipal/tax/how.html.

New York State, Department of State. n.d. Consolidation, Dissolution, and Annexation of Towns and Villages How-to Guide. www.dos.ny.gov/LG/publications/Local_Government_Consolidation.pdf.

Norris, D. 2001. "Whither Metropolitan Governance?"*Urban Affairs Review* 36, no. 4: 532–550.

Norris, D., D. Phares, and T. Zimmerman. 2009. "Metropolitan Government in the United States? Not Now . . . Not Likely." In *Governing Metropolitan Regions in the 21st Century,* edited by D. Phares. Armonk, NY: M. E. Sharpe.

Oakerson, R. J. 2004. "The Study of Metropolitan Governance." In *Metropolitan Governance: Conflict, Competition, and Cooperation,* edited by R.C. Feiock, 17–45.Washington, DC: Georgetown University Press.

———. 1999. *Governing Local Public Economies: Creating the Civic Metropolis.* Oakland, CA: ICS Press.

Oakerson, R. J., and R. B. Parks. 1988. "Citizen Voice and Public Entrepreneurship: The Organizational Dynamic of a Complex Metropolitan County." *Publius: The Journal of Federalism* 18, no. 4: 91–112.

Ohio First Suburbs Consortium. 2013a. About: Northeast Ohio Homepage. http://www.firstsuburbs.org/firstsuburbs/history.php.

———. 2013b. Northeast History. http://www.firstsuburbs.org/firstsuburbs/history.php.

Olberding, J. C. 2002. "Does Regionalism Beget Regionalism? The Relationship between Norms and Regional Partnerships for Economic Development." *Public Administration Review* 62, no. 4: 480–491.

Olson, Jr., M. 1965. *The Logic of Collective Action: Public Goods and the Theory of Groups.* Cambridge: Harvard University Press.

Orfield, M. 1997. *Metropolitics: A Regional Agenda for Community Stability.* Washington, DC: Brookings Institution.

Orfield, M., and T. Luce. 2009. "Governing American Metropolitan Areas: Spatial Policy and Regional Governance." In *Megaregions: Planning for Global Competitiveness,* edited by C.L. Ross. Washington, DC: Island Press.

Osborne, D., and P. Hutchinson. 2004. *The Price of Government: Getting the Results We Need in an Age of Permanent Fiscal Crisis.* New York: Basic Books.

Ostrom, E. 1972. "Metropolitan Reform: Propositions Derived from Two Traditions." *Social Science Quarterly* 53, no. 3: 474–493.

Ostrom, E., R. Gardner, and J. Walker. 1994. *Rules, Games, and Common-Pool Resources.* Ann Arbor: University of Michigan Press.

Ostrom, V., C. M. Tiebout, and R. Warren. 1961. "The Organization of Government in Metropolitan Areas: A Theoretical Inquiry." *American Political Science Review* 55: 831–842.

O'Toole, L., ed. 2007. *American Intergovernmental Relations.* 4th ed. Washington, DC: CQ Press.

O'Toole, L. J., and K. J. Meier. 2004. "Desperately Seeking Selznick: Cooptation and the Dark Side of Public Management in Networks." *Public Administration Review* 64, no. 6: 681–693.

Pandey, S.K. 2008–9. National Administrative Studies Project—IV. Survey. University of Kansas.

Peirce, N. 2000. "Louisville Votes Merger—First since Indy in 1969." *County News,* December 18.

———. 1993. *Citistates: How Urban America Can Prosper in a Competitive World.* Washington, DC: Seven Locks Press.

Pennsylvania Economy League, Western Division. 1990. "Regional Asset Nature of the Pittsburgh Zoo, Phipps Conservatory, and the Pittsburgh Aviary." Pittsburgh: Pennsylvania Economy League.

Peterson, P. E. 1981. *City Limits.* Chicago: University of Chicago Press.

The Pettit Company. 2011. Virginia's Counties and Independent Cities. http://www.pettitcompany.com/html/va_cities_and_counties.html.

Porter, M. E. 1998. "Clusters and the New Economics of Competition." *Harvard Business Review* (November-December): 77–90.

Posner, P. L. 1998. *The Politics of Unfunded Mandates: Whither Federalism?* Washington, DC: Georgetown University Press.

Post, S. S. 2004. "Metropolitan Area Governance and Institutional Collective Action." In *Metropolitan Governance: Conflict, Competition, and Cooperation,* edited by R.C. Feiock, 67–92. Washington, DC: Georgetown University Press.

Pound, W. 2009. "The Fiscal Condition of the States." Washington, DC: National Conference on State Legislatures.

Protasel, G. J. 1989. "Leadership in Council-Manager Cities: The Institutional Perspective." In *Ideal and Practice in Council-Manager Government*, edited by H.G. Frederickson, 114–122. Washington, DC: International City Management Association.

Reynolds, L. 2003. "Intergovernmental Cooperation, Metropolitan Equity, and the New Regionalism." *Washington Law Review* 78 (February).

Rusk, D. 2011. "Changing the 'Rules of the Game': Tools to Revive Michigan's Fractured Metropolitan Regions." *The Journal of Law in Society* 13, no. 1.

———. 2004. *Consolidating Wheeling and Ohio County: A Review of City-County Consolidation ("Unigov") Experiences Regarding Central City Health and Regional Economic Growth.* Paper prepared for Hopeful City, December 11.

———. 2003a. *Cities without Suburbs: A Census 2000 Update.* 3d ed. Washington, DC: The Woodrow Wilson Center Press.

———. 2003b. *"Little Boxes"—Limited Horizons: A Study of Fragmented Local Government in Pennsylvania: Its Scope, Consequences, and Reforms.* A background paper, December. Washington, DC: Brookings Institution.

———. 1999. *Inside Game/Outside Game: Winning Strategies for Saving Urban America.* Washington, DC: Brookings Institution.

———. 1993. *Cities Without Suburbs.* Washington, DC: The Woodrow Wilson Center Press.

Salamon, L. M. 2002. *The Tools of Government: A Guide to the New Governance.* New York: Oxford University Press.

Sanchez, T. W. 2006. *An Inherent Bias? Geographic and Racial-Ethnic Patterns of Metropolitan Planning Organization Boards.* Report, June. Washington, DC: Brookings Institution.

Sanford, P., B. Hudson, J. O'Looney, and R. Gordon. 2012. *Responding to the New Realities: Case Studies in County Governance.* Washington, DC: National Center for the Study of Counties.

Savitch, H. V., D. Collins, D. Sanders, and J. Markham. 1993. "Ties That Bind: Central Cities, Suburbs, and the New Metropolitan Region." *Economic Development Quarterly* 7, no. 4: 341–357.

Savitch, H. V., and R. K. Vogel. 2004. "Suburbs without a City Power and City-County Consolidation." *Urban Affairs Review* 39, no. 6: 758–790.

———. 1996. "Louisville and Antagonistic Cooperation." In *Regional Politics: America in a Post-City Age*, edited by H.V. Savitch and R. K. Vogel, 130–157. New York: Sage.

Sbragia, A. M. 1993. "The European Community: A Balancing Act." *Publius: The Journal of Federalism* 23, no. 3: 23–38.

Sbragia, A. M., and F. Stolfi. 2012. "Key Policies" In *The European Union: How Does it Work?* edited by E. Bomberg, J. Peterson, and R. Corbett. New York: Oxford University Press, 111–135.

Schambra, W. A. 1982. "The Roots of the American Public Philosophy." *Public Interest* 67 (Spring): 36–48.

Scheppach, R. 2003. "What Ails the States?" National Governors Association Policy Brief, January. Washington, DC: NGA.

Scherer, F. M., and D. Ross. 1990. *Industrial Market Structure and Economic Performance.* Boston: Houghton Mifflin.

Schneider, M. 1989. *The Competitive City: The Political Economy of Suburbia.* Pittsburgh: University of Pittsburgh Press.

Schneider, M., and K. O. Park. 1989. "Metropolitan Counties as Service Delivery Agents: The Still Forgotten Governments." *Public Administration Review* 49: 345–352.

Sellers, M. 2010. *County Authority: A State by State Report.* December. Washington, DC: National Association of Counties.

Shepherd, W. G. 1985. *The Economics of Industrial Organization.* 2d ed. Englewood Cliffs, NJ: Prentice Hall.

Smith, B. C. 1985. *Decentralization:The Territorial Dimension of the State.* London: G. Allen and Unwin.

Sofen, E. 1961. "Problems of Metropolitan Leadership: The Miami Experience." *Midwest Journal of Political Science* 5, no. 1: 18–38.

Southwest Pennsylvania Commission (SPC). 2013. "About US." www.spcregion.org/about_comm.shtml.

Sparrow, M. K. 2008. *The Character of Harms: Operational Challenges in Control.* New York: Cambridge University Press.

State of Arizona. 2005. An Act Amending Section 9–471, Arizona Revised Statutes; Relating to City Annexation. www.azleg.state.az.us/legtext/47leg/1r/bills/hb2602p.htm.

State of New York. 2013. The General Municiple Law, Article 17, *Petition for Annexation §703.*

Stein, R. M. 1990. *Urban Alternatives: Public and Private Markets in the Provision of Local Services.* Pittsburgh: University of Pittsburgh Press.

Steinacker, A. 2004. "Game-Theoretic Models of Metropolitan Cooperation." In *Metropolitan Governance: Conflict, Competition, and Cooperation,* edited by R.C. Feiock, 46–66. Washington, DC: Georgetown University Press.

Stephens, G. R., and N. Wikstrom. 1999. *Metropolitan Government and Governments: Theoretical Perspectives, Empirical Analysis, and the Future.* New York: Oxford University Press.

Stillman, R. J. 1974. *The Rise of the City Manager.* Albuquerque: University of New Mexico Press.

Svara, J. 2001. "Do We Still Need Model Charters? The Meaning and Relevance of Reform in the Twenty-First Century." *National Civic Review* 90, no. 1: 19–34.

Syed, A. 1966. *The Political Theory of the American Local Government.* New York: Random House.

Teaford, J. C. 1986. *The Twentieth-Century American City: Problem, Promise, and Reality.* Baltimore: Johns Hopkins University Press.

Thomas, R. D., and V. L. Marando. 1981. "Local Government Reform and Territorial Democracy: The Case of Florida." *Publius: The Journal of Federalism* 11, no. 1: 49–63.

Thurmaier, K., and C. Wood. 2002. "Interlocal Agreements as Overlapping Social Networks: Picket-Fence Regionalism in Metropolitan Kansas City." *Public Administration Review* 62, no. 5: 585–598.

Tiebout, C. M. 1956. *A Pure Theory of Local Expenditures.* Chicago: University of Chicago Press.

Tocqueville, A. de. 1953. *Democracy in America.* New York: Alfred A. Knopf.

Tsebelis, G. 2005. *The European Convention and the Rome and Brussels IGCs: A Veto Players Analysis.* Estudio/Working Paper no. 217: 1.

Turner, J.W.1995. "The Allegheny Regional Asset District: Communities Thinking and Acting Like a Region." *Government Finance Review* 111, no. 3.

University of Pittsburgh. 2012. "Metropolitan Power Diffusion Index." Press release, March 6. http://www.metrostudies.pitt.edu/Projects/Databases/Metropolitan-PowerDiffusionIndex/tabid/1321/Default.aspx.

U.S. Advisory Commission on Intergovernmental Relations (ACIR). 1995. *MPO Capacity: Improving the Capacity of Metropolitan Planning Organizations to Help Implement National Transportation Policies.* A Commission Report, A-130, May. Washington, DC: ACIR.

———. 1992. *Metropolitan Organization: The Allegheny County Case.* A Commission Report, M-181, February. Washington, DC: ACIR.

———. 1982. *State and Local Roles in the Federal System.* A Commission Report, A-88, April. Washington, DC: ACIR.

U.S. Census Bureau. "Census of Governments." Volume 1: Government Organization (various years).

U.S. Census Bureau. 2011. "2011 Public Employment and Payroll Data, State Governments, United States Total." In *2011 Annual Survey of Public Employment and Payroll,* Table. Washington, DC: U.S. Census Bureau. http://www2.census.gov/govs/apes/11stus.txt.

U.S. Census Bureau. 2012. 2012 Census of Governments. Database. www.census.gov/govs/cog2012/.

U.S. Census Bureau. 2007. 2007 Census of Governments. Database. www.census.gov/govs/cog/.

U.S. Census Bureau. 2007. 2007 Census of Governments: Finance Summary Statistics. edited by Bureau of Census U.S. Department of Commerce, 2007.

U.S. Census Bureau. 1996. Census of Governments: Finance Summary Statistics. 1996.

U.S. Census Bureau. 1982. Census of Governments: Finance Summary Statistics. 1982.

U.S. Government Accountability Office (GAO). 2009. Metropolitan Planning Organizations: Options Exist to Enhance Transportation Planning Capacity and Federal Oversight.Report to the Ranking Member, Committee on Environment and Public Works, U.S. Senate, GAO-09–868, September.Washington, DC: GAO.

U.S. Office of Personnel Management (OPM). 2011. Employment and Trends—December 2011. Table 7: Total Employment and Full-Time Employment with Permanent Appointments by Selected Agency, December 2011. www.opm.gov/policy-data-oversight/data-analysis-documentation/federal-employment-reports/employment-trends-data/2011/december/table-7/.

Walker, D. B. 1987. "Snow White and the 17 Dwarfs: From Metro Cooperation to Governance." *National Civic Review* 76, no. 1: 14–28.

———. 1986. "Intergovernmental Relations and the Well-Governed City." *National Civic Review* 75, no. 2: 65–87.

Weber, M. 1946. *From Max Weber: Essays in Sociology.* Translated and edited by Hans Heinrich Gerth and C. Wright Mills. New York: Oxford University Press.

Weick, K. E. 2001. *Making Sense of the Organization.* Malden, MA: Blackwell.

Wickwar, H. W. 1970. *The Political Theory of Local Government.* Columbia: University of South Carolina Press.

Wikipedia. 2013a. Independent city (United States). http://en.wikipedia.org/wiki/Independent_city_(United_States) (accessed January 25, 2013).

———. 2013b. Political subdivisions of Virginia. http://en.wikipedia.org/wiki/Political_subdivisions_of_Virginia (accessed January 25, 2013).

Winer, M., and K. Ray. 1994. *Collaboration Handbook: Creating, Sustaining, and Enjoying the Journey.* Saint Paul, MN: Amherst H. Wilder Foundation.

Wolman, H., and A. Levy. 2011. *Government, Governance, and Regional Economic Growth*. George Washington Institute of Public Policy Working Paper 044, April. Washington, DC: The George Washington University.

Wood, C. H. 2005. "The Nature of Metropolitan Governance in Urban America: A Study of Cooperation, Conflict, and Avoidance in the Kansas City Region." *Working Group on Interlocal Services Cooperation*, Paper 9. http://digitalcommons. wayne.edu/interlocal_coop/9.

Wright, D. S. 1988. *Understanding Intergovernmental Relations*. Pacific Grove, CA: Brooks/Cole.

Zeemering, E., and D. Delabbio. 2013. *A County Manager's Guide to Shared Services in Local Government*. Washington, DC: IBM Center for the Business of Government.

Zeigler, D. J., and D. B. Stanley. 1980. "Geopolitical Fragmentation and the Pattern of Growth and Need: Defining the Cleavage between Sunbelt and Frostbelt Metropolises." In *The American Metropolitan System: Present and Future*, edited by Stanley D. Brunn and James O. Wheeler, 77–92. London: V. H. Winston and Sons.

Zimmerman, J. 1984. "New England Town Meeting: Pure Democracy in Action?" In *The Municipal Yearbook 1984*, 102–06. Washington, DC: International City Management Association.

———. 1983. *State-Local Relations: A Partnership Approach*. New York: Praeger.

Zuckerman, M. 1970. *Peaceable Kingdoms: The New England Towns of the 18th Century*. New York: Norton.

Index

About the Authors

David Y. Miller is a professor at the University of Pittsburgh's Graduate School of Public and International Affairs (GSPIA) where he is director of the Center for Metropolitan Studies and the Congress of Neighboring Communities (CONNECT). He served for many years as Associate and Interim Dean at GSPIA. Dr. Miller's research and numerous publications focus on regional governance, regional financing of urban services, and municipal fiscal distress. Before joining the University, Dr. Miller had been Director of Management and Budget for the City of Pittsburgh, managing director of the Pennsylvania Economy League, and also a municipal manager. He is a recipient of the University of Pittsburgh's Distinguished Public Service Award and also holds an Honorary Doctor of Public Service degree from Nasson College in Springvale, Maine. He currently serves as a Commissioner on the Pittsburgh region's Metropolitan Planning Organization (MPO) and the Southwestern Pennsylvania Commission (SPC).

Raymond W. Cox III is a professor in the Department of Public Administration and Urban Studies at the University of Akron. He is the author of more than 70 academic and professional publications. Dr. Cox's governmental experience includes serving on the staff for both the Speaker of the Massachusetts House of Representatives and the National Science Foundation, and as Chief of Staff to the Lieutenant Governor in New Mexico. In 2009 he was selected to complete an unexpired term on the Akron City Council.